Power and Subversion
in *Game of Thrones*

Power and Subversion in *Game of Thrones*

Critical Essays on the HBO Series

Edited by A. Keith Kelly

McFarland & Company, Inc., Publishers
Jefferson, North Carolina

This book has undergone peer review.

LIBRARY OF CONGRESS CATALOGUING-IN-PUBLICATION DATA

Names: Kelly, A. Keith, 1972– editor.
Title: Power and subversion in Game of thrones :
critical essays on the HBO series / edited by A. Keith Kelly.
Description: Jefferson : McFarland & Company, Inc., Publishers, 2022. |
Includes bibliographical references and index.
Identifiers: LCCN 2022016574 | ISBN 9781476682648 (paperback : acid free paper) ∞
ISBN 9781476644660 (ebook)
Subjects: LCSH: Game of thrones (Television program) |
Power (Social sciences) on television. | BISAC: PERFORMING ARTS /
Television / Genres / Science Fiction, Fantasy & Horror
Classification: LCC PN1992.77.G35 P69 2022 | DDC 791.45/72—dc23/eng/20220415
LC record available at https://lccn.loc.gov/2022016574

BRITISH LIBRARY CATALOGUING DATA ARE AVAILABLE

ISBN (print) 978-1-4766-8264-8
ISBN (ebook) 978-1-4766-4466-0

© 2022 A. Keith Kelly. All rights reserved

*No part of this book may be reproduced or transmitted in any form
or by any means, electronic or mechanical, including photocopying
or recording, or by any information storage and retrieval system,
without permission in writing from the publisher.*

Front cover: photograph by Yurii Kifor (Shutterstock)

Printed in the United States of America

*McFarland & Company, Inc., Publishers
Box 611, Jefferson, North Carolina 28640
www.mcfarlandpub.com*

Acknowledgments

I would like to thank Alex J. Mack, who, as an intern at Georgia Gwinnett College, worked diligently on the volume bibliographies as well as on cataloging quoted material from the HBO television series and George R.R. Martin's novels. Another special acknowledgment goes to the folks at westeros.org, whose information on seasons and episodes was invaluable.

Table of Contents

Acknowledgments v

Introduction
    A. Keith Kelly 1

List of Seasons and Episodes: HBO's Game of Thrones 7

Breaking the Wheel: *Game of Thrones* and the American Zeitgeist
    Daniel Vollaro 13

Dangerous Nostalgia: Fantasies of Medievalism, Race, and Identity
    Robert Allen Rouse 30

Game of Victims and Monsters: Representation of Sexual and Female Violence
    Sylwia Borowska-Szerszun 48

Subversion or Reinforcement? Patriarchy and Masculinity
    Andrew Howe 68

"I'll go with anger": Female Rage in and at *Game of Thrones*
    Lindsey Mantoan 87

The Developing Verbal Power of Daenerys: A Pragmatics Analysis
    Graham P. Johnson 108

"Who has a better story than Bran the Broken?": The Power of Disability Narratives
    Jan Doolittle Wilson   131

Magic's Failure to Reanimate Fantasy
    Jason M. Embry   161

A Brief Conclusion on the Conclusion
    A. Keith Kelly   181

About the Contributors   185

Index   187

Introduction

A. Keith Kelly

HBO's television series *Game of Thrones* enjoyed enormous popularity over the eight seasons during which it aired (2011–2019). This epic fantasy, based upon George R.R. Martin's currently unfinished literary series, *A Song of Ice and Fire*, attracted tens of millions of viewers in the U.S. and hundreds of millions of viewers globally. In addition to the show's remarkable production quality, *Game of Thrones* has been extolled for striking a powerful chord with viewers for its gritty realism, its complex characters, its dynamic plots that often contained shocking twists, and for the way viewers across diverse demographics found it remarkably relatable to the current state of affairs in the real world. Now that the series has drawn to a conclusion—and the Iron Throne melted—more work can be done to analyze this television series and the ways it has influenced, and been influenced by, the cultural moments that it shared with the world. And indeed the impact of *Game of Thrones* should not be underestimated as, according to a May 20, 2019, article on Forbes.com, the "average gross audience per episode for *Thrones*, across all platforms" was 44.2 million, and the final episode of the series, Season 8, episode 6, boasted 13.6 million "viewers who watched the episode on linear TV Sunday night, a new HBO high mark, making *GoT* the most-watched program in network television history" (Fitzgerald). The number of viewers, which was already impressive, certainly will have increased since May 2019. As for the reception of *Game of Thrones*, a look at the Internet Movie Database website reveals that, as of September 2022, nearly one million IMDb users had given *GoT* a weighted average vote of "9.2/10" ("Game of Thrones"). Not only have general viewers rated the show so highly, television critics have as well, with IMDb.com noting that *GoT* has won 375 awards and had 608 nominations, including Golden Globe and Emmy Awards ("Game of Thrones"). Thus it would seem that even with the disappointment expressed by many concerning Season 8, particularly the final two episodes, the series has received a remarkably

2 Introduction

high number of positive ratings from viewers and critics alike. While some of this data may be considered soft, taken together as a whole, the inescapable conclusion is that *Game of Thrones* has resonated with audiences around the world, both the lay and the professional viewer.

The popularity of *Game of Thrones* should in some ways come as no surprise, for at its core the show is about power and has been from the moment it first aired in April of 2011. In that year, in the United States (and in many other parts of the world) the struggles for power found in our politics, our economics, our own clannish divisiveness had continued to grind its way ever deeper into an abyss. Barack Obama, ushered in as a beacon of hope and change in 2008, had really availed Americans very little when it came to facing the sweeping forces of the powerful. Five years later and on the other side of the political aisle, Donald Trump, promising to drain the swamp, merely caused the waters to grow murkier. And the battle for the proverbial Iron Throne in the United States, similar to the drawn-out fight over Brexit in the UK, and other impassioned discussions of populism, nationalism, immigration, terrorism, religion and the like from around the world, have served only to entrench our cultures more deeply into our respective identities, chanting our house words all the while. Power is the currency of our time (and perhaps all times), and it seems that wielding it, or trying to take it from those who do, is the goal of our tribalistic struggles—or at least the struggles of our leaders. And within this environment *Game of Thrones* became a mirror for our own condition, offering an entertaining vision of power depicted with even more overt injustice, brutality and heartbreak than reality. We are enthralled by it, because in spite of its dragons and swords and White Walkers it is real to us, because it is centered on the relentless struggle for power. And we should not forget that *Game of Thrones* is also about subversion—for in truth, what story about power, especially when it is shared among vying forces, is not also about subversion?

Given its tremendous success and its incredibly timely themes of political power and subversion, the genre of *Game of Thrones* might have surprised many had that success been predicted prior to its airing—who would have thought that an epic fantasy would capture the devotion of so many 21st-century viewers, many of whom remarked upon its connections with real human struggle? At the same time, genre is fundamental to the success and energy that the series generated over the course of nearly a decade. As a scholar, I have long been intrigued by notions of genre—by the conventions, tropes and, intriguingly, the subversions of established genres. While I am admittedly biased, I have often found the fantasy genre to be particularly rich in its ability to speak within a genre that has quite well-defined parameters and features, while at the same time communicating beyond it—well, good fantasy that is, and especially then when it is capable of extending beyond its typical genre readership or viewership. Without a doubt, *Game of Thrones* has far-outstripped the typical viewers of fantasy (a group that in itself has undeniably grown notably over the last two decades) and has taken on a much larger audience. The incredibly large and devoted fandom includes presidents, prime ministers, celebrities of all stripes, academics and pretty much every demographic. It is no longer simply a fantasy TV series, it is a series that enjoys mass popularity by any definition. Suffice it to say that *GoT* has a viewership that transcends typical fantasy viewership, and in the process has developed a strong relationship with that broad viewership, carrying out the contract between author and viewer in fascinating ways.

Genre has established patterns, and consequently, evokes among its audiences certain expectations. To speak in general terms, the fantasy genre—particularly epic fantasy such as *Game of Thrones*—is typically rendered as heroic, and often romantic as well. The nature of evil is fairly monolithic, and protagonists struggle against the often-overwhelming forces of it in service of a sense of goodness, or morality, or ethics, or duty, or some other set of laudable traits. The expected outcomes are generally triumphant, though often at some cost. And while dark fantasy certainly exists, and does not adhere to this pattern, it is not the dominant form—in fact its existence as a *counter* sub-genre reinforces the presence of the dominant mode. All of this is perhaps doubly true when one looks at fantasy in film and TV. High fantasy and its triumphant themes and expectations have dominated the screen market for decades ... at least prior to *Game of Thrones*.

The basic framework of *Game of Thrones* is undeniably epic high fantasy. All of the pieces were in place from the beginning, and in the first season we seemed to be traveling down a well-worn path toward a triumphant and heroic destination. Then Ned Stark's head bounced down the steps of the Great Sept of Baelor after being cut off with his own ancestral sword. Ahhh, so audiences concluded that it was an avenging son narrative (save for those of us who had read the books—we had already experienced the surprises in print). Excellent, and still in line with heroic genre expectations, until Robb Stark was stabbed at the Red Wedding along with his pregnant wife and his devoted mother. That was not supposed to happen. It sent viewers into a frenzy. But was it simply because he died? No, it was because it was not supposed to happen in *this* genre. Judging by the reactions expressed in their 2015 book, *Game of Thrones on Business*, Tim Phillips and Rebecca Claire agree:

> But the Internet-crashing shock wasn't fundamentally about death. There's loads of that on TV. What really made this stand out was that it broke the rules—the story just wasn't supposed to go this way. We'd invested in the revenge story of Robb Stark and his family who, in Hollywood narrative terms, should clearly

win the war against the Lannisters because that's the way things are done in fairy stories.

The Red Wedding episode, officially titled "The Rains of Castamere," more than any other subverts the genre and its expectations. And in spite of viewers completely freaking out (there are YouTube videos of this), the viewership of *Game of Thrones* showed an uptick. There was no "Negan kills Glenn" effect, which had deleterious consequences on the viewership of *The Walking Dead*—a dystopian show in which we assumed people would die.

And it was not just the deaths-of-characters-that-shouldn't-die that both appalled and compelled, and ultimately fascinated, millions of viewers. The show has been cited for its violence, its toxic masculinity, its gratuitous female nudity, its rape culture, its misogyny, its incest, its ruthless depictions of motherhood, and the list goes on. Again, a lot of these are not supposed to happen in high fantasy—at least not to this extent. To be sure, you don't see much of this in *The Lord of the Rings* films or books, and they are the gold standard of the fantasy genre. So why is this embraced in *Game of Thrones*? Why do all of these genre-subverting elements perhaps even explain why the show is so popular among an audience that transcends the typical fantasy one? Author, critic, journalist, leukemia-sufferer and self-avowed despiser of anything with swords and dragons, Clive James, wrote a compelling piece in *The New Yorker* in 2016. In his begrudging defense of the raw appeal of *Game of Thrones*, entitled "Thrones of Blood: Binge Watching the Most Addictive Show on Television," he observes the following:

> The real shock is not in what Joffrey's evil streak can accomplish but in what Ned Stark's virtue fails to prevent. He is a good, thoughtful man with a sense of justice, and it avails him nothing. It avails us nothing, either, who have come to depend on him. For popular art, for any level of art, this is a rare step toward the natural condition of the world. [...] Everyone in the show is dispensable, as in the real world. [Except, he notes, Tyrion Lannister, who serves as a conduit for viewers] Tyrion is us, bright enough to see the world's evil but not strong enough to change it.

Within this context of the real world, as James puts it, *Game of Thrones* and its popularity begin to make sense. Films like *The Lord of the Rings* are rousing, enchanting depictions of good triumphing over evil, of fellowship and loyalty, of hope overcoming despair, of love triumphant and hate dispelled. But, well, *The Lord of the Rings* is a fantasy, and as appealing as that vision may be, as inspiring as it is ideologically, it just doesn't strike the same chord with the grittiness of the real world that *Game of Thrones* does. *Game of Thrones* seems so real in the ideas it examines.

But ... it is still a fantasy story; it still lives in that genre where a hero prevails and good ultimately triumphs. As much as the genre and its expectations were subverted and trampled, there was still in the back of every viewer's mind that it would all end with a note of triumph. We were not certain, as we watched the final seasons unfold, who would win out in the end, but most of us were pretty sure that as catastrophic as the ending was likely to be to some of our beloved characters, the resolution would be a heroic one, befitting of the genre. We do not expect our own world to be ever heroic and triumphant, but neither do we expect it to be a futile march toward annihilation. And thus when *Game of Thrones* subverted the positive expectations natural to its genre, viewers found it more real, and were compelled to continue watching—especially since most still had in the back of their minds an ultimately optimistic ending. But true to form, the conclusion of *Game of Thrones* didn't fail to subvert the genre expectations one last time.

The collection of essays in this book seeks to explore in greater depth some of the sources, and representations, of power found in HBO's *Game of Thrones*, and to a lesser degree, its literary source, *A Song of Ice and Fire*. Likewise, the authors consider the ways that expectations and traditions, particularly as they relate to empowerment, are both reinforced or subverted as the narrative is created and received by audiences. The first two essays in the volume, from Daniel Vollaro and Robert Allen Rouse, explore the larger picture of the socio- and geo-political settings of the show, delving respectively into the immediate relevance and the problematic nostalgias that *Game of Thrones* presents to viewers. The four essays that follow, authored by Sylwia Borowska-Szerszun, Andrew Howe, Lindsey Mantoan and Graham P. Johnson, address the broad and inciteful topic of gender and power from distinctly different angles of approach. The penultimate essay, by Jan Doolittle Wilson, examines the rich and, in many ways, extraordinary presence of disability in *Game of Thrones*. The collection of essays is brought to completion by Jason M. Embry, whose essay on magic and its oddly impactful and impotent role in the series exemplifies the ultimately problematic conclusion of the series itself.

As editor, I would like to note that the contributors to this volume approach the show from a variety of perspectives as professionals—being scholars and teachers of journalism, literature, film, history and gender studies—and hail from several different parts of the world. In addition to being accomplished academics, they are also fans (sometimes painfully) of *Game of Thrones*, as am I. Our aim in this volume is to provide a collection of insights from a group of folks who have delved deeply into this remarkable television series and wish to share the resulting thoughts with fellow scholars, students, critics and really with any fans of the show who wish to arrive at a greater understanding and appreciation of what became one of the first cultural phenomena of the 21st century.

Works Cited

Fitzgerald, Toni. "'Game of Thrones' Finale by the Numbers: All the Show's Ratings Records." *Forbes*, 20 May 2019, https://www.forbes.com/sites/tonifitzgerald/2019/05/20/game-of-thrones-finale-by-the-numbers-all-the-shows-ratings-records/#e529e155f738.

"Game of Thrones." *IMDB*, 31 Dec. 2020, https://www.imdb.com/title/tt0944947/?ref_=nv_sr_srsg_0.

James, Clive. "Thrones of Blood: Binge-Watching the Most Addictive Show on Television." *The New Yorker*, 11 Apr. 2016.

Kirkman, Robert., et al. *The Walking Dead*. Beverly Hills: Anchor Bay Entertainment, 2010.

"List of *Game of Thrones* Episodes." *A Wiki of Ice and Fire*, westeros.org, https://awoiaf.westeros.org/index.php/List_of_Game_of_Thrones_episodes.

Philips, Tim, and Rebecca Claire. *Game of Thrones on Business: Strategy, Morality and Leadership Lessons from the World's Most Talked About TV Show*. Durrington: Infinite Ideas Limited, 2015.

List of Seasons and Episodes: HBO's *Game of Thrones*

Throughout this volume references to specific scenes of *Game of Thrones* are made according to Season and Episode, indicated as (S1, E1) for Season 1, Episode 1. The following chart also lists the episode titles as well as the directors and writers.

Season 1

Episode	Title	Director	Writers	Air Date
1	"Winter Is Coming"	Tim Van Patten	David Benioff & D.B. Weiss	April 17, 2011
2	"The Kingsroad"	Tim Van Patten	David Benioff & D.B. Weiss	April 24, 2011
3	"Lord Snow"	Brian Kirk	David Benioff & D.B. Weiss	May 1, 2011
4	"Cripples, Bastards, and Broken Things"	Brian Kirk	Bryan Cogman	May 1, 2011
5	"The Wolf and the Lion"	Brian Kirk	David Benioff & D.B. Weiss	May 15, 2011
6	"A Golden Crown"	Daniel Minahan	David Benioff & D.B. Weiss	May 22, 2011
7	"You Win or You Die"	Daniel Minahan	David Benioff & D.B. Weiss	May 29, 2011
8	"The Pointy End"	Daniel Minahan	George R.R. Martin	June 05, 2011

8   List of Seasons and Episodes

Episode	Title	Director	Writers	Air Date
9	"Baelor"	Alan Taylor	David Benioff & D.B. Weiss	June 12, 2011
10	"Fire and Blood"	Alan Taylor	David Benioff & D.B. Weiss	June 19, 2011

Season 2

Episode	Title	Director	Writer	Air Date
1	"The North Remembers"	Alan Taylor	David Benioff & D.B. Weiss	April 1, 2012
2	"Nightlands"	Alan Taylor	David Benioff & D.B. Weiss	April 8, 2012
3	"What Is Dead May Never Die"	Alik Sakharov	Bryan Cogman	April 15, 2012
4	"Garden of Bones"	David Petrarca	Vanessa Taylor	April 22, 2012
5	"The Ghost of Harrenhal"	David Petrarca	David Benioff & D.B. Weiss	April 29, 2012
6	"The Old Gods and the New"	David Nutter	Vanessa Taylor	May 6, 2012
7	"A Man Without Honor"	David Nutter	David Benioff & D.B. Weiss	May 13, 2012
8	"The Prince of Winterfell"	Alan Taylor	David Benioff & D.B. Weiss	May 20, 2012
9	"Blackwater"	Neil Marshall	George R.R. Martin	May 27, 2012
10	"Valar Morghulis"	Alan Taylor	David Benioff & D.B. Weiss	June 3, 2012

Season 3

Episode	Title	Director	Writer	Air Date
1	"Valar Dohaeris"	Daniel Minahan	David Benioff & D.B. Weiss	March 31, 2013
2	"Dark Wings, Dark Words"	Daniel Minahan	Vanessa Taylor	April 7, 2013

List of Seasons and Episodes 9

Episode	Title	Director	Writers	Air Date
3	"Walk of Punishment"	David Benioff & D.B. Weiss	David Benioff & D.B. Weiss	April 14, 2013
4	"And Now His Watch Is Ended"	Alex Graves	David Benioff & D.B. Weiss	April 21, 2013
5	"Kissed by Fire"	Alex Graves	Bryan Cogman	April 28, 2013
6	"The Climb"	Alik Sakharov	David Benioff & D.B. Weiss	May 5, 2013
7	"The Bear and the Maiden Fair"	Michelle MacLaren	George R.R. Martin	May 12, 2013
8	"Second Sons"	Michelle MacLaren	David Benioff & D.B. Weiss	May 19, 2013
9	"The Rains of Castamere"	David Nutter	David Benioff & D.B. Weiss	June 2, 2013
10	"Mhysa"	David Nutter	David Benioff & D.B. Weiss	June 9, 2013

Season 4

Episode	Title	Director	Writer	Air Date
1	"Two Swords"	D.B. Weiss	David Benioff & D.B. Weiss	April 6, 2014
2	"The Lion and the Rose"	Alex Graves	George R.R. Martin	April 13, 2014
3	"Breaker of Chains"	Alex Graves	David Benioff & D.B. Weiss	April 20, 2014
4	"Oathkeeper"	Michelle McLaren	Bryan Cogman	April 27, 2014
5	"First of His Name"	Michelle McLaren	David Benioff & D.B. Weiss	May 4, 2014
6	"The Laws of Gods and Men"	Alik Sakharov	Bryan Cogman	May 11, 2014
7	"Mockingbird"	Alik Sakharov	David Benioff & D.B. Weiss	May 18, 2014
8	"The Mountain and the Viper"	Alex Graves	David Benioff & D.B. Weiss	June 1, 2014

List of Seasons and Episodes

Episode	Title	Director	Writers	Air Date
9	"The Watchers on the Wall"	Neil Marshall	David Benioff & D.B. Weiss	June 8, 2014
10	"The Children"	Alex Graves	David Benioff & D.B. Weiss	June 15, 2014

Season 5

Episode	Title	Director	Writers	Air Date
1	"The Wars to Come"	Michael Slovis	David Benioff & D.B. Weiss	April 12, 2015
2	"The House of Black and White"	Michael Slovis	David Benioff & D.B. Weiss	April 19, 2015
3	"High Sparrow"	Mark Mylod	David Benioff & D.B. Weiss	April 26, 2015
4	"Sons of the Harpy"	Mark Mylod	Dave Hill	May 4, 2015
5	"Kill the Boy"	Jeremy Podeswa	Bryan Cogman	May 10, 2015
6	"Unbowed, Unbent, Unbroken"	Jeremy Podeswa	Bryan Cogman	May 17, 2015
7	"The Gift"	Miguel Sapochnik	David Benioff & D.B. Weiss	May 24, 2015
8	"Hardhome"	Miguel Sapochnik	David Benioff & D.B. Weiss	May 31, 2015
9	"The Dance of Dragons"	David Nutter	David Benioff & D.B. Weiss	June 7, 2015
10	"Mother's Mercy"	David Nutter	David Benioff & D.B. Weiss	June 14, 2015

Season 6

Episode	Title	Director	Writers	Air Date
1	"The Red Woman"	Jeremy Podeswa	David Benioff & D.B. Weiss	April 24, 2016
2	"Home"	Jeremy Podeswa	Dave Hill	May 1, 2016

Episode	Title	Director	Writers	Air Date
3	"Oathbreaker"	Daniel Sackheim	David Benioff & D.B. Weiss	May 8, 2016
4	"Book of the Stranger"	Daniel Sackheim	David Benioff & D.B. Weiss	May 15, 2016
5	"The Door"	Jack Bender	David Benioff & D.B. Weiss	May 22, 2016
6	"Blood of my Blood"	Jack Bender	Bryan Cogman	May 29, 2016
7	"The Broken Man"	Mark Mylod	Bryan Cogman	June 5, 2016
8	"No One"	Mark Mylod	David Benioff & D.B. Weiss [66]	June 12, 2016
9	"Battle of the Bastards"	Miguel Sapochnik	David Benioff & D.B. Weiss	June 19, 2016
10	"The Winds of Winter"	Miguel Sapochnik	David Benioff & D.B. Weiss	June 26, 2016

Season 7

Episode	Title	Director	Writers	Air Date
1	"Dragonstone"	Jeremy Podeswa	David Benioff & D.B. Weiss	July 16, 2017
2	"Stormborn"	Mark Mylod	Bryan Cogman	July 23, 2017
3	"The Queen's Justice"	Mark Mylod	David Benioff & D.B. Weiss	July 30, 2017
4	"The Spoils of War"	Matt Shakman	David Benioff & D.B. Weiss	August 6, 2017
5	"Eastwatch"	Matt Shakman	Dave Hill	August 13, 2017
6	"Beyond the Wall"	Alan Taylor	David Benioff & D.B. Weiss	August 20, 2017
7	"The Dragon and the Wolf"	Jeremy Podeswa	David Benioff & D.B. Weiss	August 27, 2017

List of Seasons and Episodes

Season 8

Episode	Title	Director	Writers	Air Date
1	"Winterfell"	David Nutter	Dave Hill	April 14, 2019
2	"A Knight of the Seven Kingdoms"	David Nutter	Bryan Cogman	April 21, 2019
3	"The Long Night"	Miguel Sapochnik	David Benioff & D.B. Weiss	April 28, 2019
4	"The Last of the Starks"	David Nutter	David Benioff & D.B. Weiss	May 5, 2019
5	"The Bells"	Miguel Sapochnik	David Benioff & D.B. Weiss	May 12, 2019
6	"The Iron Throne"	David Benioff &	David Benioff & D.B. Weiss	May 19, 2019

Breaking the Wheel

Game of Thrones *and the American Zeitgeist*

Daniel Vollaro

In June 2012, the producers of HBO's *Game of Thrones* were forced to apologize for putting the head of George W. Bush on a pike. The head was a fake, of course—a rubber prop—but the apology was real. The story follows a familiar script: in an interview for the DVD commentary, producers David Benioff and D.B. Weiss revealed that in the pivotal scene where Sansa Stark is forced to look upon the severed head of her father displayed on a pike on the ramparts of King's Landing (S1, E10), one of the *other* heads up on the wall is in fact a fake bust of the former Republican president wearing a wig. They intended no political statement, they insisted, though unable to contain their laughter. "We just had to use whatever head we had around" (*International*). A fan posted the picture on Reddit, and soon Benioff and Weiss were issuing a much less frivolous, far more formal apology. "We are deeply dismayed to see this," they wrote in a statement, "and we find it unacceptable, disrespectful, and in very bad taste."

So it goes in the era of social media.

The severed head scandal was an early sign that the wildly popular TV adaptation of George R.R. Martin's fantasy novels was destined to attract political analysis, both serious and silly. Soon after Season One aired, the phrase "Game of Thrones" began to show up as a clever shorthand for political conflict. By 2015, the metaphor "arrived" culturally when it appeared as the title of a *Time Magazine* cover story about the Bushes and the Clintons (Gibbs). Journalists, pundits, and magazine editors fell in love with the phrase and were soon using it to describe the political dynamics of South Africa, Saudi Arabia, Iraq, and of course, Afghanistan, a country governed by actual warlords (Nevin, Shidore, Ghosh, Nordland). Political references to *Game of Thrones* are now too numerous to count. Judy Kurtz, writing for *The Hill* in May of last year, shared some of these references, made by

American politicians including Newt Gingrich, John Delany, Hakeem Jeffries, and Elizabeth Warren, who wrote an op-ed titled "The World Needs Fewer Cersei Lannisters." The *Game of Thrones* frenzy among politicians and pundits was too much for conservative columnist Jonathan Tobin to bear. Writing in the *Federalist* last year, he begged fans to "stop making analogies between the plot and contemporary politics."

No one should be surprised. Television shows have always generated memes, stretching back to the days before anyone knew what a meme was, and the title of *this* series reads like a ready-made tagline for any political rivalry. But *Game of Thrones* is very much a creature of its historical and cultural moment. It would not have been a hit in 1991—or even 2001—because audiences had not yet been prepared for this kind of television drama (for this, we can thank the decade of HBO programming that preceded it, beginning with the *Sopranos*). It landed like dragon's feet on a castle wall in 2011 largely because its moral universe aligned so well with the American zeitgeist. The country had just survived a decade of turmoil—9/11; the "endless wars" on Terror; Katrina; the near collapse of the economy in 2008, which precipitated the Tea Party and Occupy Movements; and the resurgence of class consciousness in American politics—a decade of war, economic ruin, and institutional failure. To many Americans, their country had begun to feel like a failed state, a place where, to quote the Dylan song, "Everything is broken." Westeros, with its castles, dragons, and emergent magic, is geographically and historically alien, but its ethos—its moral architecture, the *feel* of the place—is familiar somehow. And this uncanny recognition of the place among audiences contributed to its success.

Failed State Television

Not long after George Bush's head appeared on a skewer in King's Landing, the *Atlantic* published a piece titled "HBO, your liberal Id is showing." The article pointed to a survey of 4,000 Americans that revealed HBO to be one of the most politically polarizing of America's major entertainment brands. Liberals tend to love HBO programming, the survey revealed. Republicans, not so much. The article cites the skewered head controversy alongside *True Blood*, *The Newsroom*, *Girls*, and *Veep* as evidence that the network is a bastion of liberalism (Lawson).

It is probably true that some Republicans do not appreciate polyamorous vampires, preachy television news anchors, or *Girls* who make light of their abortions, but HBO's cinematic oeuvre isn't *that* easily pigeonholed politically. Instead of wading in the shallow pool of easy comparisons to partisan politics, I'll dive into a deeper one: many of HBO's most popular and signature television series have constructed fictional worlds around failed states. I do not mean "failed state" in the modern geopolitical sense of a nation-state whose basic institutions of governance have entirely collapsed (say, Somalia). I mean that the state is either incapable of doing good or is itself the agent of corruption, injustice, and violence.

"The state" is admittedly a slippery term. In American usage, it is often deployed as an easy synonym for "government," but I prefer a broader Marxist definition which depicts the state as completely entwined with the economic system of a society rather than an entity that exists apart from the economy and is therefore capable of regulating it. Hal Draper provides an excellent definition in Volume 1 of *Karl Marx's Theory of Revolution:*

> The state is the institution or complex of institutions which bases itself on the availability of forcible coercion by special agencies of society in order to maintain the dominance of a ruling class, preserve the existing property relations from basic change and keep all other classes in subjection [251].

So the state is bigger than the government. It is the confluence of power required to govern large populations and territory that exist at the level of a "nation" or "empire" while simultaneously preserving the power of the ruling class. This power is usually exercised through institutions that represent formal divisions of labor in the society (i.e., trade guilds, the army, the police, schools, the monarchy, etc.). States can be monarchies, dictatorships, or democratic republics, but they are always hierarchically organized, and they usually protect the interests of elites at the top more assiduously than the poor and disenfranchised at the bottom. States are coercive. They possess a monopoly on violence, as defined by Max Weber and others. States use legal, judicial, and enforcement mechanisms to force compliance, as well as softer measures like education, social pressure, and even religious faith.

The near collapse of the economy in 2008 provides an excellent illustration of the scope of state power. After facilitating a profound and dangerous economic crisis through bad government policy, predatory lending practices, and the overuse of unregulated financial instruments to package loans, the agents of these decisions—representatives of the Federal Government and some of the largest banks in America—met to discuss how to solve the problem. Treasury Secretary Hank Paulson, himself a former CEO of one of the banks (Goldman Sachs) was the chief negotiator for the Bush administration. Over the next 72 hours, this small group of elites would engineer the bailout of AIG for $150 billion and TARP—the Troubled Asset Relief Fund—which would siphon $700 billion in taxpayer money towards bailing out a handful of massive banks at the center of the crisis (Cohan). The state's power—and its hierarchical power structure—was on display as it seldom is during this moment in history: the confluence of business and government interests, the influence of elite academic institutions, the existence of an actual ruling class of mostly unelected people who could control the fate of millions.

Television can be an instrument of state power or a means of critiquing it. Many historians and media scholars have used a Marxist analysis to suggest that television is just another ideological state apparatus[1]—a means of indoctrinating and controlling the public—but this is an overly simplistic perspective. Early in the history of television, the McCarthy hearings demonstrated that television could upend political power as well as support and reaffirm it. Cynthia Littleton of *Variety Magazine* chronicles the long history of television shows that tackle social problems, beginning with the early 1960s show *The Defenders*, a courtroom drama featuring a father-and-son legal duo whose cases dealt with heavy social issues like abortion and child sexual abuse. Littleton's list includes well known series such as *Lou Grant, Hill Street Blues, St. Elsewhere, Cagney & Lacey, Law & Order, Homicide: Life on the Street, The Practice,* and *The West Wing*, as well as made-for-television movies like *That Certain Summer, Friendly Fire, Something About Amelia* and *The Burning Bed*.

While sometimes creating space for social critique, many television shows also simultaneously affirm the state's power and legitimacy. The classic example is *Law and Order*, which for twenty years regularly examined social problems within the safe confines of the procedural. With its two-part format—first half focusing on the police investigation and the second, the corresponding court case—each episode was framed in the comforting notion that the "police who investigate crime and the district attorneys who prosecute the offenders" are always there, doing their jobs. This kind of state-friendly television programming is a staple of network television, where shows about cops, lawyers, firemen, and soldiers proliferate. The state is alive and well in these series—not perfect, but mostly depicted as functioning and on the side of right and justice.

HBO pioneered a very different kind of television drama, and packaged along with it, a very different posture towards state power. The origins of this new approach can be traced back to the *Sopranos*. In his book *The HBO Effect*, author Dean J. DeFino calls the *Sopranos* a narrative of "deep cynicism and ambivalence" (133). Tony Soprano, he says, is a guy who was raised in an era of "cultural cynicism"—a lapsed Catholic who believes he is surrounded by degenerates, and who follows the crudest dictates of the marketplace to prey on people (142). He is a creature of institutional failure and systemic corruption, of "an America that is irrevocably broken" (143). He is only sympathetic to the extent that the audience accepts this quasi-dystopian view on spec, or at least as a major conceit in the series' fictional world. Against this backdrop, the antihero can thrive as a character—a fixer of problems, an instrument of crude justice, or a fun-to-watch destroyer of all things straight and pretty. Without it, he would be little more than a two-dimensional character with a target painted on his back, hauled off to prison at the end of an episode of *Law and Order: Special Victim's Unit* or taken out in a drone strike on *Seal Team Six*.

HBO built some of its best dramas around the *Sopranos'* template for a moral universe. *Deadwood*, HBO's iconic take on the American Western, is an excellent example. Set in a town outside of the control of the United States government, *Deadwood*'s moral universe was more akin to Clint Eastwood's iconic *Unforgiven* than any other film made in the Golden Age of Westerns. There is no law in Deadwood, and into this vacuum pour grifters, ex-lawmen, oil barons, and corrupt government officials from the American empire. By the end of the first season, one ex-lawman (Bill Hickok) is dead and the other (Seth Bullock) has been ground through a crucible of moral ambiguity and nearly killed in a street fight. Though not rightly described as an antihero, *Deadwood*'s gangster saloon owner Al Swearengen shines like a Shakespearean tragic protagonist against this grimy, blood-spattered backdrop.

Jump ahead to early 2000s Baltimore, where *The Wire* depicts a modern American city that is every bit as lawless and violent as Deadwood, though for different reasons. Unlike the nascent frontier town, Baltimore has had its chance to build a functioning society and failed. *The Wire* is *Law and Order* without the safety net of the procedural, set free to fully explore the corruption and incompetence of the state and liberated from the expectation that criminals must always be the bad guys. Similarly, *Treme* plays out against the literally smashed-up backdrop of post–Katrina New Orleans, another failed metropolis laid low by poverty, racism, and a failed government disaster response.

David Simon, the creator of *The Wire* and co-creator of *Treme* laid bare his opinion of the American state in a speech delivered in 2013 at the Festival of Dangerous Ideas in Sydney, Australia. In it, he explicitly condemns the current neoliberal order as a failure:

> The idea that the market will solve such things as environmental concerns, as a racial divide, as our class distinctions, or problems with educating and incorporating one generation of workers into the economy after the other one that economy is changing; the idea that the market is going to heed all of the human concerns and still maximize profit is juvenile. It's a juvenile notion and it's still being argued in my country passionately and we're going down the tubes.

He went on to say that *The Wire* was about people who are deemed "worthless" in the American economy. "It was about them trying to solve, for lack of a better term, an existential crisis."

The existential crisis—the state in a state of failure—is in the background of some of HBO's most popular dramatic series in the last twenty years. In fact, it is possible to read the failure of the American state across the breadth of HBO's dramatic landscape—prisons in *Oz*; education, the media, the police, and the courts in *The Wire*; FEMA and Federal poverty mitigation in *Treme*; American empire in *Deadwood*. And while HBO's catalog is vast and variegated, its most popular shows paved the way for a new brand of scripted TV drama that builds cinematic worlds around the conceit that great stories and characters can come to life against a backdrop of societal and institutional failure.

Game of Thrones was a comfortable addition to HBO's collection of failed state television dramas. Its basic premise of warlords battling for control of a country brings to mind modern geopolitical tragedies like Afghanistan or Somalia—actual failed states. Its socioeconomic world is based on stark economic inequality. In a piece published on CNN wire in May 2014, John Blake aptly compared this television fantasy world to America saying, "There is no middle class in *Game of Thrones*. The 99% of Westeros—the peasants, innkeepers, and farmers—survive at the whim of a small group of wealthy families who treat them with indifference and cruelty." Westeros at war with itself, riven with corruption and incapable of providing security, rule of law, and justice to the people, is a moral universe not far removed from *Deadwood*, or *The Wire*'s Baltimore, or *Treme*'s New Orleans, or Tony Soprano's mobbed-up corner of northeastern New Jersey. But with dragons.

War Is the Health of the State

"Law is law," Ned Stark proclaims as he prepares to personally behead a deserter from the Night's Watch in the first episode. "The man who passes the sentence should swing the sword" Ned explains to his youngest son, Bran (S1, E1). He is upholding the "Old Way"—the way of the Northern Chieftains—which originated in a tribal past where the leaders literally embodied justice. But Ned is also defending the rule of law, which he mistakenly believes is the basis of the state's power, carried along by the honor and integrity of the nobles who protect and enforce it. Season one is a lesson in how wrong he is, as he is himself led to the executioner's block in the season finale through the treachery of people who believe, as Cersei Lannister says, that "power is power" (S2, E1).

Who is right? Which vision of state power is most accurate? *Game of Thrones* is a master class in political power and presents the issue from multiple perspectives. For Littlefinger, the recipient of Cersei's lesson, information is power. For Varys, it is an illusion, a shadow projected on the wall, and what gives it power is that people believe in it. None of these political philosophers questions the "game" itself, which is treated as simply the extant political reality of Westeros. Elites use their lineage, wealth, and military might to compete for political power, and war is often the consequence. That is the way of things.

Writing at the end of World War I, American intellectual Randolph Bourne argued somewhat sardonically that the state is a war machine that reaches its highest degree of "health" when it is organizing for war. Elites plan and start wars, but "the moment war is declared ... the mass of the people, through some spiritual alchemy, become convinced that they have willed and executed the deed themselves" (226). According to this theory, war is the organizing principle of the nation-state, and nations are at their most functional when they are preparing for or fighting wars.

This bleak depiction of the state aligns closely with the ethos of Westeros, whose elites are constantly organizing for the war. Most of them equate the health of the state with personal victory in the game of thrones. But the political "game" does not entirely explain the power of the state. For all of its warlordism, Westeros has a functioning bureaucracy, institutions, houses of worship, a kind of national library, and The Wall and its guardians of course. All of this plodding institutionalized normalcy continues to grind along in the midst of sporadic civil wars.

In the first episode, Varys explains to Ned, who is newly arrived in King's Landing, that a Small Council exists to address the "small matters" of the realm (S1, E1). Implied is the idea that the "large" matters encompass the never-ending struggle for power. Varys cares about the health of the realm "because who else will?" (S1, E1). The state manifests in two levels— the "game" which swallows the lion's share of attention, and the day-to-day affairs of the realm, which are left to a revolving door of royal aides, sycophants, political appointees, and bureaucrats who sit on the Small Council. The Small Council makes periodic appearances throughout eight seasons, often depicted in absurdly humorous discussions about taxation, sanitation, immigration, funding for wars, or the condition of brothels. In these meetings, the "peasants," are often depicted as a problem that requires a solution—like whether or not to allow them in the city walls during wartime. The men and women who make these decisions are entirely from the elite class, either nobility or their advisors. In one of the final scenes in the series finale, the newly reconstituted Small Council meets, this time with Bran as King at the head of the table. The scene is played for humor as the discussion quickly dissembles into bickering over whether to spend money on rebuilding ports or brothels (S8, E6).

The tension between the war-making capacity of the state and its duty to protect the social order is on full display in the modern era. In the decade that encompassed *Game of Thrones*, civil wars broke out in Syria, Libya, and Yemen. In each of these wars, the larger "game" is being played out by various factions while the "small" matters—the day-to-day functions of government and society, move haltingly forward, sometimes literally dodging bullets and rocket propelled grenades in the process. This dichotomy is well illustrated in Orlando von Einsiedel's stunning documentary *The White Helmets*, which chronicles a group of first responders who rescue civilians from buildings in the midst of battle, and in the siege of Sarajevo twenty-five years ago, wherein the Sarajevo Philharmonic Orchestra played concerts in a city under heavy artillery attack.

It is not necessary to look oversees to cities like Beirut, Damascus, Mogadishu, Baghdad, and Grozny to find this dichotomy in action. One might also look at the U.S. Mired its own "endless wars" in the Middle East and increasingly toxic partisan political warfare, *its* social order also appears to be faltering. The sheer volume of political parallels drawn between *Game of Thrones* and American politics as the series closed out last year suggests that writers, critics, pundits, and journalists were looking hard in this direction. From *Business Insider*, we get the cheeky "Nine Political Lessons from HBO's Hit Show *Game of Thrones*." An article on *Foreign Policy*'s website theorized that audience outrage over Dany's incineration of King's Landing was a sign that Americans are opposed to attacking civilian populations in war. Joanna Weiss of NPR called it "our best modern allegory about politics." Conversely, the *Atlantic* complained that the series had "lost its way as a political drama." In the end, everyone wanted *Game of Thrones* to say something profound about American politics.

Well, maybe not everyone. In a humorous piece in *The New Yorker*, Emily Nussbaum complained about a scene in the final episode of season 6 in which a hoard of White Walkers is streaming over a hill, then she recalls that someone on Twitter had compared the White Walkers to the threat of Global Warming. "One solid metaphor and I was on board," she wrote. "Fine, bring on the zombies."

I Want to Break the Wheel ... and Build Another Powered by Dragons

As of this moment, 1,842,669 people have signed on to the Change.org petition to "Remake Game of Thrones Season 8 with competent writers." The petition was created by fan "Dylan D" before the final season had even ended and quickly garnered over a million votes. Many of those who left comments on the site were particularly upset by the ultimate fate of

Daenerys Targaryen. All errors in grammar and spelling have been maintained in the below comments from the Change.org petition.

> Angelleyna Bresee
> 1 week ago
> I want Dany to come back to life by Jon Snows doing and all to go forward and find some satisfying ending!

The campaign highlights a deep disconnect between fans—many of whom regard Dany as a revolutionary heroine—and the show's creators, who never strayed from its grim, realpolitik depiction of political power.

> John Couch
> 4 weeks ago
> Long live the queen

> George Parker
> 5 days ago
> Then end was a huge disappointment. Killing the dragon queen was so fucked up. She really made show. The moment she was stabbed I shut the TV off and regretted watching it.

Many fans had looked to her character for heroic inspiration and saw their hopes smashed in the final episode. Some blamed the writers for shortening her arc and thus making her fall seem precipitous and unrealistic, but many others clearly hoped she would be the heroine, sweeping into Westeros to save the place from itself. A liberator. A revolutionary hero.

No matter what the legions of her fans hoped for, Dany's arc was almost certain to end badly. There is no plausible finale in which she flies off on Drogon to liberate Westeros from oppression. She is not a superhero, and she was never the moral center of *Game of Thrones*. She *is* a morally complex character—one of many—on a television series airing on a network known for serving up complex characters and moral ambiguity. Dying at the tip of a dagger was always a believable, if not likely, outcome for a character so willing to wield one (albeit it vicariously or in the form of a dragon) in the game of thrones.

Fans can hardly be blamed for believing in Dany. On the surface, she appears to represent the hope of revolutions and revolutionaries everywhere. She is an exemplar of the "strong female character" and a symbol of female empowerment. She freed the slaves of Astapor and Meereen. But she is also the daughter of nobility, and though she grew up in exile, she was raised to believe in the basic hierarchies of power common to any monarchical society. She may sound like a revolutionary at times, but she aspires to be a queen. She is no Che Guevara.

Nevertheless, her revolutionary rhetoric *is* compelling. In season 5, she has just met Tyrion Lannister, who is now himself an exile, having fled from Westeros after killing his father. As they talk—the children of two "terrible fathers"—Dany admits that she wants the Iron Throne, and Tyrion lays out the obstacles, naming the various claims to the throne by different powerful families. She listens, impatiently, and then responds. "They all say this: Lannister, Baratheon, Stark, Tyrell, they're all just spokes on a wheel. This one's on top and that one's on top and on and on it spins, crushing those on the ground. We're not going to stop the wheel. No. I'm going to break the wheel" (S5, E8). This speech apparently convinces Tyrion to follow her, but ever the pragmatist, he is clearly choosing between two types of monarchs, the lesser of evils. Dany will still be a monarch, and the state will bend to her will if she wins—she, the daughter of a family that not too long before had ruled the Seven Kingdoms.

Beyond this speech, Dany says almost nothing about what kind of reforms she will bring with her across the Narrow Sea. She freed slaves in Astapor and Meereen, but the great emancipator cannot perform the same service in Westeros, where slavery has already been outlawed. Will she smash the feudalism evident in some parts of Westeros? Will she preside over a program of land reform? Hold elections? None of this seems likely.

Dany's "break the wheel" declaration expresses a utopian aspiration, though little else she does or says suggests she has a plan for building an ideal society after her dragons tear up the old one. Her wheel analogy is reminiscent of the "end of history"—that oft-quoted tagline for a future in which political evolution ends because the ideal form of human governance has finally been realized. In the West, this fantasy of an ideal society has antecedents in Plato's *Republic*, the *Acts of the Apostles*, and Thomas More's *Utopia*. Hegel wrote of an end of history that would dawn when humans en masse become awake to the fact that they are free. Marx changed this equation by arguing that history would end when the proletariat controls the means of production. More recently, in 1992, Frances Fukuyama declared the "end of history" in the rise of liberal democracy after the fall of communism in Europe. This idea that the wheel of history can be halted or terminated recurs in Western thought, perhaps propped up by Christian eschatology, which imagines history as terminating in a triumphal end point.

It is Fukuyama's end of history that is most relevant to *Game of Thrones*. The series premiered two decades after he published *The End of History and the Last Man*—two decades in which his big idea was proved staggeringly wrong. Liberal democracy and its companion neoliberal economic system have been in decline around the world since the 1990s. History grinds on, messy and seemingly devoid of any evolutionary arc, with no idealized end in sight. The word "realpolitik" has been used to describe the political dimension of the series, and what is realpolitik but the exercise of political power without a moral compass or a clearly defined political teleology? Might is right, lurching from one messy conflict to the next. This is the zeitgeist—the spirit of the age—that gave birth to *Game of Thrones*.

The ultimate irony of Dany's break-the-wheel speech is that her family, the Targaryens, have traditionally been one of the spokes on that same wheel. And despite the fact that her own father was "the Mad King," a notorious mass murderer who had to be put down like a rabid animal by Jaime Lannister, family dynasty is never far from her mind. Dany is driven by entitlement and a strong sense of grievance. When she first meets Jon Snow, she is sitting on her family's throne in Dragonstone while her assistant rattles off her main titles in a display of power. She wants Jon to "bend the knee," and their relationship going forward is conditioned on his fealty to her. Her vanity is mixed in with her obvious sympathy for the underclass—no doubt—but watch carefully for the dictator's well-shined boot. Dany isn't promising a Hegelian revolution of the mind or a Marxist liberation of capital. There is no big idea animating this revolution. Its message is disturbingly familiar—I alone can set you free, so follow me.

Even if Dany's motivations *were* entirely revolutionary, she seems destined by weight of history to become a mass murderer. "History is replete with examples of revolutionaries becoming tyrants and war criminals," writes Michael J. Totten in his excellent post-series wrap up. "It's a story that has repeated itself with numbing regularity." He goes on to list some of the evidence—most notably the Jacobins' Reign of Terror after the French Revolution and the mass murder that followed the Russian Revolution. Not surprisingly, Dany follows the same road. For all of the angst among fans about the length of Dany's arc in Season 8, there was ample foreshadowing for her massacre at King's Landing. In Season Two, standing before the gates of Qarth, she threatens, "Turn us away and we will burn you first" (S2, E4). She commits massacres of slave masters and their employees in Astapor and Meereen. She burns Randyll and Dickon Tarly with dragon fire because they refuse to bend the knee (S7, E5). In other moments, she seems ready to cry "dracarys" and unleash indiscriminate firepower but is talked out of it by her advisors. She need not be the second coming of the Mad King to become a mass murderer in her own right. Viewed through an historical lens, her crimes against humanity are really quite ordinary and not unexpected.

The Anarchists Beyond the Wall

The symbolism is not subtle.
Drogon, the last living dragon, lumbers up through the ruins of the

Iron Keep, and upon seeing his dead mother in Jon Snow's arms, unleashes fire on The Iron Throne. Literally forged from swords, the Iron Throne is the most visible symbol of the game, the ultimate prize. Drogon incinerates it and then flies off with Dany's body (S8, E6).

On one level, the lesson is quite poignant and clear. The Iron Throne is a symbol of political ambition run amok. The quest for it killed Dany. Drogon literally illuminates this fact in dragon fire. But bathed in the afterglow of Occupy, the Arab Spring, and the Syrian Civil War, the throne takes on wider significance. It represents the state itself and everything embodied by it—hierarchy, bureaucracy, patriarchy, inequality, the monopoly on violence—all of the things under fire at the end of the first decade of the 21st century. Drogon's protest (and I think it is safe to call it that) is aimed at the very idea of the state. He is the weapon of mass destruction in revolt against the system of power that would use him to incinerate cities. If I were to put a contemporary political label on his protest, I would call it *anarchist*.

The "A" word is hanging in the background of *Game of Thrones*, quietly animating everything. For one thing, the hierarchical power structure in Westeros exemplifies everything anarchists hate about the state. Anarchism takes many forms, but most anarchists espouse a radical concept of human freedom and depict the state as a coercive force that restricts freedom and organizes society in a fundamentally unequal way. These are the facts on the ground in Westeros. "Almost everywhere in Westeros is governed badly," Totten observes, "not just by modern standards but by its own." The violent and chaos-inducing "game" is partly to blame for the bad governance, but the highly stratified, unequal social order is also a culprit. Dany's wheel analogy is so apt because it accurately depicts the plight of the common people regardless of who sits on the throne. In its brokenness, inequality, and freewheeling violence, Westeros conforms to the anarchist's grim portrait of the state.

The word "anarchy" is derived from the ancient Greek word "anarchia," meaning without a ruler (Marshall x) and for many centuries, it was used as an unambiguously negative term to describe the condition of chaos and disorder that often follows the collapse of a political dynasty. There is plenty of this kind of anarchy in Westeros, but anarchy in a modern political context has another, more positive connotation. Modern-day anarchists tend to believe that the best society must be a stateless one. Russian geographer, political activist, and writer Peter Kropotkin says it best when he defines anarchism as:

> The name given to a principle or theory of life and conduct under which society is conceived without government—harmony in such a society being obtained, not by submission to law, or by obedience to any authority, but by free agreements concluded between the various groups, territorial and professional, freely

constituted for the sake of production and consumption, as also for the satisfaction of the infinite variety of needs and aspirations of a civilized being [284].

Anarchism never shows up as a serious political philosophy in discourse that revolves around traditional political parties and partisan politics, but it is nevertheless one of the animating political forces in American history, often expressing itself in popular movements on the left. At the end of the 19th century, anarchists were key members of the coalition driving the labor movement, affiliating with socialists, communists, and labor organizer. Hundreds of American anarchists fought alongside the leftists in the Spanish Civil War in the 1930s. Anarchist ideas drove the counterculture in the 1960s and brought thousands of demonstrators to anti-globalization actions in the late 1990s and early 2000s. More recently, anarchists were early organizers of the Occupy Wall Street Movement, where they conducted experiments with alternative forms of direct democracy. Anarchists are keen to demonstrate that they can live outside of the confines of state control, living in small collectives and communities and participating in direct action protests.

While showing the negative side of anarchy, *Game of Thrones* also highlights positive alternatives to the state. The showrunners and writers clearly possessed a sophisticated palette for political philosophy that shows up in the political texture of Westeros and its environs. The state-centered politics of King's Landing—with its institutionalized religion of the Seven modeled on Catholicism—is but one political reality among several. Priscilla Walton has correctly observed that the fictional universe of *Game of Thrones* is a mashup of political ideologies and governmentalities, part medieval because the novels were inspired by England's Wars of the Roses but also mixing in other influences (she argues that the "raison d'état" of 16th- and 17th-century European monarchies is the basis for the monarchical rule of Westeros, rather than the theocratically sanctioned rule of medieval monarchy). There are city states governed by oligarchies, a nomadic tribal society akin to the Mongols, and the animistic people North of the Wall. Additionally, there are elements of democratic rule in the Night's Watch, where leaders are chosen by vote (Walton).

But the state in Westeros is tenuous. For one thing, the ring of state control appears to fray the further North one travels in the realm. In the North, the political ethos is older, more tribal, with an ancient animistic religion to go along with it (the pagan counterpoint to the Seven). The north is an honor-shame society, far less cosmopolitan, and therefore far more difficult to control from afar.

The Wall marks the official Northern boundary of the realm, and beyond it, all of the old hierarchies dissolve. There, the Wildlings live a hardscrabble existence in small bands, stateless and also more democratic than any other system of governance south of the Wall. "We don't kneel for anyone beyond the wall," Mance Rayder proclaims to Jon Snow upon their first meeting. Politically, Wildlings are the shadow version of Westeros, the "free folk" against the "kneelers" who respect abstract rituals of obedience to authority.

Some scholars have complained that the Wildlings are depicted as lacking attributes of Western Civilization. John Wilkinson writes, "the journalistic and political discourse on 'failed states' (and there are plenty in Westeros) [are] marked as exactly the negation of Western civilization" throughout the series (qtd. in Walton). Wilkinson wants us to consider that the Wildlings and the Dothraki are depicted as uncivilized when compared negatively to the norms of Western Civilization, but this is an overly simplistic critique, I think. In *Game of Thrones*, brutality reigns on both sides of The Wall. Civilization is less a moral distinction than a matter of fashion and custom (the ladies in silk dresses that Ygritte mocks when she is teasing Jon Snow in S3, E7).

What if you shift the lens through which you view the idea of civilization? Insert the new lens—an anarchist one—and a different picture emerges. Writing in *Time* in 2012, Tony Karon aptly compares the Wildlings to 17th-century pirates who had slipped both the moorings and mores of European civilization:

> Wildling culture, as depicted in *Game of Thrones*, shares some features of Caribbean pirate culture in the late 17th century, when deserters from the colonial navies of the time made common cause with freed slaves, indigenous people and others who had no stake in heeding the laws of Europe's distant crowns, and instead struck out for themselves—creating on-ship and onshore communities that transgressed many of the conventions on race, class, gender and property that prevailed in European societies at the time [Karon].

The article (amusingly titled "Where the Wildlings Are: In *Game of Thrones*, the Anarchists Have More Fun") suggests that the Wildlings are less a threat for their raids across the border than for their unwillingness to bend the knee. They flaunt the rules and norms of the Westerosi. They choose their own leaders (Karon). They live successfully, and quite happily, without the state. They call themselves the "free folk," which is a claim few South of the Wall can credibly make. David Graeber, the anarchist anthropologist and key organizer of the Occupy Movement who studied stateless societies in Madagascar, once defined anarchism as simply "living as if you are free." This seems to be the Wildling credo as well.

Game of Thrones teases other alternatives to the state. The Brotherhood without Banners, for example, functions as a kind of mutual aid society fighting for the poor and defending the common folk against the violence and deprivations of the various houses. The Brotherhood reflects the essence of anti-state politics. Like Robin Hood, or Zorro, or the hackers from Anonymous who volunteered to help Arab Spring protestors organize online, they live in the spaces created by the failure of the state to control everything. The "realm" in Westeros, for all of its sound and fury, is a failure, and the "game" an elaborate farce that pretends at the act of governing.

From the Zeitgeist

We can probably credit the German philosopher Hegel with giving birth to the concept of zeitgeist, which means "Spirit of the Times." For Hegel, art was a product of the unique spirit associated with its moment in history (Magee 262). To say that a work of art represents or reflects the zeitgeist is to say that it is saturated with the essence of its historical moment.

Game of Thrones, for better or worse, is part of the American zeitgeist. This may sound like a counterintuitive statement to make about a fantasy TV series set in an imaginary world that is loosely based on a 15th-century English civil war, but *Game of Thrones* lives up to it nevertheless. The series has attracted so much political discourse in large part because so many people see the politics and power relationships of the early 21st century reflected in it. The series was born into a period of revolt against the state, and this spirit of rebellion and disillusionment permeates it. The two years in which it aired its first and second seasons saw the rise and fall of the Occupy Movement in the U.S., the Arab Spring, the Gezi Park protests in Turkey, the "Green Wave" Movement in Iran, and the 2013 Confederation Cup riots in Brazil. It ended in the third year of the Trump presidency, in a period that has seen the rise of authoritarianism around the globe and in the U.S. Historians will likely describe this period as one of worldwide anti-state rebellion, and though *Game of Thrones* was not created with any radical political agenda, its world reflects the disillusionment of the age—with the state, the 1 percent, imperial foreign policy, and the neoliberal world order.

The series ends with a nod to anti-state politics. In the final episode, Westeros appears primed to eventually fall back into civil strife, with the North having been suddenly cleaved from the realm. How long will the other kingdoms accept these terms, or for that matter, Bran Stark as king? The power relationships have not changed fundamentally. When Samwell Tarly suggests that they allow the people to choose their leaders, he is nearly laughed out of the room (S8, E6). The future looks to be as unequal and authoritarian as the recent past.

But in the final scene, a few major characters are able to escape. Jon Snow, having been once again banished to the Night's Watch, is last seen riding out beyond the Wall at the head of a large group of Wildlings Presumably he will become the next King-Beyond-the-Wall, the chosen leader of the Wildlings Arya Stark is last seen sailing West of Westeros on a pirate ship (S8, E6). Some people, at least, will get to live as if they are free.

NOTE

1. In this article, I employ Louis Althusser's definition of "Ideological State Apparatuses" (ISAs) to delineate the nature and scope of the state. Althusser said that in capitalist societies, non-government entities such as churches, schools, the family, courts, political parties, the media, and the arts are used to ensure that fundamental ideas about power relationships are taught and reinforced. In this definition, the state permeates every aspect of human life and permeates the individual unconscious.

WORKS CITED

Blake, John. "How *Game of Thrones* Is like America." *CNN Wire*, 24 May 2014.
Bourne, Randolph Silliman. *Untimely Papers*. New York: BW Huebsch, 1919.
Carpenter, Charli, and Alexander H. Montgomery. "*Game of Thrones*, War Crimes, and the American Conscience." *Foreign Policy*, 24 May 2019, foreignpolicy.com/2019/05/24/game-of-thrones-war-crimes-and-the-american-conscience/.
Cohan, William D. "Three Days That Shook the World." *The Weekend That Changed Wall Street Forever—Dec. 15, 2008*, 15 Dec. 2008, archive.fortune.com/2008/12/12/magazines/fortune/3days_full.fortune/index.htm.
"David Graeber." *Charlie Rose*, Apr. 2006, charlierose.com/videos/10730.
DeFino, Dean J. *The HBO Effect*. New York: Bloomsbury Publishing USA, 2013.
Draper, Hal. *Karl Marx's Theory of Revolution*. Vol. 2. New York: New York University Press, 1978.
Duffy, Nancy Gibbs, and Michael. "Bill Clinton, George W. Bush and the American Game of Thrones." *Time*, 23 Jul. 2015, time.com/magazine/us/3969230/august-3rd-2015-vol-186-no-5-u-s/.
Fukuyama, Francis. *The End of History and the Last Man*. New York: Simon & Schuster, 2006.
"*Game of Thrones*." *The Economist*, vol. 416, no. 8952, Aug. 2015, p. 34.
Ghosh, Bobby. "Iraq's Top Cleric Joins Game of Thrones." *Bloomberg Opinion*, Mar. 2019, p. 1.
Hickey, Walt. "Nine Political Lessons From HBO's Hit Show *Game Of Thrones*." *Business Insider*, 7 Apr. 2013, www.businessinsider.com/political-lessons-game-of-thrones-2013-4.
Karon, Tony. "Where the Wildlings Are: In *Game of Thrones*, the Anarchists Have More Fun." *Time*, 14 May 2012, world.time.com/2012/05/14/where-the-wildlings-are-in-game-of-thrones-the-anarchists-have-more-fun/.
Kropotkin, Peter. *Anarchism: A Collection of Revolutionary Writings*. Chelmsford, MA: Courier Corporation, 2002.
Kurtz, Judy. "Winter Is Here: How *Game of Thrones* Took Over American Politics." *TheHill*, 19 May 2019, thehill.com/blogs/in-the-know/in-the-know/444260-winter-is-here-how-game-of-thrones-took-over-american-politics.
Lawson, Richard. "HBO, Your Liberal Id Is Showing." *The Atlantic*, Atlantic Media Company, 30 Oct. 2013, www.theatlantic.com/culture/archive/2012/06/hbo-your-liberal-id-showing/326810/.
Littleton, Cynthia. "A Medium With a Message: Inside TV's Long History of Tackling Social Issues." *Variety*, 14 Mar. 2017, variety.com/2017/tv/features/tv-social-issues-history-the-defenders-east-side-west-side-1202007945/.
Magee, Glenn Alexander. *The Hegel Dictionary*. London: Bloomsbury Publishing, 2010.

Marshall, Peter H. *Demanding the Impossible: A History of Anarchism*. Oakland, CA: PM Press, 2010.
Nevin, Tom. "South Africa's *Game of Thrones*." *New African*, no. 572, May 2017, p. 14.
Nordland, Rod, et al. "Infighting Among Afghan Warlords Resembles a Destructive *Game of Thrones*." *New York Times*, vol. 166, no. 57694, 19 Aug. 2017, p. A5.
Nussbaum, Emily. "The Political Resonance of *Game of Thrones*." *The New Yorker*, 9 Jul. 2019, www.newyorker.com/magazine/2016/07/04/the-political-resonance-of-game-of-thrones.
"Petition: Remake Game of Thrones Season 8 with Competent Writers." *Change.org*, www.change.org/p/hbo-remake-game-of-thrones-season-8-with-competent-writers.
Richards, Parker. "How *Game of Thrones* Lost Its Way as a Political Drama." *The Atlantic*, Atlantic Media Company, 24 May 2019, www.theatlantic.com/entertainment/archive/2019/05/game-thrones-lost-its-way-political-drama/590260/.
Shidore, Sarang. "What Lies Ahead in East Asia's Game of Thrones? Saudi Arabia's Unprecedented Purge of the High and Mighty Among the Ruling Elite along with Iran's Expanding Sphere of Influence Are Sparking Further Tensions in the Region." *India Today*, vol. 42, no. 49, Dec. 2017, p. 38.
Sinha, Sanskrity. "*Game of Thrones* Sticks George W Bush's Severed Head on Spike, HBO Apologises Amid Backlash [VIDEO]." *International Business Times UK*, 14 June 2012, www.ibtimes.co.uk/hbo-game-thrones-george-bush-severed-head-352216.
Tobin, Jonathan. "Why Daenerys's Transformation Into A Totalitarian Was Perfectly Logical." *The Federalist*, 24 May 2019, thefederalist.com/2019/05/21/daenerys-targaryens-transformation-totalitarian-perfectly-logical/.
Totten, Michael J., and City Journal. "Three Cheers for *Game of Thrones*." *City Journal*, 23 May 2019, www.city-journal.org/game-of-thrones.
Walton, Priscilla L. "'You Win or You Die': The Royal Flush of Power in *Game of Thrones*." *Canadian Review of American Studies*, vol. 49, no. 1, Jan. 2019, pp. 99–114.
Weiss, Joanna. "*Game Of Thrones* Is Our Best Modern Allegory About Politics." *Cognoscenti*, WBUR, 12 Apr. 2019, www.wbur.org/cognoscenti/2019/04/12/game-of-thrones-preview-joanna-weiss.
The White Helmets. Directed by Orlando von Einsiedel. Produced by Joanna Natasegara. Netflix.

Dangerous Nostalgia
Fantasies of Medievalism, Race, and Identity
ROBERT ALLEN ROUSE

In its final season, it was widely reported that *Game of Thrones* was attracting over *one billion* viewers worldwide per episode. While accurate viewing numbers in our increasingly complex and multiple-streaming world are notoriously difficult to nail down, even conjectured numbers like this one speak to a magnitude of influence that dwarfs all but the most widespread of previous cultural phenomena. Consumed globally across a wide range of countries, cultures, and faiths, the HBO juggernaut manifests grimdark melodrama within a fantasy world that is richly and diversely drawn, yet remains problematically nostalgic in its geographical, ethnographic, and racial provenance. The show's nostalgia for a fantasy-medieval world is multifaceted, encompassing social and political structure, the politics of racial stereotypes and gender roles, artisanal material culture, and other aspects of the fantasy-medieval setting. Such nostalgia is part of the wider appeal of medievalesque fiction, TV, and film within our contemporary culture: a phenomenon that is more and more extensively studied by scholars of medievalism. This essay examines this nostalgia by focussing on the ideological nature of the world that the show—and George R.R. Martin—creates and presents to its audience: the lands of Westeros, Essos, and beyond.

The show—and the novels that underlie its vision—engages in world-building on a grand scale, describing and visualizing not only Westeros and Essos—the quotidian West and orientalised East of their world (named Earthos by some in the *Game of Thrones* fandom/cartography community)—but also other, more exotic, lands. At once clichéd and novel, this generically familiar geographic and ethnographic conception of a medieval-fantasy past reveals much about the genre of fantasy in general and *Game of Thrones* in particular. This essay examines the nature, provenance, and contemporary resonances of this ethnographic vision of Martin's world, giving particular attention to the show's dangerous nostalgia for a worldview that is essentially Eurocentric in perspective and ideologically conservative politically, racially, and geographically. The deep-rooted racial and geographical ideologies that underpin the shape and color of the world of *Game of Thrones* are considered not only in terms of their relationship to our popular and scholarly imaginings of our medieval past, but also in relation to the very real deployment of the medieval in the identity politics of the present. The geography of HBO's *Game of Thrones* maps broadly onto the inherited ideas of race and ethnography that are endemic within the fantasy genre, owing debts both to the long history of fantasy worlds that came before, and also to the geopolitics of the contemporary world of Martin and the wider HBO creative team.

Fantastic Places and the Geographic Other

Fantastic places have no underlying reality, and as such their geographies are works of the imagination; their maps are but the lineal manifestations of the flourishes of the author's mind. In fact, fantastic worlds need not have any maps at all, yet they almost invariably do. Open up almost any fantasy novel, and you will be faced with a map in the front of the book, inscribing visibly the author's world-building in all its cartographic glory. It is almost as if fantasy maps stridently decry the very unreality of the worlds that they depict: forests are named, cities are plotted, ruins drawn, and seas charted. The map speaks to our expectation, as modern readers, that places should be mapped visually, laid out for us on an x-y grid governed by the cardinal directions, making themselves legible to our cartographically conditioned minds.

So, if not from a representation of a real world, where do fantasy cartographies and ethnographies arrive? The simplistic answer, of course, is from the hand and mind of their author. But this answer does not suffice, and for fantasy maps we need to look towards a number of important influences. First, the inherited history of cartographical thought in the western imagination; second, the lineage of maps within the fantasy genre; and third, the contemporary influences on the author themselves.

The history of western cartography is obviously an extensive area of research, and one that I don't have the space to rehearse in all its complexity here. However, from its early iteration in Ptolemy's *Geographia* (written c. 150 CE, translated into Arabic in the 9th century and then into Latin in 1406), the western geographic tradition has maintained some important tropes. First is the nature of its orientation: North lies at the top of maps,

East to the right, South to the bottom, and West to the left. Second, Ptolemy also introduced the notion of longitude and latitude, the x-y grid of the modern cartographical consciousness. Third, the tradition of center and margin: as one moves further from the cultural—and thus geographical—center of the map, one moves into increasingly exotic and culturally non-normative lands. Medieval T-O maps traditionally depicted on their outer edge Pliny's monstrous races of classical tradition, such creatures as the one footed sciapods, the man-eating blemmyae, and the lion-headed Donestre (see Friedman for the classic study on this matter). While the classical and medieval trope of the monstrous races holds a complicated relationship to our modern conception of race—which developed primarily in the post-medieval period—the geographical location of these *others* establishes a connection between geography and bodily-identity that still influences writers to this day (Heng). As we shall see, the further they travel in any of the cardinal directions from the center of the narrative (which is, I will argue, Winterfell), the characters experience greater degrees of non-normative culture.

The history of fantasy maps also plays an important role in the geography of Martin's world. In many ways Fantasy, as a genre, begins with the map, or with one map in particular. In J.R.R. Tolkien's *The Hobbit* (1937), when Bilbo travels forth from Bag End, his road may "ever go on and on," but we know where, because Tolkien—from the very first edition—gives us the map. Tolkien's map of Wilderland, from Hobbiton in the west to the Misty Mountains, Mirkwood, and to the Lonely Mountain in the east, establishes an expectation of fantastical cartography in this most itinerary of genres. It also promulgates the basic inherited orientalist model: the West is where Hobbiton and civilization reside, the East is where dragons—fantastic, deadly, and fabulous—dwell. Tolkien's maps have had a profound influence on the genre, creating an expectation for fantastic cartography in the novels and trilogies that have imitated and responded to his work over the decades. Helen Young has gestured towards the difficulty any modern writer of fantasy, creating under an almost Bloomian anxiety of influence, faces when crafting their fantasy world: the geographical models laid down by the important early writers of fantasy resist reinterpretation. It is almost unthinkable to pick up a fantasy novel and find no map inside the front cover, and these maps are, with some notable yet rare exceptions, all of a type. Turning to the world of *A Song of Ice and Fire*, and the maps that it has spawned, we can see the clear lineage of Tolkien's conception of the world: in the west lies Westeros, the home of what passes for civilization in the series; to the east lie the exotic lands, into which Westerosi travelers venture, and where they meet all manner of dangers; and in both maps, dragons lie in the utter east.

Martin's map is also, as it is for any writer, influenced by his own geo-political context. Elements of the foreign policy of the U.S. over the past 30 years can be read in the series' depiction of places such as Slavers' Bay, the Wall, the Free Cities, and Westeros itself. The remainder of this essay will examine the nature of the different regions of the world of *Games of Thrones* in an attempt to reveal the underpinning and unsettling sense of medievalesque nostalgia that it contains. Can a map be racist? As with any long-lived tradition of geo-racial representation, fantasy cartography is suspect when it comes to systemic racism. A tradition that exhibits much of the influence of a figure as racially problematic as Tolkien is bound to have some concerning elements, and the accusations of racial stereotyping and tokenism in HBO's series only further exacerbates the troubling nature of the shape of Westeros, Essos, and beyond.

The East

Essos. The great Eastern continent. The Free Cities. The Dothraki Sea. Slavers' Bay. And beyond to Qarth and Asshai. The lands of Essos are a fantastic pastiche of continental Europe, the Mediterranean, the near, middle, and far east, and the steppes of central Asia. Populated by devious merchants, heartless slavers, hirsute barbarians, dusky maidens, and inscrutable eastern magicians, Essos is to Westeros as the East has always been to Western culture: a dangerous place of slippery morals and sexual deviancy, of luxurious splendour and unthinkable poverty. Evoking both desire and disgust in the Western mind, the East is defined by an almost absurdity of excess, simultaneously attracting and repulsing the viewer.

This image of the East is familiar to us from a long legacy of Western European thought, art, and literature. The medieval *Wonders of the East* tradition—based in the exploits and explorations of Alexander the Great—constructs the East as a place of monstrous races, natural and supernatural marvels, and fabulous riches. From the earliest incarnations of Western identity, the East has haunted the collective imagination as the site and sight of the racial, cultural, and—later—religious *other*. The East has long been that against which the West figures its own identity; that which the West is not, or at least that which it fears to be. Medieval narratives contrast civilized western knights to their giant eastern opponents, avatars of rapacious greed and uncontrolled violence. The most influential theorist on the invention of the East for Western identity purposes was Edward Said, whose *Orientalism* (1978) was both a founding text in the study of post-colonialism and a trenchant reminder of the role that the East had always occupied in the imagination of the West. *Game of Thrones* revels in a form of nostalgic Orientalism that—as we have seen—is a common trope of fantasy-medieval worlds both in terms of their geography and their ethnography, providing its viewers with a world that is reassuringly conventional and familiar, while simultaneously exotic. This nostalgia is just one of the ways in which the series partakes in a desire for a conservative view of global geo-politics, appealing to fantasies of Western political primacy and cultural superiority.

One of the tropes of European Orientalism is the motif of the Western traveler in the East. From the explorations of Alexander the Great, and the late-classical literary tradition that it spawned, to the medieval narratives of *Mandeville's Travels* and the crusade romances, western texts portrayed the East as a cultural *other* against which the western traveler defined their personal and communal identity. For Alexander, and for the western Christians who later appropriated stories of his legendary exploits, the East was a world subject to conquest, incorporated into Alexander's ever-expanding empire until he reached the ultimate ends of the world. Later medieval travelers, such as the fictitious Sir John Mandeville and the heroes of the crusade romances, traverse the East with a more explicit Christian eye, figuring the East as a religious *other* in contrast to their Christian heroes. What these itinerary narratives have in common is the way in which their protagonists *produce*—as Henri Lefebvre terms it in *The Production of Space*—the Eastern space through which they move. The Western observer quite literally—and literarily—records a vision of the East that is constructed from a combination of textually-informed expectation and personal experience, *producing* the East as a product of the Western imagination—a product that is then textually consumed by Western readers and becomes part of the imaginative Western tapestry of the East.

As with these medieval orientalist narratives, our primary experience of Essos comes from the travels of the Westerosi characters who travel through it. First and foremost amongst these is Daenerys Targaryen, a character whose experiences reveal much about the show's imagined East. As the younger sister of Rhaegar and Viserys, she embodies not only the western observer of the East, but simultaneously the vulnerable western woman in the East. As such she becomes subject not only to the traditional identity dynamics of orientalism, but also to the specific threats of eastern sexuality and violence. Sold into marriage, forced to survive first as a wife and then as a leader in her own right within a strange barbarian culture, she eventually brings the East home to Westeros with her Dothraki, Unsullied, and Dragons. Throughout her narrative, Daenerys stands as our most important Westerosi traveler and observer of Essos, and her adventures reveal much about the western view of the East.

Once Were Khals:
Sexual Barbarianism and the East

Daenerys's first real encounter with Essos, after her years of exile in Pentos, is when she is sold into marriage by her brother Viserys. As part of the deal brokered by Illyrio Mopatis with Khal Drogo, the marriage would provide Viserys with Dothraki forces to pursue his claims to the Iron Throne. The Dothraki, inhabiting the steppe lands of the Dothraki Sea, are broadly modeled on Western fantasies of the Mongols: described as a horde (a term taken in part from the Mongolian term *ordo*, encampment), the Dothraki are a nomadic horse fetishizing culture that exists by raiding their neighbours and fighting amongst themselves. Chief amongst their many violent qualities is a type of sexual barbarism that summons forth the long-held fears of Western culture of the sexual prowess and rapacious nature of the East. This racialized threat, famously parodied in the words of Cleavon Little's Sheriff Bart in Mel Brooks' *Blazing Saddles*—"where the white women at?"—is one that has long been operative in the construction of both foreign and domestic racial *others* in American white culture, and HBO's presentation of the diminutive blond Daenerys's marriage night with Khal Drogo plays on these deeply-held dark fears (S1, E1).

As a part of a nostalgia for the fantasy-medieval past, the image of the sexually violent barbarian *other* is a powerful part of the construction of western—and Westerosi—masculine identity. The rape and abduction of noble western women by eastern men is a common trope of a wide range of medieval—and more recent—western literature, with the figure of the western knight—or modern equivalent—called upon for either rescue or revenge. In *Game of Thrones*, however, Daenerys is not saved by a western knight—although Jorah Mormont attempts to do so on a number of occasions, before ultimately sacrificing his life to save her in "The Long Night" (S8, E3)—but rather by taking on the role of another common avatar of Orientalism: the civilizing white savior. As we will see, this role defines much of Daenerys's interaction with the East, and it begins in a personal sense with her attempts to civilize her barbaric husband.

Daenerys's marriage night concludes with Drogo consummating their marriage in the Dothraki way, in the manner of a stallion on a mare. The nature of this consummation—being either consensual or rape depending on the book or the TV series—is one of cross-cultural shock. Traumatized by her wedding night, Daenerys seeks the advice of her servant Doreah on how to please her new husband. In a discussion that revolves around the concept of culturally specific sexual mores, Doreah advises Daenerys to take some agency in their sexual encounters, challenging her to be different: "If he wanted the Dothraki way, why did he marry you?" Consequently, in their next intimate encounter, Daenerys tells Drogo "no" when he goes to mount her, instead telling him that "tonight I would look upon your face" (S1, E2). Daenerys's literal sexual reorientation of her encounters with Drogo reconfigures their relationship into one in which she is accorded the respect and love that she expects from a marriage, within the possibilities of Dothraki culture. Daenerys here civilizes the savage, echoing a role of western white women in intercultural narratives that has a long provenance in western narratives of the East.

This role as a white savior only goes so far when it comes to sexuality in the series. When Daenerys attempts to extend her civilizing influence from the personal to the public, she sets off a chain of events that leads to tragedy, death, and despair. As Drogo's *khalasar* attacks a village of sheep-herders in Lhazar, his warriors begin to rape some of the female captives. Daenerys, coming across this scene, orders the women to be taken under her protection as Drogo's *khaleesi*, and later tells them that if they "wish to mount them, let them take them for wives" (S1, E8). By seeking to reform the public sexual behaviour of the Dothraki—as she has done with the personal behaviour of Drogo—she causes a rift within the masculine culture of Drogo's *khalasar*, leading to the deadly duel between Drogo and Mago. Wounded in this fight on behalf of Daenerys's honor, Drogo is convinced by Daenerys to accept the help of Mirri Maz Duur, one of the women that she has saved from Mago, who claims to be a godswife and a healer. Despite the objections of his bloodriders, Drogo accepts her offer, but despite her ministrations—or perhaps because of them—he continues to sicken. This leads to her offer of healing via blood magic, Drogo's death, and the death of their unborn child. Durr, as it turns out, has taken her revenge upon both Drogo and his unborn son.

Daenerys, grieving the loss of her child and the incapacitation of Drogo, is stunned by what Durr has done, and cries that her child was innocent. Durr replies: "Innocent? He would have been the stallion who mounts the world. Now he will burn no cities." In response to Daenerys's retort that she saved Durr, Durr replies: "Saved me? Three of those riders had already raped me before you saved me, girl.... So ... tell me again exactly what it was that you saved?" (S1, E10).

Against the furious anguish of the collective trauma voiced by Durr, Daenerys's attempts to play the role of the white savior leads to disaster. Her attempt to enforce a western sexual morality on the men of Drogo's *khalasar* is a misguided attempt to civilize (in a Western sense) that which will not be civilized. As Jorah Mormont warns her, this is not the Dothraki way, and not the Dothraki culture. Daenerys's tragic failure to understand the East in this episode prefigures the more significant failures that lie ahead of her as she attempts to transform Eastern society in Slavers' Bay.

Breaker of Chains: Slaver's Bay and the Crucible of the White Savior

One defining feature of Essos for the Westerosi traveler is slavery. Slavery—as the story of the exile of Jorah Mormont reminds us—is viewed as a terrible inhuman crime in the Seven Kingdoms and stands as one of the key markers of Westerosi identity. As we've seen above, Daenerys's first attempts at abolishing sexual slavery turn into a personal disaster for her and her family. This western abhorrence of slavery is explored more fully in Daenerys's adventures in Slaver's Bay, where her conquest and rule of Meereen flounders upon the rocks of her Westerosi principles and the crashing seas of her ignorance of how the East operates.

In the final act of Season One, Daenerys ascends Drogo's funeral pyre, having promised that she will lead the remaining Dothraki and their slaves as their *khaleesi*, freeing them and exhorting them to throw off their slave collars. This moment of fiery emancipation sets up a working principle for Daenerys's rule in the East; she will rule through the love of her people, and not through their servitude. Over the next few seasons she embarks on a very personal campaign of conquering masters and then freeing slaves from a number of the cities of Slaver's Bay.

The first city to fall to the Mother of Dragons is Astapor. Convinced by Jorah Mormont to travel to Astapor to purchase an army of the legendary slave warriors, The Unsullied, Daenerys launches into a passionate mission to free the slaves of the region. After taking possession of the Unsullied, and enraged by both the slavery that she witnesses and the disrespect of the Good Masters, she turns both her new army and her dragons upon the city, sacking it and freeing its remaining slaves. After the battle Daenerys grants the Unsullied their freedom: "Today you are free.... Will you fight for me? As free men?" (S3, E4). To a man they accept her offer, and take their place at the heart of her forces. From here she travels to Yunkai and defeats the Yunkai'i by having her men sneak into the city, aided by the inevitably smitten Daario Naharis. Yunkai is forced to renounce slavery and free their slaves, many of whom join Daenerys's army, calling her Mhysa ("Mother" in Old Ghiscari) (S3, E10).

Once the slaves of Yunkai are freed, Daenerys moves on to Meereen, the city of the Great Harpy. En route, they pass the bodies of 163 crucified slave children, an act intended to intimidate her army of ex-slaves. Outside the walls, she addresses Meereen, proclaiming the progress of her emancipation project: first Astapor and then Yunkai have fallen to her civilizing surge, and now Meereen will be next. As with Yunkai, Meereen falls to subterfuge as Grey Worm and a select group of the Unsullied enter the city through the sewers and lead the slaves of Meereen in a revolt against their masters. As revenge for the children, Daenerys has 163 of the masters crucified, and declares herself Queen of the city.

Her rule of the city, however, presents Daenerys with a much more complex set of problems than her conquest did. Like many occupying forces, her rule is beset by civil unrest, revenge killings, rebellions, and economic woes. There are two important contexts for understanding Daenerys's emancipation campaign: one historical and one contemporary, and both specific to the U.S. origins of the series. For U.S. viewers of the series, the spectre of slavery looms large in the representation of the East in *Game of Thrones*. Echoes of post-civil war reconstruction resound in the complaints of the starving now-workless freed slaves, and the pleas of the fighting slaves to reopen the fighting pits. Much like the post-bellum Southern U.S., Meereen presents Daenerys and her advisors with a systemic problem: how do you restructure a society and an economy that was so dependent on the free labor of a slave population? Making the situation even more fraught is the destruction of an Eastern political system by a Western outsider, an act that evokes the experiences of the U.S. in Iraq and elsewhere after the second Gulf War—and in the years since. Regime change, as Daenerys discovers, is easy; replacing the structure of that regime with a system that is sustainable is the hard part.

Love—both motherly and erotic—is her answer to what replaces slavery here; the white savior replaces one structure of servitude with another, this time based on a cult-of-personality not unfamiliar to modern students of despotism. While Daenerys is no Vladimir Putin or Kim Jong-un, her followers' loyalty to her relies upon the same sense of personal attachment as we see in other personality-cult dictatorships. And when the charismatic leader is removed—or flies off on a dragon—all societal hell tends to break loose.

While the HBO's series somewhat neatly concludes the Slaver's Bay campaign by having Daenerys place Daario and the Second Sons in charge of Meereen when she leaves for Westeros, outlawing slavery permanently and renaming Slaver's Bay as The Bay of Dragons, one holds some doubt as to the permanence of this situation. The series turns its attention elsewhere, just as one president or another may reorient foreign policy, but the problems left in the wake of Western-actioned regime change tend to linger in the East.

Daenerys's adventures in the East not only partake in a nostalgia for the sexualized, exotic East, but more problematically a nostalgia for the fantasy of the white savior. By resolving so neatly the problematic aftermath of Western intervention and regime change in Slaver's Bay, the show holds that the West—in the form of the personality-cult of Daenerys Stormborn, Breaker of Chains—can bring civilization and morality to the East, bringing it out of the dark past of slavery into the enlightened present of

Western emancipation. As geo-political events of the past few decades have reminded us again and again, this is indeed pure fantasy.

An understanding of Daenerys's adventures in Slaver's Bay in these terms perhaps helps make sense of her descent into monomaniacal tyranny in the final season of the HBO series. For those who had been watching carefully, this came as no surprise. Despite the fan outrage at this turn in her character and destiny, one has to remember that she is the daughter of a long line of inbred nobility who were dedicated to preserving genetic purity of their very white and very blond bloodline. One might even argue—if we credit the showrunners with such a degree of foresight—that the HBO series lures the unwary viewer into a false sense of nostalgia for the white savior narrative, only to reveal in the final season that such narratives ultimately underpin fascist authoritarianism.

The South

Like many fantasy worlds that follow the established Eurocentric model, Martin's Earthos gestures towards a little known and thinly described southern continent, named by the Westerosi as Sothoryos. Lying far to the southeast, and largely unexplored by those of the west, Sothoryos is home, as the prevailing geographic model suggests, to races of dark-skinned peoples who appear in Essos and Westeros primarily as a result of the translocation of peoples caused by the raids of Essosi slave-traders. Broadly analogous geographically, culturally, and racially to Africa, Sothoryos operates in Martin's imagination in a similar way: as a storehouse of exotic, material, and human raw material for the more developed peoples of the east and the west.

The Summer Islands

The most important characters that we encounter from Sothoryos are from the Summer Islands, an archipelago lying to the northwest of the continent. While the Islands are separate from the main continent, they are contiguous in racial profile, representing a more accessible part of the south. The figures who hail from the Islands signify the exotic, dangerous world of the African continent in the European imagination. In the HBO series, Salladhor Saan, for example, represents simultaneously both the late-medieval and early modern reputation of the Barbary Coast of North Africa, and the romanticised image of the black freed-slave pirates of the Caribbean. A figure of mystery, wealth, sexual licentiousness, and romance (at least in his own mind), Saan combines the seductive draw of the orientalised figure with the sexual rapaciousness of the European idea of the African. Although Saan has his origins in the Summer Islands, he lives and sails out of Lys, embodying the movement of black bodies from the Summer Islands and Sothoryos to other places, and the hybridized identities that such movement necessarily produces.

Xaro Xhoan Daxos, the wealthy merchant who attempts to acquire Dany's dragons in Qarth during Season 2, is another example of such a hybridized black body. Known as the wealthiest man in Qarth, he is a member of the ruling council of The Thirteen, but—notably—is the only non-hereditary member, and the only black member. While he is otherwise integrated into the society in which he lives and thrives, Xaro's racial otherness continues to mark him as an outsider, a figure for whom the geo-racial inertia of Martin's fantasy world persists.

The final two characters, Grey Worm and Missandei, have attracted a great deal of commentary given their roles in Daenerys's entourage. Grey Worm, taken as a child from the Summer Islands remembers nothing of them, evoking the experience of many black slaves in the Americas. Missandei is from Naath, an isle east of the Summer Islands, and while she remembers more of her homeland, she—like Grey Worm—is fully assimilated into the role of slave. As Shiloh Carroll notes, Grey Worm (and the other Unsullied) and Missandei continue to serve Daenerys "because they know no other life." Both are offered freedom, but—as I discussed earlier in this essay—freedom is often problematic for slaves who have been so since their youth.

Whether slave, pirate, or always-exotic merchant, the black bodies of HBO's *Game of Thrones* are enmeshed in a disturbing nostalgia the Martin's worldview presents. Although not voiced in the HBO series, this ideology is found in Martin's novels. Carroll notes that, in *A Dance with Dragons*, Tyrion Lannister states that all slaves are slaves through choice: "There has never been a slave who did not choose to be a slave. […] Their choice may be between bondage and death, but the choice is always there" (Martin). This ideology, Carroll argues, suggests a medieval sense of the rightful place of different peoples in the ordered world. Voiced by a nobleman, the idea that slaves must be slave, as much as smallfolk must be smallfolk, adheres disturbing to medieval ideas of the divinely ordered three estates. To find this expressed in a novel, and a major HOV series, in the 21st century is a dangerous nostalgia indeed.

Dorne: Westeros's Intimate Southern Other

Mat Hardy has written convincingly on the connection between Dorne and a mode of fantastic Orientalism that figures the Dornish as a people characterised by the cliched notion of Arabian culture. Read primarily through the Victorian legacy of writers such as Sir Richard Burton, Hardy's reads Dorne as what one might call a geographically intimate other: one that lives alongside the dominant culture rather than being located in a distant eastern land.

George R.R. Martin tells us that Dorne was inspired by "Moorish Spain, Palestine, and Wales" ("Historical Influences"). While Hardy's reading concentrates on the Moorish Spain and Palestine influences, playing down Martin's stated Welsh and Cornish influences, I want to re-center these two Celtic regions in a reading of Dorne that adheres to Westeros's geo-political resemblance to medieval Britain. Just as the other seven kingdoms bear a loose resemblance to the kingdoms of the Anglo-Saxon heptarchy, politically Dorne resembles the liminal place of Cornwall—even more so than Wales—in the politics of the realm. Cornwall was to medieval England as Dorne is to Westeros: an intimate other that performs a similar role in the identity politics of the realm. Just as the Arabic orientalism of the Dornish marks them as out as culturally other, within their own islands the medieval English found a cultural other of long familiarity: the Celts. From the earliest arrival of the English, the Celtic population had been either subsumed or marginalized, both culturally and geographically. The role of the insular Celts as other manifests linguistically: the name Welsh has its origins in the Old English *wealas*—also present in Cornwall (*weall*)—literally meaning foreigners or strangers.[1] The cultural otherness—and their treacherous nature towards the English—of the Cornish is illustrated in Sir Thomas Malory's seminal retelling of the Arthurian legends *Morte D'Arthur*, and in particular the *Tale of Tristram*. There are two major manifestations of Cornish propensity for treachery in the *Morte*: first, the involvement of King Idres in Lot's first rebellion and second, the continued problem of King Mark's relationship with Arthur's realm. Mark is *a fayre speker, and false thereundir* (Malory 365). Moreover, he is the *shamfullist knight of a kynge that is now lyvynge* (355). Idres and Mark stand as literary examples representing this characteristic of the Cornish that seems to have been popular in medieval literature. I have argued elsewhere that Martin seems to be well aware of the elegiac tone of Malory's account of the fall of the Arthurian world, an account mediated through Malory's own experience of the Wars of the Roses, and his use of the Wars of the Roses seems colored heavily by Malory's sombre tone.

Embodied most strongly in the HBO series by Oberyn Martell—and his illegitimate daughters—the intimate otherness of the Dornish acts to remind Westeros of its own internal identity divisions: while the clearly marked racial and cultural difference of figures from Essos and the Summer Islands is readily legible for the characters of The Seven Kingdoms,

Dorne reminds us that each of the Kingdoms has its own unique culture, despite the fiction of the unity that is the Iron Throne. Significantly for the racial politics of the HBO series, while Dorne remains an integral part of the Seven Kingdoms, its cultural and racial otherness sidelines it and its compelling inhabitants, making them a much less important element of the plot than in Martin's novels. Oberyn Martell exists in the HBO series only to provide a lascivious taste of intimate appeal of Dorne, before being crushed under the mailed fingers of the dominant western medievalesque culture, and Ellaria and his daughters meet similarly gruesome ends at the hands of Euron Greyjoy and Cersei. Ultimately the role of the Dornish in the HBO series is to titillate, tempt, and entertain, before being cast to the side before the more significant members of the Westerosi political system contest the eighth and final season.

The North

Fantasy worlds tend to imagine the north very much as our real-world does: as a place of ice and snow, strange beasts and stranger people. The North in *Game of Thrones* is a complex place. The narrative starts and—in many ways—ends in the North, and the central protagonists, the Starks, have the North at the heart of their identity. But the show has not one, but many different Norths. There is the once and future Kingdom of the North, ruled by the Starks; there is the North of the Night's Watch, Brandon's Gift, and the Wall; and then there is the North beyond the Wall, home to Wildlings giants, and much worse. And, just like the show's East, The North(s) of Westeros are constructed through a dangerous sense of nostalgia.

Winterfell and the Starks: The North as Center

From the very beginning of the series, the Stark family members are cast as our central protagonists, and they are synonymous with the North as a place. This positions the North—and its values—as the default (white) identity for the series and its characters; all others are judged in comparison, and—most often—found wanting. This role of the North gestures towards a form of ethnic and cultural purity: as we are often reminded, the Starks trace their heritage back to the First Men. They still worship the Old Gods, and are as embedded in the landscape as are the graven sculptures of their dead in the crypts below Winterfell. The north is a place where not only the Old Gods remain, but also the old structures of society: men live by their word, and honor is still held paramount amongst the ruling families of the North. On numerous occasions in the series the leaders of the North take principled actions over wise ones, often at great cost, but they remain true to their nature.

The nostalgia for the pure, manly, honorable, and democratic North that we find in the series is one that is vulnerable to fantasies of white supremacy. In a series that is very white, the whitest of the characters are those with whom we are most encouraged to identify: the Starks—Ned, Cat, Robb, Sansa, Arya, Bran, Rickon—and Jon Snow. Whiteness is centered in the series, and nowhere more so than in the Starks. As the key protagonists they are the normative bodies and dominant culture of the series, they attract our sympathies in their sufferings, and our joy in their successes. In Ned we see the show's first great tragic death, soon followed by his wife and oldest son, and in Arya, Bran, Sansa, and Jon we witness the triumphant end.

An Old Freedom in the Woods: Fictions of Democracy

The men of the North choose their Kings. As we move through the HBO series, we see this principle of freely chosen leadership played out in various parts of the North. Robb Stark, and later his bastard half-brother (actually cousin) Jon Snow are both acclaimed King in the North; the Night's Watch elect their own Lord Commanders (again, Jon Snow); and the Wildlings choose their own King-Beyond-The-Wall. In comparison with the Southerners of Westeros (and everyone south of the Neck is a Southerner to the men of the North), who are critiqued for their servile manner and feudal social structure, the men of the North hold themselves to be free.

This idea of a predisposition towards a more democratic system of rule in The North—and increasingly so as one travels further north—has a long and troubling history as an idea in the Western world. Eighteenth- and nineteenth-century politicians both in Britain and North America looked back to their Germanic ancestors and saw in their rudimentary political structures of Anglo-Saxon *witangemots* and Icelandic *things* a form of "democracy in the woods": a lineage of a race who—in contrast to other races—choose their leaders (Carroll 117–18). While this idea is deeply suspect as a reading of history, it has been even more problematic as a political idea in the centuries since, positing the Anglo-Saxon white races of Britain and North America as the possessors of a historical claim to democratic process and privilege. This sense of nostalgia for a never-existing fantasy of medieval polity remains powerful even to this day amongst white nationalists and other alt-right groups.

In *Game of Thrones*, we can see this sense of comparative freedom being deployed in the service of geographical and racial differentiation: the proto-democratic North is contrasted with the determinedly Feudal South of Westeros, which is then contrasted with the despotic East. This subscribes to another invidious myth: the 19th-century theory of developmental societal anthropology which held that every society would move through the same series of developmental steps, from barbarism to a classical period, then on through a medieval period to a renaissance, before finally entering the modern world. This theory was used by nineteenth-century colonial bureaucrats to classify the cultures of their respective empires into developmental stages, with often dire results for the subject cultures. The show's tacit endorsement of such a geopolitical schema, as we have seen in the civilizing of Slavers' Bay, is another aspect of its problematic nostalgia for a simpler worldview.

The Watcher on the Wall

The Wall dominates the North in *Game of Thrones*. The series starts with an ill-fated expedition north of the wall into the lands of the Wildlings, and an encounter with the ultimate *other* of the series, the White Walkers. From here on the Wall stands as a bulwark against that which is outside of Westerosi society, both the known and the legendary fears of the monstrous. The Wall draws its historical and geographical inspiration from the Roman Hadrian's Wall in the north of England, which stood between the relative civilization of Roman Britain and the lands of the Picts. As an aspect of historical nostalgia, the Wall gestures towards a time when borders were known, impervious, and well-maintained. Beyond the wall lies the barbarians, and the fantasy of a 700-foot-tall wall will keep them where they belong.

Or so one would imagine. As the series moves into its final seasons, the Wall becomes less a barrier and more a battleground as first the Wildlings and then the Army of the White Walkers breach it and move south. Here the series has the good sense to dispel its own nostalgia for the security of walls and critique their use. Walls, of course, are not just historical influences for Martin. We have to remember that Martin has written much of his series based in Santa Fe, New Mexico. Given his own geography, and the politics of the past decade or so, questions of walls are live issues. The most pertinent contemporary wall debate for Martin is, of course, the wall that lies down route 25, between El Paso and the Mexican city of Juárez. Reading Martin's Wall in the context of the ever-increasing "build the wall" rhetoric of the Mexican border suggests an encouraging nuancing of wall-nostalgia as the series progresses. The wall fails, as all walls fail, and the answers to how to deal with the *other* on the other side of the wall is to be found in negotiation and collaboration (with the Wildlings) and in a society coming together in common purpose (against the great enemy of the White Walkers). I'll discuss this last aspect more fully later in this essay, but for now let's discuss the Wildlings.

At the beginning of the series we are shown a view of the Wildlings that represents them as barbarians, eaters of men and savage warriors. While much of this remains true, the complexity and humanity of the Wildlings becomes evident first through the travels of Jon Snow beyond the wall, and later when the Wildlings ally with the Night's Watch after the defeat of Mance Rayder. As we get to know figures such as Tormund Giantsbane, we begin to see the Wildlings rehabilitated into the wider world of Westeros. Fleeing from the White Walkers, the Wildlings can be read as an analogy for environmental refugees (here reading the coming Long Winter in the place of our own climate change). Walls do not, cannot, and should not keep such fellow humans out, the show could be seen to argue, undercutting the nostalgia for the Wall that the series begins with.

The Middle

What lies at the center? Identity is, so often, defined through opposition. What we are is easiest to define by what we are not. This utility of the real, or most often the imagined, *other*, lies at the heart of group identity politics. For someone writing in Canada today, who is not Canadian, Canadian identity appears at best fragmentally construed: when I ask my students what it is to be Canadian, they hastily collect such concepts as multiculturalism, bilingualism, and tolerance—none of which stand up to much sustained scrutiny as national identifiers—before falling back on clichés of an imagined national identity such as Hockey, Moose, Winter Weather, and the Royal Canadian Mounted Police. But what really defines Canadians, as it has since at least 1812, is that they are not Americans (and by this I mean the U.S.). The U.S. stands as the Canadian *other*, acting as a key component of Canada's national identity construction.

Benedict Anderson tells us that group identity is most easily and powerfully articulated in opposition to just such an *other*, and this holds true for Martin's Westeros as it does in our own, somewhat more real, world. While the bloody civil war of the Five Kings reminds us at every step that a Man of the North is very different from a Lannister, and a Dornishman is the antithesis of a Knight of the Vale, the Seven Kingdoms come together, figuratively and then literally, in response to external threats.

In the White Walkers, the ultimate *other*, we see the men and women of Westeros come together as one (with the exception of Cersei, who has, like Lady Macbeth, thrown off the weakness of her shared humanity). In the redemptive returns of Jaime Lannister and Theon Greyjoy to the fold, the common shared identity of Westerosi overcomes the regional and family differences that have so divided the land since the beginning of the series. In the casual jokes and camaraderie that the disparate figures engage in before the battle we see their cultural commonality come to the fore. No longer are these Lannisters and Starks, Wildlings and Ladies of the Stormlands: all are now warriors of Westeros, facing the ultimate threat together.

As the battle unfolds, however, we see the removal of key non-western elements from the combined forces, such as the Dothraki. The "charge of the light-bearing brigade" exit of so many Dothraki from the series attracted a good deal of critical commentary in the days following the release of "The Long Night" (S8, E3). One of the ways to make sense of their odd tactical sacrifice is to see it in the service of Westerosi identity politics: the tragic glory of the defeat of the White Walkers is required, by the logic of identity, to return us to the core identity politics of the series. In the key figures of the battle, we see—both in those who survive and in those who sacrifice themselves for the continued existence of Westeros—a return to the white core of Westerosi identity. Western swords (and a knife) save the West, not Eastern dragons or Dothraki bloodriders.

In the embodiment of the final scene, we see the revenger's weapon that is Arya—forged in Western civil tragedy and honed through Eastern discipline—return us to the origins with a literal knife through the heart of ultimate *otherness*. Westerosi identity, as it has been throughout Martin's imagined history of the peoples of Westeros, is articulated through violence, re-inscribing the supremacy of the white North at the center of Westerosi identity.

Conclusion: Dangerous Nostalgia

Game of Thrones plays out across a fantasy landscape that is at once fantastical and familiar. Structured around long-held western notions of geographically inscribed racial and cultural difference, the series subscribes to a nostalgia for a world that centers identity in the white normative bodies of the Starks of Winterfell. Traveling further into this fantasy world we see a conservative concept of geographical distribution of race and *otherness*, and a nostalgia for the civilizing influence of white bodies as they traverse the world. Racial issues have beset the series throughout its 8-season run, with justified questions about representation, diversity, and what kind of fantasy world that HBO was presenting to its viewers. While some defended the series by invoking a sense of neomedieval reality (i.e., that the real middle ages were largely white), this idea can be countered by pointing out first that they were not (medieval Europe was quite racially diverse), and second that *this is a fantasy series*, and therefore it can create whatever world it wishes. The show very well could have subverted the traditional notion that power and identity are inherently tied to geographical conceptions of race, but it did not. The fact that the series remained doggedly monochrome in its lead characters and its stereotypical depiction of culture, speaks to a dangerous nostalgia for a world in which whiteness remains the default palette.

NOTE

1. *wealh* (a) m. (gs. Weales) foreigner, stranger, slave: Briton, Welshman (J. R. Clark-Hall, *A Concise Anglo-Saxon Dictionary* [Toronto: University of Toronto Press, 1984]). Wealum is also used to describe the Celtic Cornish—in the *Anglo-Saxon Chronicle* account for the year AD 981 there is a description of the Danish raids of that year on Padstow (Sancte Petroces stow) and the rest of Devon and Cornwall: *Her on þis geare wæs Sancte Petroces stow forhergod, and þy ilcan geare wæs micel hearm gedon gehwær be þam særiman ægþer ge on Defenum ge on Wealum.*

WORKS CITED

Brooks, Mel (writer and producer). *Blazing Saddles*. 1974.
Carroll, Shiloh. *Medievalism in A Song of Ice and Fire & Game of Thrones*. Woodbridge: Boydell and Brewer, 2018.
Clark-Hall, J.R. *A Concise Anglo-Saxon Dictionary*. Toronto: University of Toronto Press, 1984.
Friedman, John Block. *The Monstrous Races in Medieval Art and Thought*. Syracuse: Syracuse University Press, 2000.
Hardy, Mat. "The Crack of Dorne" in *Vying for the Iron Throne: Essays on Power, Gender, Death and Performance in HBO's Game of Thrones*, edited by Lindsey Mantoan and Sara Brady. Jefferson, NC: McFarland, 2018.
Heng, Geraldine. *The Invention of Race in the European Middle Ages*. Cambridge: Cambridge University Press, 2018.
"Historical Influences for Dorne," *The Citadel: So Spake Martin*, 29 Feb. 2000, http://www.westeros.org/Citrael/SSM/Entry/Historical_Influences_For_Dorne/.
Kaufman, Amy, and Paul. B. Sturtevant. *The Devil's Historians*. Toronto: University of Toronto Press, 2020.
Lefebvre, Henri. *The Production of Space*. New York: Wiley, 1992.
Malory, Thomas. *Malory: Works*, edited by Eugène Vinaver, 2nd ed. New York: Oxford University Press, 1971.
Martin, George R.R. *A Song of Ice and Fire*. New York: Bantam Books, 1996–2011.
Moseley, Charles (trans). *Mandeville's Travels*. New York: Penguin, 2005.
Ptolemy. *Geographia*. New York: Cosimo, 2011.
Rouse, Robert, and Cory Rushton. "Broken Bodies, Broken Kingdoms: The Revolutionary Failure of *A Game of Thrones*" in *The Keeper of Our Stories*, edited by Anna Czarnowus and Carolyne Larrington. London: Bloomsbury Publishing, 2021.
Said, Edward. *Orientalism*. New York: Pantheon Books, 1978.
Tolkien, J.R.R. *The Hobbit*. Crows Nest: George Allen & Unwin, 1937.
Young, Helen. *Race and Popular Fantasy Literature: Habits of Whiteness*. London: Routledge, 2015.

Game of Victims and Monsters
Representation of Sexual and Female Violence

Sylwia Borowska-Szerszun

Inspired by George R.R. Martin's bestselling yet unfinished fantasy series *A Song of Ice and Fire* (1996–), HBO's *Game of Thrones* (2011–2019) has become an international cultural phenomenon. Set in the imaginary world of Westeros and Essos, the series combines historical inspirations with the elements of fantasy in an epic-scale tale of political intrigue and dynastic struggles for power, epitomized by the Iron Throne. Usually praised for diverting from a typical high fantasy pattern of the battle between good and evil, featuring a range of multi-dimensional characters, and subverting the expectations of readers and viewers, both the novels and the TV show have received their share of criticism for the amount of violence they contain. When asked to comment on the representation of violence, especially sexual abuse, in *A Song of Ice and Fire*, George R.R. Martin has continuously repeated that it is meant to provide the story with an aura of historical realism. As he explains in one of the interviews, "[a]n artist has an obligation to tell the truth. My novels are epic fantasy, but they are inspired by and grounded in history. […] History is written in blood. The atrocities in *A Song of Ice and Fire*, sexual and otherwise, pale in comparison to what can be found in any good history book" (Itzkoff). The creators of *Game of Thrones*, David Benioff and D.B. Weiss, seem to have taken the authorial intent seriously, and the TV show has in fact become notorious for its reliance on vivid and gruesome details of violent deaths, torture, mutilation and rape. Yet, despite Martin's attempts to dismiss criticism with the claims of historical authenticity, both *A Song of Ice and Fire* and *Game of Thrones* remain strikingly presentist in their engagement with contemporary socio-political problems, including and frequently conflating the issues related to power, violence, gender and sexuality.

Graphic portrayals of violence abound in contemporary popular culture and are obviously not exclusive to *Game of Thrones*. The increasing popularity of violent entertainment in various media (film, TV, video games) suggests that "audiences both decry and demand violent media, and producers deliver on these demands" (Tamborini et al. 100), which raises concerns about the consequences of this phenomenon. My discussion of *Game of Thrones* is informed by a view that TV shows, like other media, influence our perception of and attitudes towards violence, although not necessarily in terms of explaining the cause and effect relationship between them. As M. Gigi Durham argues:

> While the media may not cause our behaviors, they are culture mythmakers: they supply us, socially, with ideas and scripts into our consciousness over time, especially when the myths are constantly recirculated in various forms. [...] They can reinforce certain social patterns and trends, and invalidate others. They can gradually and insidiously shape our ways of thinking, our notions of what is normal and what is deviant, and our acceptance of behaviors and ideas that we see normalized on television, in films, and in other forms of popular culture [Durham 148–49].

Watching a fantasy story of political intrigue and following the plots of various characters' rise to or fall from power, we are also watching a story of violence inherent in their struggles. Violence is a part and parcel of life in Westeros and Essos for men, women and children alike; it is also an integral element of political, religious, social and personal power. It affects both major and minor characters, who at different points of the narrative might change from its victims to perpetrators—a tactic that not only purposefully blurs the distinction between the "good" and the "bad" characters, but also has implications for the ways in which gendered power relations are established or subverted.

Long after its finale, *Game of Thrones* haunts its viewers with memories of the Red Wedding massacre (S3, E9), the dehumanizing torture of Theon Greyjoy (S3, E7), or the rape of Sansa Stark (S5, E6)—to mention just a few vivid examples. Each of these scripts of violence resonates with what we consider acceptable or deviant, reflects wider social and cultural patterns, and shapes our cognitive frameworks, which are "(re)produced in and through the stories we tell ourselves and others" (Shepherd 3). Situating *Game of Thrones* within the contexts of the patterns characteristic for neoliberalism and its power structures, Stéphanie Genz examines the links between the spectacle of cruelty in the TV show and "neoliberal culture of violence," which "is unconstrained by a moral compass and shaped by a demand for intense excitement, particularly in the form of extreme images of torture and death that become 'banally familiar'" (245). In consequence, the images of pain, cruelty and abuse can be perceived as "digestible spectacles for collective pleasure," inextricably linked with growing "apathy and desensitization to violence" (245) on the part of the audience. Drawing on these assumptions, in this essay I consider questions about the function of the tropes of violence for the narrative of *Game of Thrones*: are they simply employed to attract and shock the viewers or do they have ideological implications related to gendered power structures and their possible subversion? To narrow down the scope of the analysis, this essay will focus on female characters only, examining them as both victims and perpetrators of violence. Following the storylines and analyzing characterization of the most prominent women of the series, including Daenerys Targaryen, Cersei Lannister, Sansa and Arya Stark, Brienne of Tarth, and Yara Greyjoy, I will focus on two aspects—sexual and female violence—to discuss the gendered power patterns of *Game of Thrones*.

Perhaps, the most controversial aspect of *Game of Thrones* is the conflation of violence and sex, evident in the show's representation of rape, which disturbed the fans and the critics alike. Their critical voices add to the ongoing discussion about "the ethics of reading and watching representations of rape"—focusing on whether they can be interpreted as "bearing witness to a terrible crime" or rather as "participating in a shameful voyeuristic activity" (Horeck vi). The intense reactions to certain episodes of reviewers and fans imply that the manner in which sexual violence is represented on TV matters, probably even more than in the case of the novels due to distinct modes of the audience's engagement with literary and audiovisual texts. What remains in the sphere of imagination in the case of literature is explicitly displayed on screen with "its inescapable materiality, its incarnated, fleshly, enacted characters, its real locales and palpable props, its carnality and visceral shocks to the nervous system" (Stam 6). While literature relies on telling and the readers building their image of the fictional world through the mind's eye, TV depends on showing and "immers[ing] us through the perception of the aural and the visual" (Hutcheon and O'Flynn 22), which results in a greater proximity of the showing-viewing mode and makes it more difficult for viewers to distance themselves from the violence of the scene. This is not to say that the depiction of sexual violence in literary texts does not matter. Elsewhere, for instance, I argued that the representation of rape in *A Song of Ice and Fire* is highly ambivalent and problematic in itself, pointing to the main functions of the motif of rape in Martin's narrative, which include adding "realism," propelling the plot, and character (both male and female) development (Borowska-Szerszun 4–11). All of these points also apply to *Game of Thrones,* but the portrayal of sexual violence towards women in the TV narrative has proved to be even more controversial and received criticism for changing storylines and adding violence to sex scenes from which it was originally absent, which as Anne Gjelsvik demonstrates "altered gendered power relations within the fictional universe by [...] making strong female characters [...] weaker" (71).

On the whole, it seems safe to state that the problems with the portrayal of rape in both *A Song of Ice and Fire* and *Game of Thrones* are related. Furthermore, they are not limited to these particular narratives, but reflect a wider cultural problem, that is, the fact that rape is "almost always framed by a masculine perspective premised on man's fantasies about female sexuality and their fears of false accusations as well as their codified access to the possession of female bodies" (Higgins and Silver 2). This is perhaps not surprising if we bear in mind that apart from acquiring a reputation for quality content and breaking the conventions of genres, the HBO network has also "carefully carved out a niche for itself that is strongly masculine in its programming appeals" (Edgerton and Jones 322). Thus, while *Game of Thrones* features a wide range of female characters, some of them conforming to and others defying certain gender stereotypes, the series reproduces rather than challenges many pre-existing patterns that link rape with the issues of authority, power and voice. In this way, the series, like many other literary and artistic representations, "contribute[s] to the social positioning of women and men and shape[s] the cognitive systems that make rape *thinkable*" (Higgins and Silver 3, emphasis mine). It also perpetuates rape culture, which is succinctly defined by Sarah Projansky as:

> A culture in which sexual violence is a normalized phenomenon, in which male-dominant environments (such as sports, war, and the military) encourage and sometimes depend on violence against women, in which the male gaze and women as objects-to-be-looked-at contribute to a culture that accepts rape, and in which rape is one experience along a continuum of sexual violence that women confront on a daily basis [Projansky 9].

In Westeros and Essos most women, irrespective of their attractiveness or social position, face rape or threats of rape, and few of them are offered a chance to defend themselves. The most notable exceptions are Arya Stark (Maisie Williams), the show's tomboy, who manages to escape sexual abuse thanks to cross-dressing as a boy and good sword skills, and Brienne of Tarth (Gwendoline Christie), an extremely tall and muscular woman-knight, who is constantly ridiculed and scorned by men for her unfeminine appearance, lack of social graces, and choice of career path. Even Brienne, however, is shown as unable to defend herself on her own and faces the possibility of gang rape, when she and Jaime Lannister (Nikolaj Coster-Waldau) are captured by Bolton soldiers. Although she is not violated in the end, the scene in "Walk of Punishment" illustrates how the issue of sexual abuse is framed through a strongly masculine perspective, contributing to the dominant construction of gender roles.

Despite being a capable warrior, Brienne is a woman, and thus she is rapeable, which is evident in Jaime's assessment of the situation and his advice to her: "When we make camp tonight, you'll be raped. More than once. None of these fellows have ever been with a noblewoman. You'd be wise not to resist" (S3, E3). The cold remark normalizes rape as a sort of amusement and reward for the soldiers, a thing that simply happens to a woman, who is positioned as a natural and powerless victim. Brienne, however, makes it clear that she will fight even if she gets killed, which makes Jaime realize that he would do the same if he were a woman. When the captors drag her yelling and screaming to the nearby bushes, he intervenes, saying that her father would pay her weight in sapphires, "but only if she's alive, her honor unbesmirched" (S3, E3), and the would-be rapists forsake their attempt. While the scene is not particularly brutal or violent by HBO's standards, it demonstrates a number of points relevant to how *Game of Thrones* handles the trope of rape and can serve as a departure point. First, it establishes a hierarchical relationship by staging the man as "a natural predator" and the woman as "his natural prey" (Brownmiller 16). Only when Brienne refuses to play the game does Jaime's assessment of the circumstances change, as he realizes she chooses agency (associated with masculinity) over victimization (linked with femininity). Second, the scene constructs rape as business between men, with Brienne's "honor" being more profitable to the soldiers, which can be read as an echo of medieval statutes that treated rape as "an issue of property—protecting the family's land and identity, defining women as the property of the men in their family, and maintaining class and gender relations" (Projansky 4). Finally, the trope of rape is employed to demonstrate contrast between the degenerate male characters and the moral, or at least more morally complex, ones. Jaime's intervention is not particularly heroic, as an act of chivalry would be inconsistent with his character. Yet, it marks his transition from "a man without honor" (S2, E7) to a more complicated person with a sort of moral code, which strongly influences the viewers' perception of him.

The problems signaled here reappear in various combinations in the narrative's rape scripts. Sexual violation of nameless women, unimportant for the storyline, is depicted several times. The acts are framed as a background to the main scene yet treated with considerable attention to graphic detail—for instance, when the Dothraki soldiers assault women in Lhazareen village (S1, E8), or when Craster's wives/daughters are harassed by the Night Watch mutineers, a group composed primarily of former criminals. Both scenes contribute to the perception of women, especially those powerless, as "natural prey" (Brownmiller 16) at the mercy of "primitive" and "barbaric" men (the Dothraki) or socially inferior ones (the mutineers). As such, they reproduce "the dominant association of rape with the Other," perpetuating the myth that "rapes are committed by socially marginal outcasts, strangers lurking in the dark" as "the natural consequence of male resentment at being socially marginalized" (Ferreday 30). Thus, while rape in the discussed scenes is clearly staged as an atrocity of war or an abominable act, it is presented as an extreme experience and removed from a more familiar or domestic context, contradicting the argument raised by feminist activists and critics that "'regular guys' with whom one is acquainted not only *can* rape, but *are more likely* to rape than are strangers" (Projansky 113, original emphasis).

The problems related to confusing sexual violence with consensual sex combined with the use of rape for defining the male character emerge in one of the most contentious scenes in the series, in which Jaime Lannister rapes Cersei (Lena Kathren Headey) on the funeral bier of their dead son, Joffrey, in "Breaker of Chains" (S4, E3). As the scene has already been discussed in substantial detail (Gjelsvik 60–64, Ferreday 21–36), I will only highlight its most striking aspects here. The discussion in fan circles centered on the issue of the diversion from *A Song of Ice and Fire*, where sex between siblings was indubitably consensual even if disturbing, rough and angry:

> "Hurry," she was whispering now, "quickly, quickly, now, do it now, do me now. Jaime." Her hands helped guide him. "Yes," Cersei said as he thrust, "my brother, sweet brother, yes, like that, yes, I have you, you're home now, you're home now, you're home" [Martin G.R.R. 851].

In "Breaker of Chains," the dynamics of the scene are completely different. What begins as a consensual kiss, soon changes into Jamie grabbing Cersei, throwing her on the floor, tearing apart her skirts, and forcing himself on her despite her continuous protests: "No," "Please stop," "Stop it!," "It's not right." The scene concludes with the sound of his voice ("I don't care") and her grunts, which are probably meant to suggest, as director Alex Graves commented in one of the interviews, that the act was "consensual in the end" (qtd. in Martin Denise). Contrary to Graves, most viewers easily identified the scene as rape and noticed that it problematizes the issue of consent, perpetuating the "no means yes" rape myth. As Cuklanz explains,

> When mass media images depict violence as a part of consensual sex, or blur the lines between rape and consent, or depict an intimate interaction as beginning with force and ending with mutual desire, they encourage viewers to think of violence as a natural part of sex, to think of men as incapable of non-violent intimacy, and to think of women as desirous of sexual violation [Cuklanz 2014, 36].

It seems, however, that fans were enraged not so much with the fact that Cersei was raped (even though this introduces a consequential change to her motivations and character by victimizing her), but because the act was perpetrated by Jamie, which was seen as inconsistent with his character—a man caught in the process of transformation from a villain to a likeable, even if not spotless, individual (Larsson 62). Thus, rather than focusing on Cersei's experience of sexual violation by the only man she loves and trusts, the debate centered around the perpetrator, and in this way "disrupt[ed] the pleasurable narrative of a white man's redemption, spoiling his transition to a better future" (Ferreday 31). As the story develops, it becomes clear that Jaime is not to bear any consequences, and Cersei is to remain silent as if nothing happened. If handled differently, the aftermath of the scene could potentially explore a problematic scenario of "acquaintance" rape, which in real life is less frequently reported than assaults by strangers, more difficult to prove, frequently questioned by the public, and surrounded with a sense of mistrust of the victim's assessment of the situation (Burt 131–132; Cuklanz 2000, 37–38). Failing to do so, "Breaker of Chains" fits in a long tradition of silencing the victim and eliminating her point of view, which probably goes well with "male identification strategies" characteristic for much of HBO's content (Edgerton and Jones 322).

As the series progressed, criticism regarding the themes related to sexual violence towards women intensified, culminating after the episode titled "Unbowed, Unbent, Unbroken" (S5, E6) which featured Sansa Stark (Sophie Turner) being raped by Ramsay Bolton (Iwan Rheon). Referred to by numerous reviewers as "a terrible thing to witness" (Surette), having gone "too far" (Vincent and Hawkes) and "more than enough" (Hibberd), the scene pushed *The Mary Sue*, one of the most popular women-oriented geek entertainment websites, to announce that they "will no longer be actively promoting the HBO series *Game of Thrones*" (Pantozzi). In order to examine what exactly is considered "more than enough," I will juxtapose it with the scene of Daenerys (Emilia Clarke) being raped by Khal Drogo (Jason Momoa) in the opening episode of the whole series "Winter is coming" (S1, E1). Both of them are framed as perverse "wedding nights," in which men exercise their "marital right" over women, who were used as political pawns to secure political alliances through arranged marriages. For both women, the nightmare of sexual violation does not stop after the first act, but extends over time and is continuously repeated. Yet, there is also a striking contrast, regarding both visual representation and narrative functions of rape, which accounts for different reception of the scenes.

First of all, the story of the rape of Daenerys comes up at the very beginning of the series when the readers and viewers are not emotionally involved with the character yet. Furthermore, it can be somewhat clumsily justified in narrative terms, as it breaks the conventions of the genre and challenges the expectations of the audience. Despite deviating from the novel, where it was presented as consensual sex resulting from a two-page-long seduction ritual, the TV scene depicts Daenerys's reluctance and discomfort, but is not particularly brutal. The difference in power relations between male and female protagonists is visualized through the very appearance of the actors—"her fair coloring, her tininess and softness, against his dark coloring, and large, massive body" (Larsson 23). It is also emphasized by the choice of a sexual position—he takes her from behind, which brings connotations with "animalistic" and "degrading" sex and reinforces the sense of Daenerys's submission or sacrifice (Larsson 23–25). The scene is coded in racial terms, depending to a certain extent on "the stereotype of the racialized man as a rapist" (Projansky 41) assaulting the white, innocent and "civilized" woman. This impression is slightly modified, when we acknowledge that Drogo does not actually mean to harm Daenerys—it is just a "Dothraki fashion," a customary way of having sex in his culture. In narrative terms, rape is used as the initial stage of Daenerys's development. As Rikke Schubart observes, the story of the future *khaleesi* follows the familiar Beauty/Beast pattern, in which "Daenerys's task is not to transform a beast into a man, but rather to transform her own terror into pleasure, which, later still, becomes passionate love" (114). This transformation is again rendered in sexual terms. Tormented with forceful "doggy style" sex, the female protagonist undertakes to change her husband's sexual habits and manipulates him not only into face-to-face sexual position, but also the one in which she comes on top—an obvious sign of her initiative and a move towards greater equality in their relationship (S1, E2). While this rape-to-romance narrative is unsettling, it significantly contributes to the fantasy of Daenerys's individual agency, allowing her to transform victimization into empowerment. While such a trajectory may offer a sense of pleasure to female viewers, "the emphasis remains on the individual woman rising above a system that keeps her down [...] rather than in cultural revolution or innovation" (Tolmie 147). Thus, the triumph of an exceptional woman turns out illusory and fails to subvert the rape culture of *Game of Thrones*, which actually remains unharmed.

The scene of the rape of Sansa Stark can bring no sense of pleasure to the viewers at all. It commences with Ramsay ordering Sansa to undress, which she reluctantly does. Dissatisfied with her hesitancy, Ramsay rips her dress to expose her back, pushes her face-down onto the bed, pulls up the remains of her wedding dress, and cold-heartedly rapes her from behind. The position reminds one of Daenerys's wedding night, but here it is clearly meant to humiliate and degrade Sansa. From this moment on, the viewers only hear the muffled sounds of her pain, while the camera focuses exclusively on the horrified facial expression of Theon Greyjoy (Alfie Allen), who is forced to witness Sansa "become a woman" (S5, E6). Later on, the viewers see Sansa wear dark bruises, which makes it clear that she is a prisoner and a sex-slave to Bolton. Unlike in the case of Daenerys, the viewers have already invested their emotions in Sansa's character, which makes the scene all the more difficult to watch. In narrative terms, there is also little, if any, justification for this sexual violation. While the rape of Daenerys can be read as a life-changing stage of her development, prompting her to "re-vision herself as powerful rather than as victim" (Crosby 77), the abuse of Sansa is not needed to serve this purpose, as at this point of the narrative she is not an innocent and dreamy girl anymore. In fact, she has already experienced major traumatic events—her father's execution, being publicly stripped and beaten, an attempted rape during the riots, and being forced to marry Tyrion Lannister (Peter Dinklage) soon after the Lannisters and Boltons murdered her mother and brother. In short, in the perception of the audience Sansa already *is* a survivor, and rape is absolutely redundant for her storyline. Discussing the parallel scene in *A Song of Ice and Fire*, where the plot belonged to a minor character named Jeyne Poole, disguised as Arya Stark to be wedded to Ramsay to secure his claim to Winterfell, I argued that the incorporation of rape into the narrative serves to highlight Ramsay Bolton's monstrosity as well as to foreshadow Theon Greyjoy's forthcoming transformation, as witnessing the rape of the girl prompted him to overcome the fear of his oppressor and help her escape. In "Unbowed, Unbent, Unbroken" the justification behind the scene seems to be similar, yet the problem with such a rape script is that it "tell[s] more about what it means to be a man than about the experience of rape itself" (Borowska-Szerszun 8), reducing female trauma to a purely narrative function.

Discussing *Game of Thrones* and its depiction of sexual violence, many critics raise the issue of the adaptation's (in)fidelity to *A Song of Ice and Fire*, emphasizing that the TV series changes both the storyline and mode of engagement, which has ideological implications (Gjelsvik 70–71). While this is true, the issue of diverging from the source material is not the biggest problem. In fact, Martin's novels and HBO's show seem to share the same fascination with rape as "a crime that dominates public fantasies" (Horeck 4), and both of them display "the cultural fixation on the figure of the violated woman" (Horeck 8). Admittedly, turning the imagined sexual violence into watchable entertainment accounts for the perception of sex and violence coming across stronger on TV than in the novels (Larsson 18). Yet, the objectifying power of the male gaze predominating in the depiction of rape in the series mirrors the masculine perspective of the original source, which employs rape as a means of adding realism, differentiating between detestable and honorable male characters, and propelling plots. The issue of using the motif of sexual violence to trigger narrative development is ambiguous irrespective of whether the storyline concerns male or female characters, which is vividly expressed by reviewer Libby Hill:

If you watch enough prestige television, you come to realize that the most traumatic thing that could possibly happen to a man is having to suffer the pain of a woman he knows getting raped. [...] To exist as a woman on a cable drama is to understand that at some point you're probably going to be raped by someone you know or in the presence of someone you know or as a punishment to someone you know, but it's okay because in the end, it just gives you something to overcome and everyone knows that having something to overcome is the only way to prove that you are a strong woman [Hill].

Thus, even those narratives that feature women who carve out their own paths towards empowerment despite experiencing sexual violation can be read as scripts that naturalize violence against women, situating men within the position of power over them. If the creators of the show really meant to use the sensitive motif of rape in a more ethically responsible way, they would probably have to rewrite the whole storylines to restore the woman's voice and to offer another kind of a more subversive narrative, which would attempt to challenge and undermine the existing power structures instead of reinforcing them.

As demonstrated in this discussion of the representation of rape, sexual violence is strongly related to gender construction and the issues of agency and power, contributing to the perception of men as active perpetrators of violence against women. Yet, as *Game of Thrones* features a number of tough woman warriors, it is a narrative that lends itself to the analysis of another side of the coin, namely the representation of female violence. A few points worthy of consideration arise here. Is female violence depicted differently than male violence? How does the TV show construe the image of violent women? Can they pose a threat to or are they somehow accommodated within the patriarchal structures of Westeros? To examine these issues related to the representation of violence perpetrated by women, the discussion needs to be situated within a wider socio-cultural context.

Female violence is traditionally considered as something unnatural. In fact, a greater portion of academic research in social and legal studies has examined women as victims of violence than as perpetrators of violence, which can be only partly justified by the fact that female violence is a rarer phenomenon (Weare 340). The underlying assumption of men's violence and women's non-violence reflects gender-related power discourses, which perpetuate the idea that passivity, kindness, and gentleness are inherently feminine. Consequently, violence and aggression are predominantly viewed as "culturally appropriate means for men to exert dominance and control," whereas "dominant constructions of femininity discourage women from employing violence in the same manner" (Meyer 2). In her discussion of legal and media narratives of murders committed by women, Belinda Morrissey demonstrates that, as result of such gender assumptions, female murders are typically viewed as "more traumatic for heteropatriarchal societies than those of men" (2), which parallels Siobhan Weare's observation than "when women commit violent crime, [...] some of the fundamental social structures based on appropriate gendered behaviour are contradicted and challenged" (338). Thus, when women are violently criminal, they not only break the law, they also step out of the appropriate feminine role, which has serious implications for the understanding of their agency. Morrisey and Weare further argue that in order to accommodate female violence within the existing power structures, socio-legal and media discourses employ various strategies to diminish or even deny agency of violent women, and that these mechanisms are strongly linked with the portrayal of the female killer's image.

The first of these strategies is "vilification" or "monsterization," which exposes "the evil nature" of the violent woman and transforms her into a monster that acts, but not as a human being. It is linked to the process of "mythification"—a narrative script relating female violence to "mythic evil" associated with characters such as Medea or the evil witch, who are "designed to increase fear and elicit harsh responses" (Morrissey 25). Both strategies work to distance the female offender from the society, create the impression of her otherness, and deny her agency through making her appear non-human. They result in the image of the "bad" woman, someone inherently wicked, and often equipped with "an 'extra element' of bad that goes beyond [her] actual crime" (Weare 346). This extra element of bad, Weare argues, can also be perceived as a result of the violation of gender norms, which indicates that the violent woman fails to perform an appropriate version of femininity. The last strategy of denying agency is referred to by Morrisey as "victimism," which paradoxically emphasizes "the powerlessness of the oppressed" (Morrisey 25). This is particularly visible in the perception of battered women who kill their violent partners, which is typically presented "only as a direct response to being battered by them" (Weare 351). The image of the victim can also be conflated with the stereotype of the "mad woman" (Weare 351), which has a long history in gender related discourse and results from the association of women with irrationality, emotional instability, and impulsiveness. When a woman is given the label of the mad one, she is seen as losing control due to some form of abnormality or extreme emotions, and thus her responsibility and agency are refused. These three mechanisms—making murderesses appear as victims who have been so victimized that they did not realize what they were doing when they killed, crazy women incapable of taking rational and autonomous decisions, or mythological or inhuman personifications of monstrous evil—serve to minimize the challenge the violent woman might pose to the construction of gender norms. Morrisey explains that through insisting on her lack of agency, the violent woman "is returned to her place of passivity and silence" (Morrisey 351), which is considered appropriate for the dominant framework of femininity.

Although social and legal discourses construe violence as unnatural for women, the images of active and violent women abound in popular culture, especially in action, adventure and crime genres. The late 1990s and 2000s saw a growing popularity of "action babes" or "tough babes," such as Xena, Buffy, and Lara Croft, who have been characterized by Yvonne Tasker and Lindsay Steenberg as a "combination of violent subjectivity and eroticized spectacle" (173). On the one hand, the rise of heroines depicted as active agents, who do not need to be rescued and can fend for themselves, may reflect the change in the roles attainable to women in real life and offer a vision of a more powerful femininity. On the other hand, "action babes" may be "further fetishized as dangerous sex objects" (Brown 47), doing little to subvert gender stereotypes. The latter possibility seems to inform certain predictable images of female toughness in popular entertainment. As Sherrie A. Innes notes: "The stereotypical female heroine can be muscular but not so much so that she presents a threat to the males with whom she stars. Her muscularity might be impressive for 'a girl,' but she is no challenge for the 'boys'" (Inness 8). The same could probably be said about female violence. It may be allowed, but only when it serves justified reasons and within limits the audience are willing to tolerate.

Unlike "action babes," the female warriors of *Game of Thrones*—Brienne of Tarth, Arya Stark, Yara Greyjoy (Gemma Whelan) and Ygritte (Rose Leslie)—are not portrayed in a way that would conflate their potential for violence with sexual display. Out of them only Ygritte, whose story line is the shortest, is depicted as a woman who easily combines violence with femininity. These two qualities go together in this case, as Ygritte is a Wildling born beyond the Wall among the Free Folk, a non-hierarchical society that values individual skills over gender norms. Physically attractive, yet not oversexualized, Ygritte is a fierce, independent woman, confident in both her archery skills and her body, for whom fighting and sexuality are equally natural. In conversations with her lover Jon Snow, she constantly questions his assumptions about femininity, which emphasizes that gender ideas depend on his upbringing, and thus are culturally constructed. Bravery, autonomy and resilience are defining qualities of the figure of Ygritte, yet she also shows capacity for empathy and love. Capable of defending herself but not overtly aggressive, she is a woman who resorts to violence when needed, but does not use it to gain power or authority for her own sake. While Ygritte offered a reassuring image of female independence, without making her appear masculine or hyper-sexualized, her storyline was too short to make a lasting change in the perception of gender relations in the series.

In contrast, the depiction of the other three woman warriors in HBO's TV show relies heavily on the emphasis of the masculine traits over feminine ones. Brought up in a harsh reality of the Iron Islands, evoking connotations with the Viking Scandinavia, Yara Greyjoy is a product of her culture that celebrates violence, lives off plunder, and takes pride in paying the "iron price," i.e., fighting for and taking what they want by force, rather than trading and negotiating. She is not only a fighter, but also a competent military leader esteemed by her soldiers, whose loyalty she earned through her daring deeds, risk-taking, and behaving just like one of them. She is not ridiculed for her masculine behavior, as "she assumes the signifiers of male military power in order for her position in the military hierarchy to be clearly understood by those around her" (Tasker and Steenberg 186). Quite disturbingly, just as she leads her men to war, she also leads them to a brothel in Volantis, where she is shown kissing a barely clad sex-slave and simultaneously making fun of the castrated Theon (S6, E7). The scene contrasts Yara's virility with Theon's impotence and plays on butch and *femme* lesbian stereotyping to deny Yara's femininity and once again highlight her masculine traits. Interestingly, Yara's non-heteronormative sexuality, which is just another addition to Martin's narrative, contributes to the perception of the relationship between women and violence as unnatural, perpetuating just another myth about femininity:

> We have, then, woman as innocent, gentle, caring, nurturing, and incapable of committing violence—the angel, the mother, the virgin, the Madonna, and yet still the "other." We also see woman as evil, sexual, dangerous, the vampire, the black widow, the whore, the vamp, the "other." A woman who is capable of aggression and violence becomes the masculine woman, the lesbian, the "other" [Gilbert 1294].

Brienne is masculinized in a completely different way than Yara, as she functions as the "other" among both men and women. Among women, she looks anomalous due to her physicality—she is "neither decorative nor a sexual object" (Carroll 2014: 225), which highlights her exclusion from the sphere of appropriate femininity. Yet, contrary to Yara, she is not readily accepted in the company of men, either. Towering over most of them and stubbornly repeating "I am no lady" (S2, E3), she is not simply a female fighter, but a true knight errant in the world where chivalry has lost its meaning. Stronger than most men and fighting better than them, she is considered a freak and constantly ridiculed for attempting to act like a man, which corresponds with Paula Ruth Gilbert's observation that "men see violent women as an oddity, comic, insane or laughable" (1286). While Yara is construed as a "buddy" type and operates with a bravado in a male-dominated environment, Brienne appears eccentrically unsuited in the company of other knights, who have much lower moral standards. As a paragon of knightly virtue, she is neither aggressive nor brutal, but always loyal, honorable and fully committed to her quests, which she places above her personal wants and desires. "Brienne's assumption of knightly regalia," Tasker and Steenberg write, "suggests a complicated kind of crossdressing; neither disguise nor burlesque, but an outward indicator of her inner commitment to chivalric ideals" (178). The construction of Brienne's character is unusual, as it combines the elements of exceptional womanhood and exemplary knighthood, which challenges the gender binary oppositions between lady-like femininity and hegemonic masculinity (cf. MacIness, 86–87).

Unlike Yara and Brienne, Arya Stark, the cycle's tomboy, occupies a liminal space and is "defined as in-between: a boyish girl, not yet a mannish woman" (Tasker and Steenberg 183). Her narrative is the one of finding her own path to maturity, and she is constantly depicted as caught between fleeing danger and seeking revenge. From the outset of the series, Arya rejects a conventional aristocratic femininity, and desires to learn how to fight. Arya's most important teachers are Syrio Forel, who instructs her in the very beginning and makes her believe "there is only one thing we say to Death: 'not today'" (S1, E6), the Hound, from whom she learns the most about "the grammar of violence and its place in Westeros" (Tasker and Steenberg 184), and the Faceless Men, who pushes her to abandon her identity and become a merciless killing-machine. Although Arya learns the skills of an assassin, she never forgets her Stark background and becomes a force of vengeance, becoming "increasingly sociopathic in her appetite for violent revenge" (Tasker and Steenberg 185). Unlike other female warriors in the series, Arya is depicted as cold-heartedly committing acts of violence (e.g., stabbing in the eyes and in the guts, slitting throats) in the scenes that feature gory detail and lots of blood. Deadly efficient, ruthless and reveling in her vendetta, Arya defies the stereotype of female violence as result of either victimization or madness and is offered a triumphant hero moment, when she single-handedly kills the Night King and becomes a savior of Westeros (S8, E3). The trajectory of her tomboy narrative also diverges from a typical pattern, where the liminal figure of a tomboy is seen as stage of preparation for appropriate femininity, as the tomboy character usually abandons her masculine clothes and behavior when she finds the right man (Tasker and Steenberg 183–184). Arya does become a woman, but on her own terms. This is evident in the scene of her sex with Gendry (Joseph Dempsie), when she is depicted as both strong and vulnerable, unlacing the ties of her leather armor herself, opening up emotionally, and removing—for a very short moment—all her defenses (S8, E2). Her control over her sexuality and her life becomes even more visible in the scene in which she refuses Gendry's proposal. When he kneels down and asks her to marry him, she bends to kiss him and gently maneuvers him to stand on his feet again, saying: "You'll be a wonderful lord, and any lady would be lucky to have you. But I'm not a lady. I never have been. That's not me" (S8, E4). Yet, Arya's subversive potential for changing the power structures of Westeros is mitigated in the end, as she sails off to the West. Deservedly becoming an exceptional woman, who makes her own decisions and forges her own fate, she takes a step to move out of the system, which is not capable of accommodating her the way she is.

Undeniably, the creators of *Game of Thrones* gave much attention to characterizing and developing the storylines of violent women in the show, especially Brienne and Arya. However, in the end these women are not in a position to change anything but their own fate. While this gives them individual agency, and their use of violence is crucial to forging this agency, they are not challenging to the whole system of gender relations, which remains largely untouched. Yara becomes a ruler of Iron Islands—a position she always aspired to; Brienne is dubbed a knight and becomes a commander of the Kingsguard—a function that allows her neither partner nor children; and Arya just leaves the stage. Even though all of these women transgressed against the norms that discourage women from employing violence to exert control and dominance in the same way men do, they turn out to be unthreatening to the system, which remains modified only in political terms—from absolute to elective monarchy. Those who decided to fit in stayed; those who did not left. This is emphasized in the last scene of the series, when the Free Folk leave to live their lives north of the Wall, the show symbolically making a full circle. The same episode features the scene in which the new Small Council of King Bran the Broken, led by Tyrion Lannister, discusses the need to restore King's Landing. When rebuilding brothels is mentioned as a priority, Brienne, the only woman on the council, observes that ships take precedence over brothels, which is dismissed with an anecdotal joke. Thus, Brienne can play the game, but only if she plays according to the rules defined by men. The brothels, symbolic of gender power structures, are to stay just as they were, and Brienne is to remain a silenced woman in the man's world.

In his article on the reception of female violence in film, Doug Meyer demonstrates that when dealing with violent women viewers make a difference between legitimate and illegitimate forms of violence. "Viewers," Meyer writes, "are the most likely to code women's violence positively when a film justifies the characters' actions. In other words, film viewers evaluate violent women by critiquing their motivations for committing violence" (Meyer 65). This probably explains why the mechanism of monsterization, mythification, or victimization were not applied in the portrayal of violence committed by Ygritte, Yara, Brienne, and Arya. Although their motives range from self-defense to revenge, they can be seen as fully justified within the narrative. In the portrayal of Yara, Brienne, and Arya the creators additionally resorted to emphasizing their diversion from appropriate lady-like femininity through presenting them as mannish women, and yet equipping them with attributes such as selflessness (Brienne) or caring for their families (Yara and Arya). The images of Cersei Lannister and Daenerys Targaryen diverge from this pattern, as both of them are a dangerous combination of masculine and feminine traits contained within attractive female bodies, over which they exercise full control. Despite completely different motivations, both of these influential women aspire to the highest power, desiring to become queens of all Westeros, and both of them are eliminated in the end.

As much criticism has already been devoted to the portrayal of Cersei and Daenerys at earlier stages of the narrative, in this essay I will only highlight the issues that are most important to the representation of female violence. From the very beginning of *Game of Thrones* Cersei has been consistently shown as a woman who would do everything to achieve her personal aims and the position of power, becoming a short-sighted tyrant in skirts and combining all the worst qualities stereotypically attributed to women (manipulative sexuality, irrationality, instability, jealousy, etc.) and men (alcohol abuse, cruelty, ruthlessness, arrogance, etc.). Daenerys, on the other hand, was depicted predominantly as the mother of dragons and slaves. The double-edged metaphor of motherhood allowed to reconcile two aspects of her personality—the violent one, evoked through the association with monsters and accounting for her success as warrior queen, and the nurturing one, which propelled her to avoid combat when unnecessary and embrace all her subjects, especially the powerless. Throughout the narrative she was also shown as continuously learning how to reconcile personal desires with the demands of the state, which was meant to prepare her for firm and effective leadership. Thus, in contrast to Cersei, she combined the positive archetypes of masculinity (courage, independence, assertiveness) and femininity (caring, compassion, mercy).[1] Irrespective of these differences, however, both Cersei and Daenerys are portrayed as monstrously violent women—the former cold-heartedly blowing up the Sept of Baleor to avoid conviction and take revenge on her enemies (S6, E10), and the latter flying on a dragon and burning King's Landing despite its surrender. It can be disputed whether Daenerys's madness was satisfactorily implied in the narrative, yet her storyline demonstrates that "[o]vert aggression by a woman is also a cultural transgression—threatening not only to the social structure but also to the mythology that separates women into demons and angels. If an angel suddenly turns into a demon, punishment can assume apocalyptic proportions" (Gilbert 1287). This falls in line with Shiloh Caroll's observation that *Game of Thrones*, in contrast to the novels again, tends to depict Daenerys as requiring men to control her violent tendencies, which gives the disturbing undertone to her storyline "that a woman's failure to listen to a man's advice [...] is evidence of madness and said woman must be stopped by any means necessary, then replaced by a man" (Carroll 2020, 180).

The treatment of Cersei and Daenerys indicates that *Game of Thrones* had no place for female leaders at the very top of its structures. However, the narrative of Cersei was consistent in this respect, as the series followed Martin's novels in highlighting all the misogynistic attitudes towards female leadership and making her the evil queen of the cycle. Although her violence could be partially explained through the victimization she experienced in the Walk of Punishment (S3, E3), the cold-blooded massacre she orders has "a vital role in maintaining notions of feminine evil" (Morrissey 7), and the viewers generally agree that she deserved what she got. In Daenerys's case, her Targaryen blood, i.e., a history of insanity in her family, the connection with dragons symbolizing monstrosity, and emotional distress which she experiences in the last season, are all hastily combined to account for her outburst of violence. This outburst is consequently framed as loss of control and disruptive release of tension—a stereotypical way of perceiving female aggression. On top of being presented as mad, she is also monsterized and mythified in a way female killers frequently are. Morrissey explains the logic behind such portrayal in the following way: "if she is portrayed as a mythic, inhuman personification of wickedness, then the radical implications of her acts are muffled, her challenge to oppression nullified, at least as far as the dominant purveyors of cultural meaning are concerned" (170). Following those viewers who found Daenerys's quick descent into madness as unjustified in psychological and narrative terms, I read her annihilation as a deeply internalized fear of the only leader in *Game of Thrones* who acted on the behalf of the underprivileged and had a true potential for changing the gender structures. Like Slavoj Zizek, I see Daenerys as not only a strong female leader but also "the only social agent who really fought for something new, for a new world that would put an end to old injustices" (Zizek). Such a combination proved too difficult for the creators of the show to handle, and so the mother of dragons and slaves, a woman with too many prospects for the subversion of the existing power structures, had to be annihilated, ironically through the hands of her lover, who "saved" her from herself.

Captivating a vast international audience, *Game of Thrones* can clearly be perceived as contemporary popular culture mythmaker that both reflects and shapes our ways of thinking about violence. As such it has had a huge potential for shifting and subverting ideas about gender, power and violence. Yet, the scripts of sexual violence against women developed in the series confirm a masculine-centered perspective, normalizing rape and doing little to offer women a real voice. Consequently, the representation of rape follows a dominant pattern that equips men with agency and reinforces the perception of women as passive and helpless victims. Even the rape-to-power narrative of Daenerys Targaryen is problematic, as it portrays overcoming the effects of sexual violation as a stage of development, without which she would be incapable of growing to her role as a leader. If we believe that "who gets to tell the story and whose story counts as 'truth' determine the definitions of what rape is" (Higgins and Silver 1), *Game of Thrones* fails spectacularly in changing these definitions. As for the representation of violent women, who are potentially dangerous as they might challenge the assumptions of male agency and female passivity, it can be concluded that it does not have a lasting influence on gender hierarchy in Westeros. While some viewers may rejoice in the fact that Yara, Brienne and Arya survived and managed to carve out their own paths, all of them function as exceptional women, who have little influence over the fate of Westeros after all. The story of Daenerys's vilification, on the other hand, reflects the fear of powerful women, reinforces the connection between female aggression and madness, and invalidates the idea that a truly influential female leader can come up to the mark. Thus, a woman can get some power, especially over her own life, but not the power to shape and change the existing socio-cultural *milieu*. She can acquire some authority, especially in the margins of the kingdom, i.e., in Iron Islands (Yara) or in the North (Sansa), but not the authority that would allow her to become a ruler and protector of the whole realm. Initially hailed for its representation of a range of diversified female characters, *Game of Thrones* eventually failed them, leaving the impression that their subversive potential was safely contained.

Note

1. For a more detailed discussion of the representation of female power in the depiction of Cersei and Daenerys in *A Song of Ice and Fire*, focusing in particular on how it resonates with medieval tradition, see Borowska-Szerszun, "Westerosi Queens: Medievalist Portrayal of Female Power and Authority in *A Song of Ice and Fire*," pp. 55–59, 64–68.

Works Cited

Borowska-Szerszun, Sylwia. "Representation of Rape in George R.R. Martin's *A Song of Ice and Fire* and Robin Hobb's *Liveship Traders*." *Extrapolation*, vol. 60, no. 1, 2019, pp. 1–22. DOI: 10.3828/extr.2019.2.

Borowska-Szerszun, Sylwia. "Westerosi Queens: Medievalist Portrayal of Female Power and

Authority in *A Song of Ice and Power*" in *Queenship and the Women of Westeros: Female Agency and Advice in Game of Thrones and A Song of Ice and Fire,* edited by Zita Eva Rohr and Lisa Benz. London: Palgrave Macmillan, 2020, pp. 53–76.

Brown, Jeffrey A. "Gender, Sexuality, and Toughness: The Bad Girls of Action Film and Comic Books" in *Action Chicks: New Images of Tough Women in Popular Culture,* edited by Sherrie A. Inness. London: Palgrave Macmillan, 2004, pp. 47–74.

Burt, Martha R. "Rape Myths" in *Confronting Rape and Sexual Assault,* edited by Mary E. Odem and Jody Clay-Warner. Lanham, MD: SR Books, 2003, pp. 129–144.

Carroll, Shiloh. "Daenerys the Unready: Advice and Ruling in Meereen." in *Queenship and the Women of Westeros: Female Agency and Advice in Game of Thrones and A Song of Ice and Fire,* edited by Zita Eva Rohr and Lisa Benz. London: Palgrave Macmillan, 2020, pp. 169–185.

Carroll, Shiloh. "'You Ought to be in Skirts and Me in Mail': Gender and History in George R.R. Martin's *A Song of Ice and Fire*" in *George R.R. Martin's A Song of Ice and Fire and the Medieval Literary Tradition,* edited by Bartłomiej Błaszkiewicz. Warsaw, Poland: Wydawnictwa Uniwersytetu Warszawskiego, 2014, pp. 247–259.

Crosby, Janice C. *Cauldron of Changes: Feminist Spirituality in Fantastic Fiction.* Jefferson, NC: McFarland, 2000.

Cuklanz, Lisa M. "Mass Media Representation of Gendered Violence" in *The Routledge Companion to Media And Gender,* edited by Cynthia Carter, Linda Steiner and Lisa McLaughlin. London: Routledge 2014, pp. 32–41.

Cuklanz, Lisa M. *Rape on Prime Time: Television, Masculinity, and Sexual Violence.* Philadelphia: University of Pennsylvania Press, 2000.

Durham, M. Gigi. *The Lolita Effect: The Media Sexualization of Young Girls and What We Can Do About It.* New York: Overlook Press, 2008.

Edgerton, Gary R., and Jeffrey P. Jones. "HBO's Ongoing Legacy" in *The Essential HBO Reader,* edited by Gary R. Edgerton and Jeffrey P. Jones. Lexington: University Press of Kentucky, 2008, pp. 315–330.

Ferreday, Debra. "*Game of Thrones,* Rape Culture and Feminist Fandom." *Australian Feminist Studies,* vol. 30, no. 83, 2015, pp. 21–36. DOI: 10.1080/08164649.2014.998453.

Genz, Stéphanie. "'I'm not going to fight them, I'm going to fuck them': Sexist Liberalism and Gender (a) Politics in *Game of Thrones*" in *Women of Ice and Fire: Gender, Game of Thrones, and Multiple Media Engagements,* edited by Anne Gjelsvik and Rikke Schubart. London: Bloomsbury Academic, 2016, pp. 243–266.

Gilbert, Paula Ruth. "Discourses of Female Violence and Societal Gender Stereotypes." *Violence against Women,* vol. 8 no. 11, 2002, pp. 1271–1300. DOI: 10.1177/107780102237405.

Hibberd, James. "*Game of Thrones* producers: 'Not one word' changed due to criticism.'" *Entertainment Weekly,* 1 Apr. 2016, www.ew.com/article/2016/04/01/game-thrones-season-6. Accessed 26 Oct. 2019.

Higgins, Lynn A., and Brenda R. Silver. *Rape and Representation.* New York: Columbia University Press, 1991.

Hill, Libby. "*Game of Thrones* recap: Another brutal wedding, another vicious rape." *Salon,* 18 May 2015, www.salon.com/2015/05/18/game_of_thrones_recap_the_honor_of_your_presence_is_requested_at_another_brutal_wedding. Accessed 18 Oct. 2019.

Hutcheon, Linda, and Siobhan O'Flynn. *A Theory of Adaptation.* 2nd ed. London: Routledge, 2013.

Innes, Sherrie A. "Introduction. 'Boxing Gloves and Bustiers': New Images of Tough Women" in *Action Chicks: New Images of Tough Women in Popular Culture,* edited by Sherrie A. Inness. London: Palgrave Macmillan, 2004, pp. 1–17.

Itzkoff, Dave. "George R.R. Martin on *Game of Thrones* and Sexual Violence." *ArtsBeat. New York Times Blog,* 2 May 2014, artsbeat.blogs.nytimes.com/2014/05/02/george-r-r-martin-on-game-of-thrones-and-sexual-violence/. Accessed 20 Oct. 2019.

Larsson, Mariah. "Adapting Sex: Cultural Conceptions of Sexuality in Words and Images" in *Women of Ice and Fire: Gender, Game of Thrones, and Multiple Media Engagements,* edited by Anne Gjelsvik and Rikke Schubart. London: Bloomsbury Academic, 2016, pp. 17–38.

MacIness, Iain A. "'All I Ever Wanted Was to Fight for a Lord I Believed in. But the Good

Lords Are Dead and the Rest Are Monsters'": Brienne of Tarth, Jaime Lannister, and the Chivalric Other" in *Queenship and the Women of Westeros: Female Agency and Advice in Game of Thrones and A Song of Ice and Fire,* edited by Zita Eva Rohr and Lisa Benz. New York: Palgrave Macmillan, 2020, pp. 77–101.

Martin, Denise. 2014. "Breaking Down Jaime Lannister's Controversial Scene with Last Night's *Game of Thrones* director." *Vulture,* 21 Apr. 2014, www.vulture.com/2014/04/game-of-thrones-director-on-the-rape-sex-scene.html. Accessed 15 Oct. 2019.

Martin, George R.R. *A Storm of Swords.* New York: Bantam Books, 2011.

Meyer, Doug. "'She acts out in inappropriate ways': Students' evaluations of violent women in film." *Journal of Gender Studies,* vol. 18, no. 1, 2009, pp. 63–73. DOI: 10.1080/09589230802584295.

Morrissey, Belinda. *When Women Kill: Questions of Agency and Subjectivity.* London: Routledge, 2003.

Pantozzi, Jill. "We Will No Longer Be Promoting HBO's *Game of Thrones*." *The Mary Sue,* 16 May 2015, www.themarysue.com/we-will-no-longer-be-promoting-hbo-game-of-thrones. Accessed 19 Oct. 2019.

Projansky, Sarah. *Watching Rape: Film and Television in Postfeminist Culture.* New York: New York University Press, 2001.

Schubart, Rikke. "Woman with Dragons: Daenerys, Pride, and Postfeminist Possibilities" in *Women of Ice and Fire: Gender, Game of Thrones, and Multiple Media Engagements,* edited by Anne Gjelsvik and Rikke Schubart. London: Bloomsbury Academic, 2016, pp. 105–130.

Shepherd Laura J. *Gender, Violence and Popular Culture: Telling Stories.* London: Routledge, 2013.

Stam, Robert. *Literature and Film: A Guide to the Theory and Practice of Film Adaptation.* Hoboken: Blackwell, 2005.

Surette, Tim. (2015). "*Game of Thrones* 'Unbowed, Unbent, Unbroken'" Review: The Attack on Family, Values." *TV,* 8 May 2015, www.tv.com/shows/game-of-thrones/community/post/game-of-thrones-season-5-episode-6-unbowed-unbent-unbroken-143182259771/. Accessed 18 Oct. 2019.

Tamborini, Ron, et al. "'Violence Is a Many-Splintered Thing': The Importance of Realism, Justification, and Graphicness in Understanding Perceptions of and Preferences for Violent Films and Video Games." *Projections,* vol. 7, no. 1, 2013, pp. 100–118. DOI: 10.3167/proj.2013.070108.

Tasker, Yvonne, and Lindsay Steenberg. "Women Warriors from Chivalry to Vengeance" in *Women of Ice and Fire: Gender, Game of Thrones, and Multiple Media Engagements,* edited by Anne Gjelsvik and Rikke Schubart. London: Bloomsbury Academic, 2016, pp. 171–192.

Tolmie, Jane. "Medievalism and the Fantasy Heroine." *Journal of Gender Studies,* vol. 15, no. 2, 2006, pp. 145–158. DOI: 10.1080/09589230600720042.

Vincent, Alice, and Rebecca Hawkes, R. "Rape on TV: Has *Game of Thrones* gone too far?" *The Telegraph,* 18 May 2015, www.telegraph.co.uk/culture/tvandradio/game-of-thrones/11612290/rape-game-of-thrones.html. Accessed 20 Oct. 2019.

Weare, Siobhan. "'The Mad,' 'The Bad,' 'The Victim': Gendered Constructions of Women Who Kill within the Criminal Justice System." *Laws,* vol. 2, 2013, pp. 337–361. DOI:10.3390/laws2030337.

Žižek, Slavoj. "*Game of Thrones* tapped into fears of revolution and political women—and left us no better off than before." *Independent,* 21 May 2019, www.independent.co.uk/voices/game-thrones-season-8-finale-bran-daenerys-cersei-jon-snow-zizek-revolution-a8923371.html?utm_source=reddit.com.

Subversion or Reinforcement?
Patriarchy and Masculinity
ANDREW HOWE

Much has been written about patriarchy in HBO's *Game of Thrones*, specifically about the intersections between power and gender structures that exist throughout the show. Strong female characters abound, but the preservation of male power is often linked to female victimization, and in the end a male ends up ruling in King's Landing—notionally Brandon Stark, but really Tyrion Lannister—despite the narrative seemingly headed towards enveloping a female ruler. These accusations hold merit, more so for the show than the books, but a larger, overall picture of gender exists, one of nuance that simultaneously criticizes and reinforces certain aspects of patriarchy and toxic masculinity. This essay examines the features of masculinity valued by such a society—e.g., physical strength, assertiveness, and ability to wield power—and the manner in which various characters and plot developments either subvert or reinforce the patriarchal system. Analysis is benchmarked somewhat to a medieval viewpoint, but more so to contemporary political realities that both George R.R. Martin and the showrunners, Benioff and Weiss, have faced as storytellers. This essay references numerous characters, although several are more prominently featured. Numerous reversals in power are explored, especially involving those in the early part of the series who either control the realm or seek to increase their power, such as Robert Baratheon, Tywin Lannister, and the "Five Kings." Groups with complex masculine codes—such as the Dothraki and Unsullied—are also examined, particularly as those codes relate to their gender performance. Theon Greyjoy's story arc is also surveyed, particularly the manner in which he transitions from sexual exploiter to victim of sexual violence. Character arcs for Ned Stark, his son Robb, and his nephew Jon Snow are also explored. These three characters chart similar but ultimately different paths through a gender landscape where honor and ethics can be dangerous amidst situations that require fluid thinking but decisive action. Masculinity is a set of socially and culturally-determined behaviors and attributes, ones that are not restricted to male characters. Thus, Brienne of Tarth is examined for her difficulty in dealing with gender dysphoria; more to the point, the difficulty that *others* have in adjusting to the subversion she threatens to introduce into the gendered social order. And finally, the essay examines the frequency of rape as depicted in this medievalesque world particularly as employed in many different situations as a form of patriarchal control seeking to perpetuate male dominance.

The purposeful and studied linkage of his characters and plot developments to real world analogues in *A Song of Ice and Fire* constitutes one of Martin's most notable departures from the fantasy genre. Daenerys reminds of Joan of Arc in her "birth" upon Drogo's funeral pyre—her experience of course voluntary, and unlike her progenitor resulted in a physical rebirth rather than a spiritual one via martyrdom—and in the religious devotion she inspires in those she leads into battle. The Dothraki are based on Mongols and other nomadic tribal peoples of the steppes of Asia, Central Europe, and North America, many of whom relied heavily upon the horse in order to dominate these lands. The Wall is based upon the Great Wall of China and, especially, Hadrian's Wall in England, the latter built to keep the fierce Picts and other tribal groups from making incursions into the Roman-held lands of Britannia. More controversially, in depicting a massive civil war set in a world of antiquity with traditional gender values, Martin necessarily had to negotiate aspects of storyline appropriate to such a world. In exploring the intersections between masculinity, violence, and power, Martin sampled from different time periods and locations, each with different views of gender, kinship, and sexuality. It is therefore difficult to link his characters and plot developments—or those of the HBO show—directly to their historical antecedents other than in how each fits within the larger project of patriarchy on display.

Of course, the enormous sprawl of this fictional world and the amount of time it has taken him to write it have inevitably introduced problems involving consistency. Compound Martin's at times inconsistent approach to gender with an even more inconsistent portrayal within the HBO show—not to mention the problem of showing visually what might not be as difficult to read textually—and the difficulty in finding a coherent message about masculinity within *A Song of Ice and Fire* and *Game of Thrones* becomes obvious. Martin's universe is so massive and so loaded with signs—many of which are emotionally coded—that many readers infuse their own ideas, presuppositions, and even values into the text. Despite what amounts to a project of eisegesis about a text which has produced large amounts of scholarly criticism—as well as countless opinion pieces in the blogosphere—there are still quite a number of takeaways regarding patriarchy and masculinity. Gabrielle Bruney indicts the show's tendency "to mount its action upon the stage of women's bodies" (Burney), and Harriet Williamson reminds us that some of the shows excesses exist commonly in the real world, bravely noting that, as a sexual assault survivor, she has difficulty watching a show with so many rape scenes (Williamson). In identifying a narrative device whereby monologues filled with information are delivered in brothels—so that gratuitous sex scenes can be included as backdrop—Myles McNutt even coined a phrase now part of the lexicon: "sexposition" (McNutt). Other critics, however, have focused upon the larger system of patriarchy and its gradual undoing at the hands of increasingly powerful female characters. Alyssa Rosenberg has written extensively about masculinity and power in the gender politics of *Game of Thrones*, noting how women are able to break free of toxic masculinity and stifling patriarchy, but not without significant—if not permanent or, in the case of Cersei and Dany, fatal—cost (Rosenberg).

Suspicion about power and patriarchal structures pervades both the books and the HBO adaptation. King Robert is powerful physically, Lord Tywin due to the strength of his strategic mind. Robb Stark gains power, even if only for a brief period of time, due to his family name and the manner in which he uses it to inspire his men. As Linda Antonsson points out, however, all three of these men fail:

> Characters are quite directly indicated to be great men: Tywin Lannister is called the greatest man to come along in a thousand years; Robert, during the war, is described in larger-than-life terms; Robb Stark is hailed as the Young Wolf personally responsible for the string of military victories.... No matter how much characters in the Seven Kingdoms, and the readers of the novels, might romanticize these "great men," might romanticize their past and present wars, might find endless virtues to praise, they're all brought down to the earth: Tywin is killed on the privy, Robert's gutted by a boar, Robb Stark is betrayed and his corpse desecrated [12].

Antonsson—who along with Martin and Elio M. García Jr., co-authored *The World of Ice & Fire*—makes good points. Furthermore, warning signs for each character's downfall appear long before their fate. Robert is one of the strongest men in Westeros, second only to Gregor Clegane and possibly Lyle Crakehall, known as Strongboar. A minor book character absent from the HBO series, Strongboar is nevertheless notable in that he doubles Robert. A tactless carouser who relies on brute strength in combat, Strongboar's impulsiveness is not well suited for anything other than the heat of battle. When it comes to fighting wars, men such as Robert Baratheon and Strongboar are necessary. However, in the peace that inevitably follows, they are ill-suited for leadership, although due to the medieval structure of the world the winners of such battles gain lands and titles. On their way to King's Landing, Robert even admits as much to Ned, noting that his skill set was tailor-made for the rebellion but not for what came after.

Linda Antonsson also mentions Robb's downfall, which similarly involves aspects of masculinity. Although Robb proves his mettle, both in uniting the northern families and in his battlefield exploits, he duplicates some of Robert's problems. Robb relies on his skill in battle to win the war, not realizing that some victories are best accomplished with words and ravens rather than with swords. The political maneuvering of three older and wiser men—Tywin Lannister, Walder Frey, and Roose Bolton—prove his undoing. Notably, the show never depicts any of these three directly participating in fighting. Robb also duplicates his father's mistakes, naively believing that such things as Guest Rite will protect him and his men at Edmure Tully's wedding. Robb may be outclassed by these three older men, but that is not to suggest that the narrative validates Tywin's obsession with patrilineal succession, Roose's cruelty, or Walder's family loyalty. In fairly short order, two of these men are destroyed by their own progeny (Roose so that Ramsay can ensure his own succession, Tywin due to Tyrion's desire for revenge) and the third is killed by Arya Stark, who relies upon Walder's lechery to allow her, wearing the mask of a scullery maid, to get close to him. And Robb is not the only one of the five kings to be undone, in part, by aspects of masculinity. Joffrey Baratheon does not fully appreciate the manner in which cruelty translates to enemies, and that cruelty in high enough quantities allows boldness to overcome fear in such enemies. In a subversion of patriarchy, two of the five kings end up killed by a woman, but unlike Stannis who is done in by a powerful warrior in the personage of Brienne of Tarth, Joffrey gets poisoned by an elderly woman, Lady Olenna Tyrell. Brienne's execution of Stannis in Season Five serves as a form of gendered divine justice, Olenna's more a statement about the futility of Joffrey's use of power against that of a wily matriarch. It should be noted that Littlefinger acts as a silent partner in this scheme. As a character who neither benefits from a family name nor embraces a martial approach, he must out-think his opponents. Littlefinger's only real foray into the traditional realm of masculine competition, in fact, is the duel he fought many years ago over Catelyn Tully, a contest in which he was soundly defeated and permanently scarred.

Balon Greyjoy, on the other hand, is undone by his younger brother, Euron. Whereas in the books a faceless man kills Balon (presumably as hired by Euron), in the HBO show Euron serves as the literal agent of Balon's demise, the act of throwing his elder brother over a bridge direct commentary about patriarchy. Despite the fact that the Iron Islands elect their leader through the Kingsmoot, the recent practice in the islands was for patrilineal succession, giving Euron every hope that he would be the one to replace his brother. Such principles of succession also play a role in the murder of Renly Baratheon, who in the show cannot perform sexually with his wife Margery. Stannis predicates his claim to the throne on patrilineal succession, in his case with the medieval practice of primogeniture, where it is not the firstborn child but the firstborn *male* who should rule (practiced everywhere in Westeros but Dorne). Stannis has a daughter, although the show indicates that his wife Selyse has had a number of stillborn sons, an added flourish which highlights the importance of sons when houses and even kingdoms are at stake. The books contain an additional sub-plot with interesting implications for Stannis' embrace of traditionally patriarchal notions of royal succession. Gendry in the show is an amalgamation of two characters, the book Gendry (Arya's friend) and another one of Robert's bastards, Edric Storm, from whom Melisandre leaches blood to defeat Stannis' enemies. Edric's backstory occurs in the wake of Robert's Rebellion, when during Stannis and Selyse's wedding festivities a drunken Robert carried one of her maids up to the marital bed in order to break it in. Conceived during this union, Edric becomes one of few bastards that Robert officially recognizes. Selyse attributes her inability to conceive a male heir to this defilement of their marital bed. In cutting out the character of Edric the show loses this critique of Robert. However, Benioff and Weiss include numerous other attacks on traditional patriarchy.

Tywin Lannister constitutes the final character parsed in Antonsson's quote about the failures of traditional power in Westeros. In many ways, he stands as one of the most fascinating figures in this fictional realm. As a character, Tywin exhibits few of the traditional markers of masculinity valued in Westeros. Not feared for his physical prowess, he is instead a thinker, strategic and cautious and very much Robert's antithesis. His economic success bolsters his political acumen, in particular through the Lannister gold mines. Despite achieving success through these channels, Tywin is one of the most respected men in all of Westeros, perhaps because he has been so very successful over such a long period of time, and so thoroughly reversed the lot of his own house. Although it appears as backstory, his father was quite weak, to the point that he allowed himself to be bullied by his own bannermen. Tywin began restoring the Lannister power even before inheriting Casterly Rock, during the rebellion of several families. As memorialized in the song "The Rains of Castamere," the Reynes defied the Lannisters, sealing themselves in a mine shaft they knew could be defended with ease against the invading army. Tywin had a river diverted into the mine, drowning the entirety of House Reyne, including women and children. Although he played a role in subsequent military campaigns, after the destruction of House Reyne he is most well-known for settling conflicts through political and economic means. In this way, much like his rival Ned Stark, he does not conform to Westerosi models of traditional masculinity.

Tywin might thus seem like a refreshing departure from the norm when it comes to depictions of patriarchy, but he is anything but, a truth that is underscored in his failure to survive the machinations surrounding the consolidation of Lannister rule following King Robert's death. First of all, those with facility at statecraft incentivize would-be usurpers to hatch even craftier plans, and Tywin does not realize that Littlefinger and Lady Olenna conspire to replace Joffrey with Tommen, whom they feel Margaery can control. In "The Climb," Tywin believes that he has defeated Olenna in her political maneuvering but, in reality, all he does is ensure that she will take the next step, and murder Joffrey. Tywin's threat to Olenna is very revealing, as it becomes clear that despite having two sons, he is just as concerned as Stannis about the laws of primogeniture. In arranging marriages for his children, Tywin goes a step further in the autocratic approach he takes in the face of their objection, very much in line with the Roman concept of *pater familias*, where the father had absolute power over all family members. Tywin believes that Jaime should rule after his death. The only problem is that the Mad King appointed Jaime to the Kingsguard as a rebuke to the growth of Lannister power. Although he may have been insane, Aerys II realized that this appointment meant Jaime would no longer be Tywin's heir. Many years later the shoe is on the other foot, with Tywin threatening to put Ser Loras on the Kingsguard in order to ensure Olenna's compliance. This departure from the books provides another critique of patriarchal succession, as it can be weaponized by those competing for power (in the books, Loras joins the Kingsguard, as unlike in the show he has two older brothers and is not the heir to Highgarden).

Tywin is fascinating for his blind spot: his other two children—neither of whom he views as good enough to be his heir—are much closer to him in their strategic capacity, although he is singularly and wholly fixated on Jaime. Tywin dismisses Cersei due to her gender, and Tyrion due to his deformity (and some book readers have theorized because he suspects that Tyrion might not be his son). These two characters, however, are consistently depicted—along with Varys, Littlefinger, Doran Martell (at least in the books), and perhaps a couple more—as playing the game of thrones on a very deep level. At least in the show, were it not for Drogon it is very likely that Cersei would have been the last ruler standing in Westeros, and Tyrion routinely out-thinks his opponents. However, in Tywin's mind both have handicaps that preclude them from ever ruling effectively. As Ian Ross notes, Tywin's view of his youngest son fits into Martin's larger thesis regarding how those with physical deformities are diminished by those around them:

Despite his talents and credibility, Tyrion's size causes his father to see him as a stain on the pride of the Lannister name. Maimed characters like the scarred Hound, one-handed Jaime, or castrated Theon are consistently mocked, underestimated, or shunned for their physical deformities by those in power [171–172].

As becomes increasingly evident as the realm devolves into chaos—much as occurred during parts of the feudal period in medieval Europe—Westerosi chivalry is paper thin and easily pierced during times of peace, let alone civil war. Characters in this world, much as our own, are held to impossible gender standards and forced to live with the judgment and scorn of those around them lucky to have been born into or acquired positions of privilege. As Ross goes on to note, however, such characters are eventually validated in both print and on screen:

> Therefore, we see that instead of creating a world of shining knights for us to cheer, David Benioff and D.B. Weiss (and of course George R.R. Martin) create a world that punishes physical deviation from hegemony in the extreme. However, much more importantly, the series also props these characters up as the secret heroes and architects of this world by providing characters with new means of wielding power [172].

In the show at least, despite being a paraplegic and unable to produce an heir, Brandon Stark becomes the King, at least in name. Despite his size, Tyrion Lannister becomes Hand of the King, but as the ending suggests the actual King in everything but name. Theon Greyjoy and the Hound are given the two biggest redemption stories, further evidence that traditional masculinity is not necessary for, and often exists as an impediment to, power. Heroism, bravery, and other such positive attributes are not solely reserved for those who easily slot into traditional roles of patriarchy.

It is also instructive to explore how certain groups are depicted when it comes to notions of gender and power. The show's widely disparaged "Dornish subplot," as it has become known, introduced four powerful women to the narrative, one noted for her political prowess (Ellaria Sand), the other three for their skill in fighting (Obara, Nymeria, & Tyene Sand). These characters showed initial promise but devolved into cartoonish depictions before ultimately serving as a vehicle for a revenge plot involving mothers and daughters. The end of this narrative arc also served as a backdrop for one of Dany's early forays into "Mad Queen" territory when, in response to these four either being captured or killed, she mounts an attack on the Lannister supply train and burns both Randyll and Dickon Tarly for their refusal to kneel. The Dornish subplot was unpopular amongst the show's audience for the reasons noted above, but amongst the book readers for another: the elision of Arianne Martell, Doran's oldest child. The Dornish observe the laws of primogeniture but not patrilineal succession, which means that Arianne is heir to Doran's throne. Omitting Arianne from the show in favor of Trystane undercuts the project of critiquing patriarchy in that it elides the only Westerosi system of governance where women can inherit, doubly so in that Arianne is intelligent and calculating. The omission of Sarella Sand, one of the book's additional Sand Snakes, is also troubling. Although not yet confirmed, it is widely believed that Alleras, one of the initiate maesters Sam Tarly meets in the Citadel, is actually Sarella. If so, that means that she has passed as male for over a year at the Citadel, forging several links on her way to becoming a female maester in what is supposed to be an all-male order and subverting the medievalist view that knowledge is a domain reserved solely for men.

Aside from the Dornish, the Dothraki and the Unsullied fascinate from a gender standpoint, particularly as contrasted with one another. Much of the time, the Dothraki are represented as extremely patriarchal. The culture is nearly uniform in its martial outlook with rank earned by one's facility as a fighter. Where one sits at a meal indicates status, those who are infirm or crippled sitting far from the fire alongside the elderly, who instead of being venerated for their wisdom join the others who cannot fight. The hair braid represents another marker of status among Dothraki men. Should he lose a fight, a Dothraki fighter cuts off his braid, a symbolic act of castration signifying shame. The longer the braid, the higher ranking the Dothraki, his entire value represented in a phallic symbol of power built solely upon his ability to ride a horse and swing an *arakh*. However, as Valerie Frankel points out, although the Dothraki are depicted as the most unrelentingly patriarchal group in this world, they are in one respect ruled over by old women (124). Former *khaleesis*, the wives of dead *khals*, make up the *dosh khaleen*, which governs certain aspects of the Dothraki culture and interprets their prophecies. The Dothraki are migratory, and historically such cultures kept time by the lunar cycle, in so doing attaching notions of spirituality to the female menstrual cycle. Due to the Dothraki's martial nature, most of the older voices—presumably wiser in benefitting from experience—would come from women who have grown to old age. Despite the *dosh khaleen*, however, the Dothraki are not matriarchal, rather a strongly patriarchal culture that, once a year, pays lip service to listening to their female elders. The episode "Book of the Stranger" establishes that the power of the *dosh khaleen* only extends so far, with the *khals* making the final decisions, ones rooted in adolescent squabbling over status and property. Drogo's death is also significant in that he does not die in battle but instead distally from an infection acquired following a fight with one of his lieutenants (proximally, Dany smothers him with a pillow). As the fiercest Dothraki in living memory, Drogo falling off his horse and brought low by blood poisoning testifies as to the emptiness of his pride and futility of his masculinity.

Most of the societies and cultures depicted in this fictional world feature female empowerment of some form or another. Although there are clear gender divisions amongst the Wildling clans, clearly women from north of The Wall have more agency in choosing their partners. Also, Wildling women fight alongside men, and the commander of Mance Rayder's vanguard, Harma Dogshead, is female (although, in a troubling twist in the show, she is completely undone at Hardhome when faced with the knowledge that children can be turned into wights). A woman—Chella, of the Black Ears—leads one of the hill tribes in the Mountains of the Moon area of the Vale. The Unsullied represents the only sub-culture that does not have female leadership, and that is because they have no female members, although Grey Worm and his compatriots remain wholly and completely devoted to Dany. As a group, the Unsullied serve as a ready counterpoint to the Dothraki, well-disciplined and from all appearances completely unmotivated by status or material gain. They do not rape and plunder after victories in battle, as do the Dothraki. Although the Unsullied may not be the most realistic portrayal of eunuchs—a well-documented side effect of castration is weight gain, in part due to lower testosterone levels—there are real world precedents for warrior eunuchs, although most were relegated to the arena of politics. As Sarah Bond notes, it is the very obsession with patrilineal primogeniture that ensured many eunuchs' elevated status, from antiquity through the medieval period and even, in a few areas, into the modern era: "One of the attractive things about eunuchs used either as soldiers or as court servants was the lack of sexual and reproductive threat; they would never have sons that could threaten the allegiance of their fathers or put the court at risk" (Bond). In particular, Varys' claim that he owes his allegiance to the realm resonates with this aspect in history. In the absence of a family that can carry forth his legacy, Varys' impact will be on the world he leaves behind, hopefully one devoid of a vain or cruel ruler whose power flows solely from inherited power.

As Benjamin Bartu notes, castration has often been dismissed both in history and in Westeros as an eastern, foreign ritual, although the truth is much more complicated (74). Although largely eliminated from both east and west by the early modern period, eunuchs were part of the Ottoman Empire until its dissolution following World War I, and Allesandro Moreschi, the last *castrati* opera singer, performed into the 20th century. Historically, most eunuchs were cut early in their lives, although one stands out in *Game of Thrones* for his recent status: Theon Greyjoy. Grey Worm and the other Unsullied were castrated early in life, Varys as an older child. Ramsey Bolton emasculates Theon, however, as an adult and after the latter has had direct, sexual knowledge. Carolyne Larrington also points out that Theon's is extra-judicial in nature, unlike many of the castrations in Essos (205).

Theon's physical emasculation is presaged by Robert's crushing of the Iron Islands during Balon Greyjoy's ill-advised uprising, and later by Theon's treatment at the hands of his father and sister. Theon labors under a difficult yoke, as he is the youngest and now only son of Balon, his older brothers killed in the uprising. He grew up a ward of House Stark, in essence a hostage ensuring that Balon Greyjoy did not attempt another rebellion. As Larrington notes, "His position as hostage compromises his sense of honour, particularly in the face of his father's unyielding view of what constitutes Greyjoy honour" (18). Theon finds himself stuck between two honor codes, one espoused by a biological father he barely knows, the other by the man who raised him to adulthood. As Myke Coyle points out, the PTSD that Theon suffers post-emasculation relates distally to the continual reminder during his adolescence of his prisoner status and due to the poor treatment he received from the Stark siblings, even when he saves Bran from the wildlings (Coyle 82–83), the young Stark himself a sort of eunuch figure given his injuries. Theon's mis-treatment continues when he finally returns to Pyke in "The Night Lands," as his sister humiliates him—perhaps justifiable considering he tries to seduce her—and his father derides him as a "girl" for dressing in northern fashion.

Trauma connects to both role and performance, and Theon is forced by the agent of his emasculation to play the part of Reek, his role as sexless servant even more humiliating given the lothario persona he previously embraced. Grey Worm moves in the other direction, from slave to general. He gains rather than loses power and can choose to leave but instead opts to serve Daenerys. Varys plays multiple roles, pretending to be an obsequious servant while in reality attempting to play kingmaker. Theon exists as a pure victim, however, moving from Greyjoy heir apparent to Ramsay's plaything. The tortures of the flesh, despite their excessiveness, pale in comparison to the complete evacuation of his character in so thoroughly embracing his Reek identity. As Colt J. Blunt notes, Theon displays not only symptoms of PTSD, but also sensory deprivation, conditioned response, and Stockholm Syndrome (75–76, 80). Theon redeems himself, however, by fighting for his sister and protecting Bran. His transformation begins at the Kingsmoot, a rare example of democracy in Westerosi governance. Although he gives an impassioned speech promoting his sister's claim, as a woman she has even less of a chance of being elected than does he. Much of Theon's redemption comes about because of his skills as a fighter: he wins a fight with a member of his crew—fortuitously, because being kicked in the groin does not affect him—thus allowing him to regain control of his men. At the Battle of Winterfell he keeps the wights at bay in the godswood long enough for Arya to have the epiphany that she must kill the Night King. Before he dies, Bran validates him as a "good man," a problematic conclusion given the fullness of his arc as a serial womanizer and former purveyor of patriarchy.

Varys, on the other hand, appears to have no sexual interests whatsoever. His mission of benefitting the realm consistently benefits from a lack of personal desire, despite his attempts to acquire power. As Bartu further notes:

> Varys is also, notably, the only one of the three eunuchs never depicted in physical combat. He is also one of the only men in the entire series depicted as having no thirst for participating in violence himself.... Just as Theon loses a fundamental part of his fighting nature when he is castrated, Varys has either lost that part of himself as well or never possessed it in the first place. His physical characteristics place him within a space that so few "intact" men get to inhabit in the world of Westeros, where he can operate without having any expectation of military performance placed on him [73].

It should be noted that Varys on the show is quite different from Varys as depicted in the books. In the latter, he wears loose-fitted clothing to hide the fact that he's muscular and powerful, and he is proficient with weapons, killing Pycelle and mortally wounding Kevan Lannister. The character Strong Belwas further establishes the book's greater complexity when it comes to eunuchs and power. This character—who does not appear in the show—is a former pit fighter from Meereen who attaches himself to Dany's cause. He claims to have never lost a match and counts his victories by the number of scars on his body, as he allows each opponent to cut him once before dispatching them. Although many of his claims likely involve self-aggrandizement, the ease with which he kills the champion of Meereen—in the books, Belwas and not Daario Naharis takes up this challenge—suggests that at the very least, he is a highly skilled fighter. Strong Belwas, Varys and, despite his former status as a chauvinist womanizer, even Theon Greyjoy bring complexity to the representation of masculinity by demonstrating how physical emasculation does not necessarily result in actual disempowerment, subverting how power in the narrative is both constructed and perceived.

Further complexity exists in the portrayal of knighthood in *Game of Thrones*. At the beginning of the narrative, chivalry appears to be alive and well in both the print and screen versions of Westeros. All is not as it appears, however, and the ideals of courtesy, honor, and manners are in short order demonstrated to be a facade. As Charles H. Hackney notes, "One must search high and low to find knights who genuinely embody such ideals. The majority of Westerosi knights are often brutal, often uncouth, often dishonest, often impious, often lecherous, and certainly no friend to the smallfolk" (132–133). Hackney also notes that numerous characters in Westeros lament the loss of a chivalry that pervaded earlier times, but that

Martin's novella *The Hedge Knight* demonstrates that the knights of the past were just as inconsistent in their application of these ideals (134). And Martin's *Fire and Blood*, the first installment of his multi-volume history of the Targaryen family, does so on a more massive scale. In *Game of Thrones*, much of the disillusionment regarding the chivalric code comes through Sansa Stark's storyline, first in learning about Loras Tyrell's trick of jousting on a mare in heat to help him unseat Gregor Clegane, and later—and more seriously—in the way that Joffrey treats her once he is king.

Instead of representing the pinnacle of chivalry, the Kingsguard—at least under Joffrey, after the dismissal of Barristan Selmy—represents its very antithesis in their treatment of Sansa, their interactions with the people of King's Landing, and in the attempt to kill Tyrion during the Battle of Blackwater Bay. Ken Mondschein argues that the numerous depictions of failed chivalry fit within a consistent thesis:

> George R.R. Martin is rather cynical about knighthood. There are no paragons of chivalry in this world: Boros Blount is a coward who beats Sansa Stark on Joffrey's orders; Amory Lorch and Gregor Clegane are monsters; Jorah Mormont is a slaver and a traitor; Dontos Hollard, who images himself a hero out of legend, is a lecherous, drunken sot [11].

Stacey Goguen makes the connection between this aspect of Westerosi masculinity and Sansa Stark even more strongly, noting how this character represents more than just the prism through which Westerosi chivalry is exposed as false, but also serves as an example of how the code conspires to disenfranchise women:

> Chivalry treats (highborn) women as having a childlike status and then assumes that the status is a natural trait. Just as Sansa has been taught and encouraged to take on certain childish traits, chivalry encourages women to be vulnerable and dependent. It also encourages other people (especially knights) to treat women as if they are in a perpetually vulnerable state [210].

Perhaps the characters who best live up to Sansa's vision of the chivalric code are her father and half-brother. Eventually, she ends up viewing that it was just these qualities of honor and fair play that led to the death of one, and the subsuming of the other's ambition to that of Daenerys Targaryen.

Larrington notes that the Stark ancestral sword, Ice, both introduces Ned into the story as an authority invested in meting out death, while serving as the eventual agent of his own mortality (48). Ned carries out his own executions, in part due to a high-minded ideal he explains to Bran, but really due to a ritual that dates back to the First Men, from whom the Starks descend. The implication is that "real men" swing the sword, and later in the show we see Robb carry out this sentence after Rickard Karstark's betrayal, although unlike Ned he is unable to perform the coup de grace cleanly due to Ice's massive size. Many honor codes exist throughout the narrative—most with traditions designed to perpetuate patriarchy—and no two are the same. Ned's code, for instance, differs from that of the Dothraki. Ned's code may be more consistent but his rigid adherence to such aspects of chivalry—honor, tradition, justice—hinder him from moving against Cersei when she and Littlefinger conspire against him. They outmaneuver him effortlessly, and he loses his power just a few short months in King's Landing despite having ruled the north for over a decade. Traditional codes of masculinity mean nothing in the arena of shifting alliances, with men such as Littlefinger and Varys better suited for playing power politics. Ned fails completely, as does Robb, perhaps not as rigid as his father but nearly as much so. Robb's downfall comes in the form of, much like Ned's, not fully understanding what motivates those around him and trusting that those with competing agendas will follow the same code of conduct. Walder Frey, deeply insulted by Robb's abandonment of the Stark-Frey marriage pact, sides with the Lannisters and making plans for Robb and his men to be slaughtered despite the age-old protections of Guest Rite. To Robb, this ritual serves as a protection; to the Freys, as well as the Lannisters and Boltons, it represents an easily removed impediment to concluding a costly and ongoing civil war. When it comes to power, rigidity rooted in tradition and honor can facilitate a strong group identity; however, it can also mean that competitors willing to try various avenues are more able to usurp that power.

Jon Snow was raised as Ned Stark's son and embraces the Stark code, but he is more fluid in his outlook than his adoptive father and brother. As Larrington notes, the north is a lot rougher than the rest of Westeros, and thus a place where warriors can thrive and knights are not needed (57). This assertion does not seem to apply to Ned. He tells Jaime Lannister that he does not fight in tournaments because he does not want his opponents to know his fighting capacity, but in reality there are no tournaments in the north for northern knights to fight in. Despite the lack of a need for knights, Ned still adheres to a knight's code. Larrington's point rings truer for Jon, and it applies rather strictly to the Night's Watch. Martin based this group on several chivalric knight organizations—most notable of which were the Knights Templar—but in many ways the Watch is anything but chivalric. Honor, justice, and all other such features are completely and utterly subsumed by the central project of protecting the realm from the wildlings. The Night's Watch does have codified rules and expectations, but these are less about chivalry and more about an agenda whose pursuit validates all actions, no matter how heinous they would be considered in the rest of the Seven Kingdoms. With the Night's Watch, the ends truly do justify the means, with a 1000-year distrust of the wildlings giving context to the actions of the brothers who murder Jon (Bowen Marsh and Wick Whittlestick in the novels, Ser Alliser Thorne and Olly in the show). In some situations, Jon is much more fluid than were Ned and Robb, able to adapt to new situations despite his desire to follow the code exemplified by his father. In other moments, however, he is just as rigid, such as when he cannot bring himself to kill the unarmed Ygritte, despite orders to do so. Although he has an attraction to her, the primary reason he disobeys Qhorin Halfhand remains that his code will not allow him to kill an unarmed woman.

Jon represents a study in contrasts in that sometimes he allows a traditional code of masculine behavior involving honor and tradition to govern his actions, while at other times he does not. Both approaches serve to place him in danger, and both save his life, the quintessential example being the plot point of forging an alliance with the wildlings, an action which precipitates his murder by Night's Watch brethren but that also saves not only his life but perhaps those of the entirety of Westeros as the Wildling army aids in the fight against the Night King. Jon is better equipped to survive the upheavals that grip Westeros following Robert's death, facing surprise after surprise but having a code of conduct that guides his actions much of the time, while having the fluidity to change when necessary. This duality stands in marked contrast to his adopted father, captured and executed with his own sword, which is subsequently melted down and remade into two Valyrian blades, both of which offer interesting sub-plots involving masculinity. Joffrey names his sword Widow's Wail, an unfitting moniker in his intention to assert his dominance in the military arena when in reality he is a coward who orders others to do his fighting. The other sword is Oathkeeper, given to the character who best exemplifies chivalry, with the possible exception of Ned Stark and Barristan Selmy (Hackney 135). This character is, ironically—but perhaps not surprisingly, given the narrative's indictment of traditional norms of masculinity—a woman: Brienne of Tarth.

Brienne perhaps represents the ultimate fish-out-water character in Westeros. There are plenty of other women who take on aspects of masculinity, if not patriarchy (Spector 182), and plenty of historical antecedents from which Martin no doubt drew in creating these characters: Joan of Arc, Mary Reed, Mademoiselle La Maupin, Anne Bonny (Frankel 46). At the most basic level, such characters adorn themselves with outward markers that suggest masculinity: Arya cuts her hair short and wears pants; Asha/Yara wears pants and openly flirts with women; Dany's sartorial choices gradually embrace a more masculine look as she moves east toward Meereen; and, Cersei keeps her hair short after it is shorn prior to her walk of atonement. Brienne's difference, however, lies in the depth and magnitude of her gender dysphoria. Arya has always been the Westerosi version of a tomboy, although some of her choices are so that she can blend in with the Night's Watch recruits while escaping King's Landing. Asha/Yara from the moment she is introduced, and Daenerys after a time, are quite comfortable with their sexual identity, as is Cersei.

Brienne stands out amongst this group of characters in the utter confusion evident in her POV chapters in *A Feast for Crows* and in Gwendoline Christie's portrayal of the character in the show—confusion not only about the role she is trying to carve out for herself but, more to the point, the effect it has on others. As Caroline Spector notes, those who encounter Brienne routinely deride her for the very character attributes that would be admired in a man: "Because her actions fall consistently and fully outside the social norms, Brienne provides a stark lesson on how women who dare to take male power for their own are judged and treated not only in Westeros but in all conventionally patriarchal societies" (180). Brienne thus differs from the other female characters in the narrative who usurp masculine power in that her size and strength allow her to not only compete, but also excel, in the world of physical competition. Throughout *Game of Thrones* there are countless examples of women empowered at the expense of men—Melisandre tying down Gendry in order to leach his blood, Dany making Daario disrobe in an example of the female gaze, to name a few— but Brienne's defeat of the Hound in hand-to-hand combat certainly stands as the most visceral example. The greatest battle she fights, however, lies in asserting her chosen identity against entrenched views regarding traits traditionally associated with masculinity, and reserved for men.

It should be noted that Arya treads some of this ground before Brienne even makes an appearance in the narrative. Arya's introduction showcases her boredom at domestic pursuits such as needlepoint and her facility with the bow & arrow. Spector notes that this character's subversion of patriarchy begins before she enters King's Landing: "When Arya defends Mycah against Joffrey, she steps outside the bounds of acceptable behavior, and in doing so, takes a piece of traditionally male power for herself" (173). Unlike Brienne, Arya enjoys a series of mentors—notably, all male—who guide her through her gender dysphoria. Syrio trains her in the sword, but many of his lessons double as instructions for how to role play (e.g., "My tongue lied, my eyes shouted the truth"). Yoren encourages her to embrace the role of "boy" in order to keep her safe. The Brotherhood Without Banners and, in particular, the Hound serve as protectors and even tutors in how to survive during a time of internecine conflict. And quintessentially, Arya receives training in how to embrace and fit into different roles at the House of Black & White. Brienne is gifted no such road map, both text and show making it clear that no one accepted her as is until she met Renly. Of course, it is Jaime Lannister with whom her journey will ultimately achieve fruition. Brienne's relationship with this foil, friend, and ultimately—if only for one night—lover exhibits tremendous complexity, full of inspired gender moments where Brienne is allowed to step outside her proscribed role but also missteps where traditional aspects of patriarchy are underscored.

When they first meet, Catelyn Stark tasks Brienne with escorting Jaime to King's Landing. Her prisoner, he must fence with words in order to diminish her and try and gain the upper hand. Later, they share a moment of victimization when she is nearly raped and his hand is cut off after coming to her rescue. The first seeds of attraction occur in the baths of Harrenhal, when for the first time Jaime sees her as something more than just a masculine woman: "Seeing each other naked thrusts sexual tension into their relationship, especially because Brienne's nakedness comes as a surprise to them both in its sudden exposure and in its undeniable evidence of her femaleness" (Moyce 65). In many ways, Brienne serves as Jaime's antithesis, at least when it comes to notions of chivalry. She embraces the code despite being told that she should act her place. Jaime, on the other hand, is noted as being one of the most proficient knights in the realm, but one who committed the ultimate non-chivalric act of murdering his king and who has continued to act in ways unbecoming of a knight, including pushing Bran out a window for witnessing his liaison with Cersei and murdering his cousin, Alton, during a failed bid to escape imprisonment. Incongruously, this epitome of what a knight is *not* supposed to be finally knights Brienne, although given their relationship and his journey of redemption, this scene is one of the final season's most poignant. However, in a reversal greatly maligned by the show's fans, Jaime seduces Brienne and subsequently abandons her for Cersei following the Battle of Winterfell. She handles this rejection with grace, lauding Jaime in the White Book, where the accomplishments of the Kingsguard are recorded. Brienne has travelled a long road in her bid to live with gender attributes normally reserved for men. She goes from being a victim of societal derision and near victim of rape to being the only female knight in the realm and the captain of Bran's Kingsguard, who in her final scene holds the power to define legacies in deciding how Jaime Lannister will be remembered.

Brienne is far from the only character in Westeros or Essos subjected to sexualized violence, rape being an all too common method of power and control employed throughout the narrative. Another essay in this book collection explores violence against women, but the subject must be addressed here vis-à-vis excessive masculinity and the manner in which these depictions threaten to undermine the thesis that traditional masculinity is inevitably destructive. As Alyssa Rosenberg perceptively notes, rape is portrayed in many different ways throughout the series, simultaneously the lynchpin for the overthrow of the Targaryen dynasty following the supposed abduction of Lyanna Stark, a method of humiliation and control employed by powerful men and entire cohorts such as the Dothraki, and a crime so disruptive to society that those guilty of it are threatened with either castration or exile to the wall (19). It can be a fine line between a depiction of rape as the apotheosis of toxic patriarchy and an implicit support of rape culture. Rosenberg supports the former by noting that the show consistently associates the act with some of the narrative's true monsters: Gregor Clegane and Ramsay Bolton weaponize rape, Roose Bolton asserts his First Night rites, and Joffrey employs the threat of sexual violence, all of these moments both about the assertion of control and personal satisfaction (22–25). Other examples encompass numerous typologies, from cultural rituals of conquest (Iron Born, Dothraki) to sexual violence as a form of punishment (Tywin ordering the violation of Tyrion's first wife), from assault for personal satisfaction (Polliver and the innkeeper's daughter) to depictions of intimate partner violence (Jaime and Cersei at Joffrey's wake, Craster and his daughter-wives).

Rosenberg concludes her excellent study of sexual violence by noting how, in the books, Martin situates depictions of rape within a greater, and largely consistent, textual indictment of destructive patriarchy:

> Unpunished rape is a sin that carries implications far beyond individual victims and perpetrators, a crime that comes back to haunt the society that permits and enables it. This is the one moment in the novels when the characters acknowledge an argument that Martin's been building for us all along: rape produces damage that lingers beyond a single act, a single victim. It can produce monsters and contribute to the destabilization of entire societies [26].

Rosenberg's make a good case, as Martin's depictions are less about sensationalism and more about the long-lasting destructiveness of the ultimate excess of patriarchy. The same cannot be said for how the show handled this subject. Perhaps part of the reason the show's depictions were more sensational revolved around the visual nature of the depictions, but that does not explain the gratuity of representation from Dany's wedding night with Drogo, to Sansa's wedding night with Ramsay, to Jaime forcing himself on Cersei against the corpse of their dead son. The numerous depictions of rape in Martin's text represent the finishing touches of a thesis developed over thousands of pages: patriarchy perpetuates structures of male dominance that inevitably result in sexual exploitation and violence. The depictions of rape in the show, however, are much more problematic, sensationalized in such a way that—along with some of the problematic gender reversals evident in Season Eight (particularly involving Daenerys)—they threaten to undermine the show's greater trajectory of suspicion when it comes to the destructiveness of masculinity and patriarchy.

There are many other topics that might be explored when it comes to depictions of masculinity in *Game of Thrones*: parent/child and sibling relationships; the role of alcohol in violence and sexualized violence; bullying; depictions of same-sex sexuality (including the paucity of such depictions on both page and screen); the intersection of masculinity and race; romantic and non-romantic love; and others. The narrative encompasses a fictional world that spans (thus far) five books and eight seasons, featuring hundreds of characters involved in thousands of interactions in dozens of cultures spread across two continents. The complexity of the fictional universe and its sprawl across multiple decades and several forms of media make it difficult to come up with a *singular* conclusion as to whether or not traditional patriarchy as a system, and masculinity as its core feature, stands indicted or supported. Despite this caveat, a central goal involves demonstrating the long-lasting harm perpetuated by individuals and groups who use privilege, violence, and even sexualized violence to control those around them. This world teems with victims of such a system, people who for no fault of their own are either forced to accept their victim status or step outside their personal honor codes or comfort zones in order to survive, forced to either accept the gender roles expected of them or risk censure, or worse, for displaying their true identity. In this way, George R.R. Martin's *A Song of Ice and Fire* consistently subverts patriarchy, although its HBO adaptation, replete with numerous problematic depictions of sexualized violence and plagued by character reversals, offers a more conflicted message.

Works Cited

Antonsson, Linda, and Elio M. Garcia. "The Palace of Love, the Palace of Sorrow" in *Beyond the Wall: Exploring George R.R. Martin's A Song of Ice and Fire*, edited by James Lowder. Dallas: BenBella Books, 2012. pp. 1–14.
Bartu, Benjamin. "A Few Broken Men: The Eunuchs and Their Names" in *Vying for the Iron Throne: Essays on Power, Gender, Death and Performance in HBO's Game of Thrones*, edited by Lindsey Mantoan and Sara Brady. Jefferson, NC: McFarland, 2018. pp. 69–78.
Blunt, Colt J. "The Breaking of a Man: Torture and Transformation" in *Game of Thrones Psychology: The Mind Is Dark and Full of Terrors*, edited by Travis Langley. New York: Sterling Publishing, 2016. pp. 71–83.
Bond, Sarah. "What *Game of Thrones* Gets Right and Wrong About Eunuchs and Masculinity." *Forbes*, 20 Aug. 2017, www.forbes.com/sites/drsarahbond/2017/08/20/what-game-of-thrones-gets-right-and-wrong-about-eunuchs-and-masculinity/#6e58df3bc55f. Accessed 8 Dec. 2019.
Bruney, Gabrielle. "*Game of Thrones*'s Treatment of Women Tarnish Its Legacy." *Esquire*, 11 Apr. 2019, www.esquire.com/entertainment/tv/a27099255/game-of-thrones-treatment-of-women-controversy-legacy/. Accessed 1 Dec. 2020.
Coyle, Myke. "Art Imitates War: Post-Traumatic Stress Disorder in *A Song of Ice and Fire*" in *Beyond the Wall: Exploring George R.R. Martin's A Song of Ice and Fire*, edited by James Lowder. Dallas: BenBella Books, 2012. pp. 73–88.
Frankel, Valerie Estelle. *Women in Game of Thrones: Power, Conformity and Resistance*. Jefferson, NC: McFarland, 2014.

Goguen, Stacey. "'There are no true knights': The Injustice of Chivalry" in *Game of Thrones and Philosophy*, edited by Henry Jacoby. Hoboken: John Wiley & Sons, 2012. pp. 205–219.

Hackney, Charles H. "'Silk ribbons tied around a sword': Knighthood and the Chivalric Virtues in Westeros" in *Mastering The Game of Thrones: Essays on George R.R. Martin's A Song of Ice and Fire*, edited by Jes Battis and Susan Johnston. Jefferson, NC: McFarland, 2015. pp. 132–149.

Larrington, Carolyne. *Winter Is Coming: The Medieval World of Game of Thrones*. London: I.B. Tauris, 2016.

McNutt, Myles. "*Game of Thrones*—You Win or You Die." *Cultural Learnings*, 29 May 2011, cultural-learnings.com/2011/05/29/game-of-thrones-you-win-or-you-die/. Accessed 1 Dec. 2020.

Mondschein, Ken. *Game of Thrones and the Medieval Art of War*. Jefferson, NC: McFarland, 2017.

Moyce, Audrey. "Brienne and Jaime's Queer Intimacy" in *Vying for the Iron Throne: Essays on Power, Gender, Death and Performance in HBO's Game of Thrones*, edited by Lindsey Mantoan and Sara Brady. Jefferson, NC: McFarland, 2018. pp. 59–68.

Rosenberg, Alyssa. "Men and Monsters: Rape, Myth-Making, and the Rise and Fall of Nations in *A Song of Ice and Fire*" in *Beyond the Wall: Exploring George R.R. Martin's A Song of Ice and Fire*, edited by James Lowder. Dallas: BenBella Books, 2012. pp. 15–27.

_____. "The arguments about women and power in *Game of Thrones* have never been more unsettling." *The Washington Post*, 9 Aug. 2017, www.washingtonpost.com/news/act-four/wp/2017/08/09/the-arguments-about-women-and-power-in-game-of-thrones-have-never-been-more-unsettling/. Accessed 1 Dec. 2020.

Ross, Ian. "Avatars and Identity Performance: Disembodied Self in Virtual Spaces" in *Vying for the Iron Throne: Essays on Power, Gender, Death and Performance in HBO's Game of Thrones*, edited by Lindsey Mantoan and Sara Brady. Jefferson, NC: McFarland, 2018. pp. 171–181.

Spector, Caroline. "Power and Feminism in Westeros" in *Beyond the Wall: Exploring George R.R. Martin's A Song of Ice and Fire*, edited by James Lowder. Dallas: BenBella Books, 2012. pp. 169–188.

Williamson, Harriet. "The Sexual Violence in *Game of Thrones* Has Gone Too Far." *Grazia*, 19 May 2015, graziadaily.co.uk/life/opinion/ok-sexual-violence-game-thrones-gone-far/. Accessed 1 Dec. 2020.

"I'll go with anger"
Female Rage in and at Game of Thrones

Lindsey Mantoan

Near the conclusion of Season Seven of *Game of Thrones*, as fans have endured growing tension between Arya and Sansa Stark sowed by Petyr Baelish, Sansa cautions Arya, "You're angry. Sometimes anger makes people do unfortunate things." Arya replies, "Sometimes fear makes them do unfortunate things. I'll go with anger" (S7, E6). Little did fans know, the Stark sisters were putting on a public performance for Baelish's benefit and—audiences learn later—quietly plotting his downfall.

This exchange provides an excellent example of the ways in which women—on screen and off—navigate their personal and political anger. The 2010s might well be remembered as the decade of female anger, and the consequences of ignoring it. From discourses about "likeable women" (see Nilsen) to critiques of what it means for a woman to have "angry face" (see Barrett), women are awakening to their own anger and the ways in which patriarchal systems ingrain self-censorship in them, and men are awakening to the realities that women feel anger just as much as they do, if not more (see, for example, Chemaly xv). Since the election of Donald Trump, female anger has become a popular narrative in the U.S. from arenas spanning television to government. From the Women's March in January 2016 to the many articles citing female anger as the reason unprecedented numbers of women ran for office in 2018 (see, for example, Tackett), U.S. women are channeling their fury at the patriarchy into political action in both the fictional stories people consume and the ballot box. In 2018, three books on female anger explored the relation between rage and political power: Rebecca Traister's *Good and Mad: The Revolutionary Power of Women's Anger*, Soraya Chemaly's *Rage Becomes Her: The Power of Women's Anger*, and Brittany Cooper's *Eloquent Rage: A Black Feminist Discovers Her Superpower*. And yet, Olivia Goldhill argues that the most memorable anger of the year came from Brett Kavanaugh at his Senate confirmation hearings following his nomination to the Supreme Court, and she cautions that anger stemming from personal slights might derail a political movement aimed at subverting hierarchical systems of power and social movements. Anger represents a complicated political tool.

While the U.S. continues to struggle with recognizing the political authority of angry women and the overwhelming amount of emotional labor women do to enable men to live with more privilege, *Game of Thrones* suggests that female rage can transform an entire continent and opens space for women who have been pushed past their breaking point to reshape the seven kingdoms. The show's antiquated notions of gender in early seasons were made palatable to viewers because of its setting in a fictional medieval realm where the chivalric code reinforced female passivity. In its later seasons, women violently subverted patriarchal norms and occupied, at least temporarily, some significant positions of power, including Cersei Lannister, Queen of the Seven Kingdoms; Yara Greyjoy, Queen of the Iron Islands; Sansa Stark, Queen in the North; and Daenerys Targaryen, Queen of the Seven Kingdoms.

For all these titles and the sparks of feminism audiences thrill to, pealing back the historic patriarchy of Westeros revealed ... more patriarchy. Despite Sansa's trueborn birth and the fact that she won the Battle of the Bastards, Northerners name Jon Snow their king. Jon Snow might be the protagonist of the show's later seasons, but Chaim Gartenberg points out that he "fails almost perpetually, blundering his way from one situation to the next until someone—usually a more competent woman, including but not limited to Ygritte, Melisandre, Sansa, Arya, and Daenerys—bails him out of his latest problem. Then he's rewarded, and the cycle repeats again" (Gartenberg). After he's crowned, he heads off to Dragonstone while Sansa stays home and feeds the North. Demonstrating the gender dynamics that Lockman points out in domestic U.S. households, Jon seems oblivious to the labor the women in his life have done in order to advance his political position, such as Sansa feeding, clothing, and sheltering the people of the North while he's away, or the ways in which Daenerys allowing him to ride one of her dragons prompts male characters to list dragon-riding as evidence of his king-like qualities. For eight seasons, the show dangled the promise of a subversion of patriarchal systems of power, only to double-down on those systems in its disappointing conclusion. All told, Westeros's attitude toward female anger largely mirrors contemporary U.S. attitudes. The show is instructive in that it offers us much to learn from, both in its strong representations of righteous female anger, and in its blunders on the same front. Chemaly writes, "Anger is usually about saying 'no' in a world where women are conditioned to say almost anything but 'no,'" and this holds true in both Westeros and the U.S. (Chemaly xix).

In what follows, I analyze the ways in which female anger operates in the political and cultural landscape of the U.S. in the 2010s and in *Game of Thrones*, attending to its consequences and also its absence or erasure. I argue that *Game of Thrones*' showrunners missed opportunities to imbue female characters with a wide range of emotions, particularly anger, in the face of injustice and inequality. I conclude by critiquing the real-world implications of the ways in which *Game of Thrones* represents the relationship between political power and female anger. Given the many excellent edited collections published earlier during the series' nine-year run, I focus primarily on the final two seasons.

The Power of Female Anger in the U.S. and in Westeros

One of the most high-profile examples from the 2010s of the political power of women's anger, and the consequences of failing to acknowledge it, came during the U.S. House of Representatives impeachment hearings for President Donald Trump. Testifying before the House Intelligence Committee, Fiona Hill, the former senior director for Russia and Europe at the National Security Council, detailed Ambassador to the European Union, Gordon Sondland's, "domestic political errand" in Ukraine and its connection to the delay in disbursement of U.S. aid per Trump's request that the Ukraine investigate his political rival Joe Biden's son. Explaining that she had several "testy encounters" with Sondland, that she was "actually, to be honest, angry with him," Hill then testified, in front of Congress, that "often, when women show anger, it's not fully appreciated. It's often, you know, pushed onto emotional issues perhaps, or deflected onto other people" (quoted in Reston). That Hill entered into the official transcript of a presidential impeachment hearing the frequent dismissal of female anger turned her into a hero and an internet sensation.

Female anger has also swelled in the domestic sphere, too. The women's movements that led to dual-career households have failed to uphold its promise of actual gender equality in both the professional and personal world, with women stepping back from their careers as soon as kids enter the picture and men leaning into theirs (see Miller). In "What 'Good' Dad's Get Away With," Darcy Lockman demonstrates the ways in which fathers—especially those who espouse liberal ideas regarding gender parity—have cultivated a studied obliviousness toward household chores and parenting duties. Women feel frustrated and angry at the persistent inequality shaping their lives, and men remain as blithely unaware of this anger as they are of the pile of laundry quietly growing in the corner. Studies show that in two-career heterosexual households, women still do more than twice the domestic chores (see Berman).

So, it makes sense that angry women would proliferate on screen, as well. Even before the 2016 election of Donald Trump, a surge in angry women on television subverted the traditional representations of complacent, unempowered female characters in favor of a furious titular superhero on *Jessica Jones*, rebellious inmates on *Orange Is the New Black*, and singing lawyers belting their rage on *Crazy Ex-Girlfriend*. Lili Loofbourow's article in *The Week*, "All hail the angry women of 2016," celebrates that "Our screens overflowed this year with women who'd just about had it. Women whose varieties of fury ranged from intense irritation to murderous bemusement to quiet hatred and pure reactive rage." She traces the origin of this new representation of female emotion to the first decade of the 21st century and shows such as *Buffy the Vampire Slayer*, *The Fall*, and *The Good Wife*, but notes that the TV women of the 2010s express a fuller range of emotions not previously available to them, thereby subverting typical representations of women. According to Loofbourow, "Rage and resentment aren't beautiful emotions, and ours is not a culture that trains us to sympathize with un-beautiful women. It's a sign of something—Progress? The crisis of the present?—that so many have graduated from glowing to glowering on our screens, and that their anger is presented not as a reason to abandon but to join them" (Loofbourow). The photomontage that accompanies her article boasts images from *Empire*, *Insecure*, and *One Mississippi*, and only two shows are represented an impressive four times: *Westworld* and *Game of Thrones* (featuring images of Sansa, Arya, Lyanna Mormont, and Cersei).

The trajectory of progress winds and dips, never directly shooting upward in a straight line, and even in 2019, three years later, showrunners struggled to display female anger. Liz Feldman of *Dead to Me* reported that she received notes from the studio that her lead character (played by Christina Applegate) was too angry. Her response: "I was angry that there was fear around her anger. [...] An angry woman is powerful. An angry woman rejects the notion that women are the weaker, gentler sex. An angry woman is uncontrollable. And as we know now, she's also very relatable." With her show renewed for a second season, Feldman asserts that the character's anger will only grow. But even while *Dead to Me* was renewed, shows like Marti Noxon's *Dietland*, dubbed by some "a feminist version of Chuck Palahniuk's *Fight Club*," was cancelled after a single season. Although *The Atlantic* claimed in 2018 that "everyone in Hollywood is looking for a Marti Noxon now," a showrunner unafraid to showcase "the fight-back part" of female anger, audiences and studios alike only intermittently lean into the full range of human emotions when displayed by women.

These arenas—political, domestic, entertainment—are, of course, related. What the citizenry sees on screens help them imagine future possibilities, and in turn the political and domestic realities—power structures and oppressions they generate—shape the stories artists tell on television, in books, and on stages. Jill Gutowitz writes in *Elite Daily*:

> Trump's America has engendered a backlash—a nasty-lash, if you will. My anger is being met by the wrath-driven art of female creators like Patty Jenkins (*Wonder Woman*), Margaret Atwood (*Alias Grace, The Handmaid's Tale*), and Jenji Kohan (*GLOW*) and god, it feels good to watch. I'm seeing my darkest rage-filled fantasies played out in gruesome revenge plots. […] If 2017 has taught me anything, it's that women are furious, and that feeling is nothing to shy away from. In fact, quite the opposite: We are so unconscionably justified in our rage against the Trump administration, sexual harassment, and rape culture. It was only a matter of time before this anger came pouring out in massive, guttural fits of hostility, and that time is now [Gutowitz].

The same day that the Nigerian Army rescued 5,000 people—mostly women and children—from terrorist group Boko Haram, 26 June 2016 ("Nigeria"), Cersei Lannister blew up the Sept of Baylor in the Season Six finale "Winds of Winter," and her act felt like an important demonstration of the rage that's essential for liberation from patriarchal oppression.

Furious Westerosi Women: Character Anger and Its Absence

Anger, experienced with equal frequency across gender, gets discounted and villainized when displayed by women. Yet Chemaly defines anger as "one of the most hopeful and forward thinking of all our emotions. It begets transformation, manifesting our passion *and* keeping us invested in the world. It is a rational *and* emotional response to trespass, violation, and moral disorder" (Chemaly xx). Certainly, the world of *Game of Thrones* is filled with trespass, violation, and moral disorder; arguably the entire premise of the narrative is the relation between power and these wrongs. Westerosi culture, like many contemporary societies, operates on a binary gender schema and draws sharp distinctions between men and women, firmly situating men at the top of power hierarchies and subjugating women. Much like 21st-century women, when the women of Westeros experience trespass, violation, and moral disorder, they might feel anger, or the more intense sister emotions of rage and fury. And Westerosi women, like their real-world counterparts, struggle to express their anger, which the men (and sometimes other women) around them often discount as madness or overly emotional behavior from unstable women and/or mothers.

Game of Thrones has a middling track record of representing female anger, with Season Six, more than any other, meaningfully demonstrating what female anger is and how it might transform into political power. Cersei blowing up the Sept of Baelor and Daenerys burning down Vaes Dothrok serve as clear examples of female rage and its intersection with political power: both women suffered violation, trespass, and moral disorder—from individual men and from patriarchal systems—and both deployed their rage not only to overthrow individuals, but also to subvert entire systems of oppression. These women have channeled their rage into political action, staking their claim to authority and power *outside of their status as mothers*. For a show that spent at least five seasons awash in sexism, Season Six demonstrate that pissed off women make excellent warriors, rulers, villains, and heroes. Characters in the show and fans watching at home typically interpret Daenerys' famous speech about breaking the wheel as a commentary on dismantling powerful Houses and monarchs who abuse their smallfolk, but implicit in her mission is dismantling the patriarchy.

Alas, the promise of Season Six is not borne out in the final two seasons. The scene I began this essay with, Arya and Sansa discussing anger and fear, stands as but one example of how the show denies healthy female anger in favor of shock value. The suspense the writers played with as they pitted sister against sister in Season Seven, and the payoff in the season finale as they put Baelish on trial and executed him, came at the expense of displaying Arya and Sansa's anger at his machinations. The writers preferred a prolonged catfight between the Stark sisters and a sudden and shocking death for Baelish to allowing audiences the opportunity to witness Sansa and Arya (and, one presumes, Bran) recognize Baelish's strategy and collaborate to circumvent it. How satisfying and important it would have been to see the many talents—and emotions—of the Stark sisters put toward eliminating their most insidious enemy.

The anger audiences do see from Sansa in the final two seasons comes across as petulant and small, such as when Daenerys suspends her war with Cersei and brings her armies and dragons to Winterfell and Sansa asks how she can be expected to feed this massive influx of fighters and two dragons. In light of the looming battle with the Dead, one could reasonably expect Sansa to be at the very least grateful for additional armies fighting on her side; her anger at having to feed them diminishes her as a character. *Game of Thrones* is more comfortable with Sansa's emotions when they relate to grief than to anger, like when the camera lingers on her tears for Theon after he dies in the battle of Winterfell, but denies her even a single line of angry dialogue when Tyrion announces that the Lannister army would be arriving at her home—instead, a chorus of angry male voices rumbles in the background (S8, E1).

Female anger, when it is shown in the final two seasons, most often becomes evidence of madness. As I wrote in a CNN article, "For six seasons, 'Game of Thrones' cultivated fans' admiration for Daenerys Targaryen, the

Mother of Dragons and Breaker of Chains—and for six seasons, kept her far away from the Iron Throne she sought to claim. Once Daenerys landed in Westeros and launched her military campaign, however, the show began to frame her ambition as evidence of her unfitness to rule" (Mantoan, "Momentous Fate"). As soon as a strong, angry woman who, up to this point, has been viewed by characters and fans as the equivalent of the modern social justice warrior (although also an obvious example of the white savior trope) gets proximate to the real center of power in this world, the show subverts fans' admiration of her and instead represents her as callous and out of touch. This subversion lacks the innovativeness of the show's genre subversions when it unexpectedly kills off certain characters; instead, it becomes yet another tired representation of angry women as unhinged.

Because audiences and even critics have been conditioned toward negative reactions to female anger, it can be hard to recognize how problematic the show's representation of Daenerys is in its final season. Those who criticized Daenerys for her reaction to Jon's parentage (see, for example, Emily VanDerWerff, who writes, "the way she freaks out makes clear that this is so much more about her own desire to sit on the throne than anything else") demonstrate the ways in which we have all been subsumed into patriarchal responses to female anger and ambition. Daenerys has devoted her life to questing for the Iron Throne, and in blink of an eye, one of the worst tacticians in Westeros has a better claim than her. Jon Snow says repeatedly that he doesn't want a crown, and suddenly people in Westeros—and those watching at home—began throwing their support behind him rather than her. The show even hinted for a while that Daenerys might be pregnant with Jon's child, in which case, the story could have circumvented any direct conflict between the two; their child could rule, which would reduce Daenerys to a womb and evacuate her of the political and military authority she's acquired over seven seasons of subverting expectations of women, commanding her own armies, and building a coalition of diverse allies.

While fans love to draw sharp lines between Cersei and Daenerys, their character arcs share many parallels, including their struggles against misogyny and their complicated roles as mothers. Cersei Lannister held the title "Queen" for more than a decade, but as wife and mother to actual rulers, her power was illusory and her reality involved her husband raping her, her lover Jaime raping her (see Lyons), a religious fanatic imprisoning her and forcing her to walk naked through the streets, and her son the King (Tommen) issuing a new decree about trial protocol that all but guaranteed she would be executed. Framed as a mother who values her children above all else, Cersei's loss of all three of them explains to viewers why she finally made the bold move to *take* the title of Queen of the Seven Kingdoms when she had no actual claim to it and a woman had never held that title before—Rhaenrya Targaryen briefly occupied the Iron Throne during the Targaryen civil war called "Dance of the Dragons," but never held that title (See George R.R. Martin's *Fire and Blood*). Parenthood so dominates Cersei's storyline (and barely registers on Jaime's, as Anna Nordberg demonstrates in her article "In the World of *Game of Thrones*, Mothers Have Power, but They Pay a Terrible Price for It") that Cersei's pregnancy in the final two seasons generated fan theories about Tyrion promising her Daenerys would name Cersei's child her heir, if only Cersei would pledge Lannister armies to fight in the North (see, for example, Busch) and speculation about how she might navigate paternity, given the triangle between her, Jaime, and Euron.

Cersei's dying words, "I want our baby to live," reframes her from an absolutist monarch to a protective mother. Her quest in the final two seasons, to create a dynasty for her baby and protect it at all costs, creates virtually the only path for viewers to empathize with her and does work to justify her actions. Anger simmers underneath her haughty veneer as she conducts negotiations and ascribes to a political realism war strategy (meaning, the ends justify the means) throughout Season Eight. But, as Chemaly argues, "Women's anger is usually disparaged in virtually all arenas, except those in which anger *confirms* gender-role stereotypes about women as nurturers and reproductive agents. This means we are allowed to be angry but not on our own behalves. If a woman is angry in her 'place,' as a mother or a teacher, for example, she is respected, and her anger is generally understood and acceptable" (xviii). The writers thus displace Cersei's rage from the many moral wrongs and trespasses she's personally endured, and map it instead onto her maternal need to protect her unborn child.

Cersei's eleventh-hour pregnancy, one of the only dynamic plotlines for her character in Season Seven (the other two are her relationship with Euron and her strategies to maintain power as Queen of King's Landing, which are given short shrift, to say the least), gave the fans fodder to theorize: was she really pregnant? If not, how abhorrent that a woman might ever make up such a thing—only a monster would lie about pregnancy. Describing the way children function vis-à-vis the storyline of *Game of Thrones*' mothers, Nordberg writes: "there's the strength of knowing you'd do anything to protect your child; there's the vulnerability of knowing that no matter what, you cannot guarantee their safety." Cersei's storyline, and Daenerys' to a smaller extent, demonstrates the ways in which women are humanized by their children and, in particular, by the loss of them. A mourning mother presents a more legible storyline than a woman enacting violence on her own behalf. Thus, when the men they love abandon them (which somehow also costs them political power), Cersei and Daenerys both turn to their sole remaining child as their last hope. Miraculously, in the final hours of this epic series, Cersei's motherly turn transforms her back into a sympathetic character as she's dying, whereas Daenerys' anger at watching Euron brutally slaughter Rhaegal, and her frustration at her inability to kill Euron in return gives proof of her declining power and descent into madness (S8, E4).

Nevermind that Daenerys should have been justifiably furious at Tyrion, her Hand, for his abysmal strategic advice; at Varys, her Master of Whispers, for utter failure to acquire and share vital intelligence regarding the location and movement of enemy armies across Westeros; and at the two of them for their treason in plotting to overthrow her. This absence of rage is one of the most conspicuous denials of female anger in the last couple of seasons. Conferences between Tyrion and Varys wherein they express doubts about Daenerys' fitness to rule began in Season Seven, after she burns Randall and Dickon Tarly alive. This scene of their conspiracy occurs only a couple of episodes after this exchange between Varys and Daenerys:

> VARYS: I will serve you well. I will dedicate myself to seeing you on the Iron Throne because I choose you. Because I know the people have no better chance than you.
> DAENERYS: Swear this to me, Varys. If you ever think I'm failing the people, you won't conspire behind my back. You'll look me in the eye as you have done today and you'll tell me how I'm failing them.
> VARYS: I swear it, my Queen [S7, E2].

Only once does Varys look Daenerys in the eye, as he'd vowed, and tell her he thought she was failing the people, and it's after he's had multiple conversations with Tyrion suggesting overthrowing her. Instead of acting as a hands-on advisor offering real solutions (any meaningful suggestion other than "don't attack King's Landing" would have been welcome advice for Daenerys and viewers alike), Varys sows doubt and writes secret letters that undermine her and prop up Jon Snow. Varys wholly fails Daenerys not only as an advisor but also as a Master of Whispers, the de facto intelligence officer of an administration, by allowing Euron Greyjoy's massive armada to sneak up on Yara's fleet (S7, E2), on the ships that carried the Unsullied to Casterly Rock (S7, E3), and on Daenerys' fleet after the Battle of Winterfell (S8, E4). The show never provides Daenerys an opportunity to confront him about his poor performance as her Master of Whispers or to vent her anger at him. Rather, she represses all her anger at all the wrongs she's endured until it erupts in the penultimate episode, when the show frames her attack on King's Landing, after its armies have surrendered, as unhinged and immoral.

Likewise, the show denies Daenerys significant anger at Tyrion for his dreadful strategizing, which costs her dragons, armies, allies, and, possibly, her life. It was Tyrion's idea to send Jon Snow North of the Wall to capture a wight and bring it to King's Landing, advice that resulted in Viserion's death and a baffling timeline in terms of writing that left fans shaking their heads (Alan Taylor, director of "Beyond the Wall" (S7, E6), ultimately made a statement about the timeline that included the admission, "there was some effort to fudge the timeline a little bit by not declaring exactly how long we were there [North of the Wall]. I think that worked for some people, for other people it didn't" (quoted in Otterson)). Meghan O'Keefe argues that the ultimate destruction of King's Landing is in fact all Tyrion's fault for giving Daenerys ruinous advice that led to significantly more death and destruction than if Daenerys had marched on King's Landing as soon as her army landed in Westeros—as all of her female advisors had urged her to do. Indeed, I wrote something similar back in 2018: "As grim as it is, in military strategy, there is some wisdom in striking an opponent in a swift and brutal attack that ends the war as soon as possible." Indeed, this military strategy, known as political realism, finds that "any degree of restraint in war produces higher cost in the long run—human, material, financial—because it prolongs the conflict" (Mantoan, *Vying*, 51).

Instead, her male advisors (including, later, Jon Snow) continue advising Daenerys not to use her military advantages, and apart from some small verbal expressions of frustration, Daenerys swallows her fury. After Euron sinks Yara's ships and captures her and Ellaria, Daenerys receives the news stoically, her hands clasped in front of her (more on this posture below). It's not hard to imagine a male monarch receiving such news with vocal or physical outbursts of rage and frustration. When word reaches Daenerys about Jaime's clever moves with his military at Casterly Rock and the annihilation of her ships there, she paces the beach, saying, "enough with the clever plans. [...] What kind of queen am I if I'm not willing to risk my life. [...] I'm at war. I'm losing" (S7, E4). Her advisors again stifle her suggestion to storm King's Landing, with Jon Snow telling her if she uses her dragons she'll be "more of the same" kind of ruler she pledges not to be.

The muzzling in this scene isn't confined to her desire to deploy her dragons; her anger also feels muzzled. The show allows her to act frustrated, but not to feel anger; she's denied the opportunity to raise her voice, to bellow at Tyrion for his weak advice that has been bested *again* by his siblings, or to rain down accusations at Varys for not getting wind of the Lannister army's movements. Instead, Jon tells her not to use her dragons and she looks on, trapped and, with norms in both Westeros and the contemporary U.S., unable to express anger—to *feel* her own anger. Chemaly writes that "Men more frequently associate feeling powerful with experiencing anger, but women, notably, associate powerlessness with their anger" (xv). This powerlessness has two facets: the anger derives from a lack of power, and in turn, censorship of anger (whether self-imposed or external) produces more powerlessness.

The list of restrictions on Daenerys' options grows with every loss, and Cersei and the Night King's unscrupulous approach to war amplifies her feelings of powerlessness. The Night King operates by no code, and Cersei lied about aiding the North in their fight against the Army of the Dead, then hid behind the innocent people of King's Landing, using them as a shield against Daenerys' dragons and armies. Her strategy leaves Daenerys with few options to take the throne beyond deploying dragons and producing mass casualties. Summing up Daenerys' predicament: She rescued Jon Snow and the other men foolish enough to go North of the Wall to capture a wight and lost a dragon/child in the process; she suspended her campaign for the Seven Kingdoms to fight for the North, suffering the loss of her Dothraki army and most of her Unsullied, and endured Sansa's derision and the North's "low-key racist" attitude toward Missandei and Grey Worm rather than heart-felt thanks and gratitude (Abad-Santos). And, "as Winterfell celebrated its victory over the Night King, men praised Jon for riding a dragon into battle—and ignored entirely that Daenerys has been doing that for years. […] After the Dothraki were slaughtered, she's the one who took off on a dragon to fight the dead while Jon encouraged her to wait; as is so often the case in the real world, a woman leads and a man gets the credit" (Mantoan, "Momentous Fate").

There are consequences to denying women both equality *and* anger at inequality. After the penultimate episode of the series, "The Bells" (S8, E6), Alex Abad-Santos wrote: "And now, with Euron having killed her dragon Rhaegal and Cersei having executed Missandei in the wake of Ser Jorah's death, Dany's circle of trusted friends and loved ones has shrunk again. Mad queen be damned—at this point, could anyone really blame her for wanting to lash out? I wouldn't" (Abad-Santos). It's no coincidence that "Mad Queen" becomes Daenerys' moniker in the wake of her destruction of King's Landing; Daenerys at the conclusion of "The Last of the Starks," when Cersei beheads Missandei, is a study in what "angry face" looks like. The creators of *Game of Thrones* reveal a distinct lack of imagination, however, when they have Daenerys light King's Landing on fire. There are so few examples in both real life and on screen of women expressing healthy anger, and *Game of Thrones*, a show that importantly subverted expectations on multiple levels, instead perpetuates flat representations of women.

Not every critic even agrees that Daenerys torching King's Landing demonstrated her insanity, with Matthew Yglesias finding: "Daenerys has an objective—to induce the Lords of Westeros to bend the knee and acknowledge her supremacy—and her attack on King's Landing in 'The Bells' was well-calibrated to achieve that objective. […] If Daenerys had simply allowed King's Landing to surrender without consequences only after she evaded its air defenses, then every other recalcitrant lord in the Seven Kingdoms would have incentive to resist her" (Yglesias). In "The Strategic Case for Burning King's Landing," Robert Farley, a war strategist, echoes these assertions: "For Queen Daenerys Targaryen, seizure of King's Landing and the deposition of the usurper Cersei no longer cuts it. Aegon Targaryen (Jon Snow) has a better claim to the throne; he has a base of operations, a narrative of legitimacy, and his own army. Even if Jon doesn't want to be King, people who dislike Daenerys will fight in his name. Dany is no longer the presumptive Targaryen heir and can no longer rely on her family's right to the throne. She can rely on Drogon, however" (Farley).

Yet while multiple critics find exemplary political and military strategy in Daenerys burning King's Landing, her fascist speech amidst the rubble of King's Landing positions her as a foreign dictator and leaves viewers no option for sympathy for or identification with her (S8, E6). The aesthetics of the scene, with row upon row of ordered soldiers occupying the foreground as a strong (wo)man speaks from a raised dais next to a massive red banner, parallels aesthetics seen in Leni Riefenstahl's Nazi propaganda film *Triumph of the Will*—aesthetics recreated for General Hux's speech in *Star Wars: The Force Awakens*. Audiences have been trained to associate these aesthetic choices with the fascist enemies of the "good guys" in television and film.

With this background, the scene in which Daenerys gives her victory speech is shockingly anti-immigrant, with the audience positioned against her as she speaks to people of color from over the sea in a foreign language. She addresses the Unsullied as former slaves, and when she speaks of liberating all of Westeros, low, ominous music signals to viewers how morally wrong her understanding of liberation is. Jon Snow, Arya Stark, and Tyrion Lannister stand in for the audience in this scene, and their fear and distrust signals how audiences are meant to feel about Daenerys as she praises and thanks formerly enslaved people and people of color. Reframing Daenerys as a fascist dictator suggests that it was her anger that transformed her into a villain.

After the speech, Tyrion reminds Jon, and by extension the audience, that Daenerys has slaughtered slavers and misogynist Khals who "would have done worse to her[…]. Everywhere she goes, evil men die, and we cheer her for it" (S8, E6). But with these words, Tyrion implies that Daenerys has always been a murderer and the audience was always wrong to support her dismantling of unjust systems and the men who prop them up. Transforming the woman who has fought against oppressive systems into the leader of an oppressive system pessimistically implies that women cannot legitimately fight for justice. Then, in addition to stripping a hero character of rationality and ethics, she is stripped of agency and perspective when her death scene is framed through someone else's point of view. It's heartbreaking, not only on a narrative level but also on a meta level, that after eight seasons, Daenerys Targaryen dies and the focus of her death scene is on Jon Snow's inner conflict and loss.

Real-World Anger: The Fury of Female Fans

Which brings us to *my* anger—and the anger of many fans of the series—at the way the writers undercut everything that was compelling and complex about the show in the final two seasons—the contractions and inconsistencies, the failure to see complex prophesies through to the end, and the nonsensical relations among time, space, and travel. I vented my fury in a CNN.com article that posted the morning after "The Bells" aired, writing: "In its last few episodes, the show has devoted more energy to granting its major characters a curtain call than grappling with the complex aspects of power that formerly guided the narrative. Fans invested in the slipperiness of prophesy continue trying to imbue every action with significance but it's likely there is none, and this final season lacks the subtlety and commitment to carry through Martin's intricate vision" (Mantoan, "For Longtime Fans…").

Fans were angry that the actors were put in awkward positions again and again as they were asked to defend the final season (see Rosen). The writers went into hiding until, oddly, six months after the finale aired when they were at the Austin Film Festival and they admitted they had very little idea what they were doing, saying: "everything we could make a mistake in, we did" (Bradley). One of the most astute articles deconstructing the source of fans' outrage, written by Zaynep Tufekci in *Scientific American*, argues that the storytelling shifted from a sociological one to a psychological one: "For Benioff and Weiss, trying to continue what *Game of Thrones* had set out to do, tell a compelling *sociological* story, would be like trying to eat melting ice cream with a fork. Hollywood mostly knows how to tell psychological, individualized stories. They do not have the right tools for sociological stories, nor do they even seem to understand the job" (Tufekci).

And yet I would distinguish the more general anger at the poor storytelling of the last two seasons from, specifically, female anger at the conclusion of the series. My feelings watching the conclusion—in particular, scenes like the treasonous discussion between Tyrion and Varys in "The Last of the Starks" as they evaluate Jon's claim to the Iron Throne—were overwhelmingly ones of anger at the way the female characters were treated by men—both on screen and in the writers' room. My frustrations over

Cersei's diminished role in the final season—both her scant screen time and her lack of any meaningful impact on the trajectory of the narrative's events—was matched by Lena Headey herself, who has said she "wanted a better death" for Cersei (Rosen). She also reports that they had filmed a scene for Season Seven in which Cersei loses her baby, which Headey describes as "really traumatic," saying, "it would have served her differently" (Sharf). I had mixed feelings when I read this; on the one hand, including this scene would have doubled-down on the positioning Cersei as a mother first and a queen second, justifying her anger as on behalf of her child, not herself. I join Chamely when she dreams of "a culture that no longer conflates the word *woman* with *mother* and the word *mother* with *sacrifice*" (Chamely 119). But on the other hand, Cersei, a female character with a complex character arc over seven seasons, had little character development—or even *action*—in Season Eight, and this scene would have elevated her status as a character of consequence in the show's conclusion.

Watching Cersei's demise when bricks fell on her, as she clutched Jaime and said she didn't want to die, broke my heart not because a beloved character/villain's storyline was over, but because her death was unceremonious and she was rendered weak and powerless, mothering over Jaime's injuries even while he took the lead in trying to locate an escape path and physically propped her up despite his Euron-inflicted wounds. In "And What of My Wrath," a title taken from Cersei's line to Ned Stark back in Season One, Sara Fredman advocates for Cersei as a model for a female antihero, if only she been on a different show. According to Fredman:

> David Benioff's assertion that Cersei's love of her children is the only thing that humanizes her is possibly the best example of the way in which the *Game of Thrones* writers misunderstood their characters and their audience. It overlooks the other reasons the show gave us to root for Cersei and betrays an ignorance of the extent to which enduring patriarchy might itself be, for at least a portion of its audience, humanizing. It reveals an inability to grasp the possibility that the mother and the monster can be the same person. For a show dedicated to demonstrating just how thin the line is between good and evil, *Game of Thrones* was surprisingly blind to Cersei's potential to become a compelling antihero, to be humanized by something other than her children [Fredman].

Cersei's autonomy has never been assured and her storyline in the final two seasons lacks complexity or intrigue. Fans (and, it would seem, at least some of the actors) wanted at least one scene between Cersei and Daenerys, given that the final season was framed as a showdown between the two, and were denied even this simplest of expectations—a subversion of expectations that weakened the show's conclusion.

Instead, the show's dramatic shortchanging of its core female characters left Cersei bereft of the cunning plots audiences had come to expect from her. One of my friends vented on social media after "The Bells" aired that it was unbelievable that Cersei's strategy when Daenerys came for King's Landing was: "all we need is one good shot." Ian Sandwell of *Digital Spy*, echoes my friend's critique, calculating that Lena Headey, one of the strongest—if not *the* strongest—actors on the show, graced the screen for a mere thirty minutes across the six episodes of Season Eight. Sandwell writes, "It's bad enough that Cersei didn't just wipe out Dany's tiny army at the end of episode four, but it appears that she had no plan at all. Yes, she was arrogant and complacent, and had Euron and his Iron Fleet and the Golden Company, but a cunning plotter like Cersei would have had a back-up plan" (Sandwell). For a narrative with such careful early plotting and intricate character development of Cersei to abandon the wildfire cached underneath King's Landing and her ability to scorch the land to protect herself reveals the writers' either disregard for or lack of skills at writing women. In the wake of her wildfire strategy at the end of Season Six, Cersei's pose as she stood in the window of the Red Keep, drinking wine and smirking, became iconic. In Season Eight, it became mundane through overuse as multiple episodes saw Cersei looking out the same window, her hands clasped in front of her, doing little else.

Indeed, the show stages both queens (Cersei and Daenerys) in a "neutral" pose that positions their hands clasped in front of them, a pose that signals nerves, discomfort, defensiveness, or self-restraint; it's not a posture that broadcasts confidence or flexibility. Perhaps this choice relates to a lack of weapons—the resting position of many of the men on the show involves a hand or arm on a sword hilt. As a director myself, I can attest that hands are some of the hardest things to direct and position. But giving the two most "powerful" women on the show identical resting postures reveals more than simple parallels between the characters; it also demonstrates that women in power would only ever be awkward, uncomfortable, or restrained—by convention, by patriarchal systems, by the men surrounding them, and by their internalized understanding of their position in the political hierarchy. This posture restrains the person in question from gesticulating, drawing a weapon, or fully embodying the wide range of human emotions, including anger.

Kevin Fallon of the *Daily Beast* writes, "for everything *Game of Thrones* has done to change the face of television as we know it, failing women is its ugliest legacy" and he locates this failure in the show's lack of inclusion on the production level: "the total number of women employed as either a writer or director over the course of eight seasons and 73 episodes of arguably the most influential television series of the modern era [is] just four" (Fallon). The consequences of leaving women outside the room are wide-sweeping on both a narrative and real-world level. Looking at the final episode alone, Sansa Stark may have been named Queen in the North, but Sophie Turner has only a few lines of significance in the seventy-nine-minute finale that sees three women argue over Jon Snow's fate (Sansa, Arya, and Yara) until the sensible and measured Davos Seaworth brings them to heel and reframes the conversation. After that, the men dominate the speech that follows, with Yara's only contribution affirming Bran as King. By Paul Tassi's count in *Forbes*, women in Season Eight have only 22 percent of speaking lines, the lowest of any *Game of Thrones* season, a surprising statistic, "especially since it was supposed to be a conflict between two queens, Cersei and Daenerys, and two of three remaining Starks were also women" (Tassi).

When they did have lines, women in the show were given some infuriating things to say—dialogue that alienated and angered female fans. Perhaps the most egregious example is Sansa's line to the Hound during "The Last of the Starks" (I would posit this was one of the most misogynist episodes in *GoT* history) after he says that none of her misfortunes would have happened if she'd just left King's Landing with him years ago. Her response: "Without Littlefinger and Ramsay and the rest, I would have stayed a little bird all my life" (S8, E4). It's baffling that writers (even male ones) in 2019 could suggest that rape is necessary for a woman to grow stronger. In this moment, *Game of Thrones* joins a long list of shows that uses violence against women as a narrative tool. As a viewer, I seethed when I heard Sansa, one of the strongest women on television, connect her personal growth to surviving sexual violence. As Elis de Guerre writes, "nothing could be further from the truth, and it is irresponsible for Benioff and Weiss to suggest otherwise" and, "And as a survivor myself? I'm livid with Benioff and Weiss, the show's creators and writers, for giving such an inaccurate line to a character who deserves better" (de Guerre). Actress Jessica Chastain tweeted, "Rape is not a tool to make a character stronger. A woman doesn't need to be victimized in order to become a butterfly. The little bird was always a Phoenix. Her prevailing strength is solely because of her. And her alone" (quoted in Fallon). It seems plausible that had more women been involved in the production of *Game of Thrones*, painful missteps like this could have been avoided.

This same episode has Brienne of Tarth sobbing as she begs Jaime Lannister, "Stay. Stay with me, please. Stay." One of my frustrations with this dialogue is its lack of persuasive rhetoric—Brienne might not be the most poetic of speakers, but better writing would have her give a more creative plea. Critic Nell Scovell attributes this uncharacteristic weakness in Brienne to the lack of female representation in the writing room, tweeting: "A female writer would have fought to the death to not have the weepy Brienne of Tarth scene in the last episode" (quoted in Fallon). Further, the series finale reduces Brienne, the realm's first female knight, to historian of Jaime's life, with the camera lingering much longer over the scene in which she inks his deeds into the Book of Brothers, the history of the Kingsguard, than her contributions as the only woman at the table during the Small Council meeting (I believe a more true-to-character Brienne would have stayed in the North as Queensguard to Sansa anyway).

Female fans are also furious that the show deployed the death of, as Ava DuVernay describes Missandei, "the one and only sister on the whole epic, years-long series," in order to advance the story of a white character (quoted in Fallon). For a translator, Missandei barely had any lines in this or any season, yet won the hearts of many women, especially women of color. And not only did the largely white group of *Game of Thrones* writers and directors kill off the only woman of color, but they made her die in chains. The writers leave Missandei passive for most of Season Eight, with her two biggest moments being to defend Daenerys to Sansa in the crypt of Winterfell and her final word, "*dracarys*," encouraging the queen she serves to torch King's Landing.

Then there's Yara, one of the few women allowed to express her anger. When Theon rescues her from Euron's ship, her first move is to topple him with a savage head-butt, venting her fury at his weakness when Euron captured her. While physical violence is arguably an unhealthy method of expressing anger, in the world of the Iron Islands—and Westeros at large—it blends in with what men are allowed—even expected—to do. Yara's shortchanging comes later, in the Dragonpit when the leaders of Westeros are debating the land's future. Her only lines are to bicker with other women about Jon Snow's fate. Sansa announcing "the North will remain an independent kingdom, as it was for thousands of years," was significant, but it strains credulity that Yara wouldn't immediately chime in proclaiming the Iron Islands an independent kingdom as well (and that the new Prince of Dorn wouldn't do likewise).

Indeed, that entire scene was infuriating to watch for me and for many female fans, and the absence of righteous anger from the female characters in the scene demonstrates that, to the end, the writers of the show misunderstand the significance of angry women. Tyrion propping up Bran Stark for King of Westeros, the least capable leader among them, angered me for many reasons; Bran has no experience in matters of state, has never governed any group of people, and has done nothing to earn this position. It makes little sense that the Three Eyed Raven would also be its leader, as opposed to its living archive. The confusion of this choice only deepens during the subsequent Small Council meeting when he points out that he still needs a Master of Whispers—*why*? The one person in the world who can see anywhere, anytime, still needs a spy? I have similar questions about his being named King in the first place and his bratty line, "why do you think I came all this way" (S8, E6)—Bran's abilities seem to have clued him into his being named king, but left him incapable or uninterested in meaningfully helping with pretty much anything else (spying on the Night King before and during the Battle of Winterfell, say, or protecting King's Landing from destruction). Based on past actions, Bran has demonstrated little ability to unite a land broken by war.

That Tyrion suggests Bran over Sansa, whom he, Jon, and Arya have spent the season pronouncing one of the smartest people they know, was baffling. And that the show never allows Sansa, easily the most qualified person in the circle, the opportunity to refuse the title of Queen of the Seven Kingdoms angered many fans, with Emily Dreyfuss of *Wired* writing:

> If the point of that roundtable was to show us that Sansa was clearly the boss (when she tells Edmure Tully to "sit down," you know she's already the Queen) and yet the men don't respect her, and thereby make a comment on what it's like to be a woman seeking election in modern day America, then great, fine, it succeeded in making its point. Sansa got treated the way women around the world get treated every day: overlooked and passed over and then placated by being "given" an inferior role [Dreyfuss].

The political commentary embedded in this moment extends past Sansa as an individual to women as rulers more generally. In the history of Westeros, only two women have ever claimed the title of Queen of the Seven Kingdoms, and both were tyrants. The clear message here seems to be that women aren't capable of ruling such a vast and diverse land. It's great that Sansa becomes a queen, but the writers signal to audiences that female leaders must stay in their place (in the North, in this case).

Chemaly finds that women have been conditioned to believe "anger was experienced in isolation and not worth verbally sharing with others. That furious feelings are best kept to oneself" (xiii). It's therefore significant and refreshing how many women have taken to very public outlets to express their anger at *Game of Thrones*' treatment of women, both onscreen and in its exclusion of female writers and directors. As Season Eight progressed, fans began asking if Daenerys might prove to be a worse villain than Cersei, but that was the wrong question; rather, they should have asked what it might look like if women and mothers stopped putting their skills in the service of the men and children around them and started leading on their own terms. It's a shame we weren't given a chance to see Sansa rule the North in her own right.

Why does all this matter? After all, *Game of Thrones* is just a television show, and the massive outpouring of energy on behalf of fans angry at the show arguably could do more important work in the world if directed at real injustices. But for an entire decade, *Game of Thrones* was the world's most popular show, and the fact that the show appealed to non-fantasy fans indicates it bore important connections to real-world situations and dynamics. Fallon writes, "One could argue that a responsibility comes with popularity. No show is as popular as *Game of Thrones*, and there may never be one as popular again. Airing at a time when representation and that responsibility have blanketed industry discourse, it's dismaying that a show this popular isn't mentioned as a vehicle of progress, but instead as an example of the problem" (Fallon). The series had some truly shining moments of empowerment (female and otherwise), but the final seasons demonstrate that those moments were exceptions, not fundamental changes to the system. It's significant that Fallon, a man, writes so persuasively—and angrily—about the ways in which *Game of Thrones* failed in its responsibility to represent and include women. Allyship matters. Perhaps if there had been more women and allies in the writers' room, there would be less cause for rage.

That's why it's disappointing that HBO cancelled the only *Game of Thrones* prequel helmed by a woman (Jane Goldman), the publicity for which emphasized that it starred Naomi Watts, which had been in development the longest of any of its prequel options. Instead, HBO issued a straight-to-series order for *House of the Dragon*, which will be helmed by George R.R. Martin, Ryan Condal, and frequent *Game of Thrones* director Miquel Sapochnik—all men. It seems as though the network has learned little from the rage fans expressed about the ways in which the original series excluded women.

Indeed, critics and scholars from Fallon to Chemaly to Rebecca Traister demonstrate that the trespass, violation, and moral disorder women experience in real life—and the related wrongs they grapple with in the stories we tell and consume—will take sustained effort to overcome. It's vital that we "stand with our angry sisters, rage-filled shoulder to rage-filled shoulder, staring out into a future we hope can be better" (Grey). Because what we see on screen helps us imagine how to subvert existing patriarchal power structures in the real world, and the identification and catharsis that women experience when watching female characters express fury on screen is essential to sustaining a political movement.

Works Cited

Abad-Santos, Alex. "*Game of Thrones*' Mad Queen theory, explained." *Vox*, 5 May 2019, www.vox.com/2019/5/5/18530451/game-of-thrones-season-8-episode-4-daenerys-dracarys-mad-queen. Accessed 14 Jan. 2020.

Barrett, Lisa Feldman. "Hillary Clinton's 'Angry' Face." *New York Times*, 23 Sept. 2016, www.nytimes.com/2016/09/25/opinion/sunday/hillary-clintons-angry-face.html?_r=0. Accessed 13 Jan. 2020.

Berman, Jillian. "Women's unpaid work is the backbone of the American economy." *MarketWatch*, 15 Apr. 2018, www.marketwatch.com/story/this-is-how-much-more-unpaid-work-women-do-than-men-2017-03-07. Accessed 13 Jan. 2020.

Bradley, Laura. "*Game of Thrones* Creators Chose a Weird Time to Confirm They Had No Idea What They Were Doing." *Vanity Fair*, 28 Oct. 2019, www.vanityfair.com/hollywood/2019/10/game-of-thrones-david-benioff-d-b-weiss-panel. Accessed 14 Jan. 2020.

Busch, Caitlin. "*Game of Thrones* Fans Think Tyrion Made a Deal with the Devil." *Inverse.com*, 29 Aug. 2017, www.inverse.com/article/35976-game-of-thrones-tyrion-jon-daenerys-child-heir-cersei-plan-theory. Accessed 15 Jan. 2020.

Chemaly, Soraya. *Rage Becomes Her: The Power of Women's Anger*. New York: Simon & Schuster, 2019.

De Guerre, Elis. "What *Game of Thrones* Gets Wrong about Sansa Stark and Abuse." *The Daily Beast*, 7 May 2019, www.thedailybeast.com/what-game-of-thrones-gets-wrong-about-sansa-stark-and-abuse-in-the-last-of-the-starks. Accessed 16 Jan. 2020.

Fredman, Sara. "And What of My Wrath?" *LongReads.com*, 30 May 2019, longreads.com/2019/05/30/and-what-of-my-wrath/. Accessed 15 Jan. 2020.

Gartenberg, Chaim. "Westeros deserves a much better hero than Jon Snow." *The Verge*, 3 May 2019, www.theverge.com/2019/5/3/18528437/game-of-thrones-got-season-8-jon-snow-hero-westeros-daenerys-bad-leadership-dragons?fbclid=IwAR1u_eU1t7scRJTCRtJG-VL0kqGJuszZGIA2u1oOSVEz8NRlW_7viBPXUtA. Accessed 13 Jan. 2020.

Gilbert, Sophie. "Is Television Ready for Angry Women?" *The Atlantic*, June 2018, www.theatlantic.com/magazine/archive/2018/06/marti-noxon/559115/. Accessed 10 Jan. 2020.

Gray, Emma. "The Enduring, Messy Power of Rage-Filled Women." *Huffpost*, 2 Oct. 2018, www.huffpost.com/entry/angry-women-good-and-mad-rebecca-traister-rage-becomes-her-soraya-chemaly_n_5bb27285e4b027da00d65113. Accessed 22 Jan. 2020.

Gutowitz, Jill. "Angry Women in TV & Movies Are Finally Getting Our Close-Ups." *Elite Daily*, 24 Nov. 2017, www.elitedaily.com/p/angry-women-in-tv-movies-are-finally-getting-our-close-ups-5538671. Accessed 13 Jan. 2020.

Farley, Robert. "The Strategic Case for Burning King's Landing." *Slate*, 13 May 2019, slate.com/culture/2019/05/battle-kings-landing-got-military-analysis-tactics.html. Accessed 14 Jan. 2020.

Feldman, Liz. "Dead to Me Creator on Why It's Time for TV to Embrace Angry Women (Guest Column)." *Hollywood Reporter*, 13 June 2019, www.hollywoodreporter.com/news/dead-me-creator-why-time-tv-embrace-angry-women-1217407. Accessed 13 Jan. 2020.

Fitzpatrick, Kevin. "George R.R. Martin Admits *Game of Thrones* Wasn't 'Faithful' to His Preferred Ending," *Vanity Fair*, 5 Oct. 2019, www.vanityfair.com/hollywood/2019/10/game-of-thrones-ending-george-rr-martin-faithful. Accessed 13 Jan. 2020.

Fredman, Sara. "And What of My Wrath?" *Longreads*, May 2019, https://longreads.com/2019/05/30/and-what-of-my-wrath/. Accessed 14 Oct. 2020.

Lockman, Darcy. "What 'Good' Dad's Get Away With." *New York Times*, 4 May 2019, www.nytimes.com/2019/05/04/opinion/sunday/men-parenting.html. Accessed 13 Jan. 2020.

Loofbourow, Lili. "All hail the angry women of 2016." *The Week*, 28 Dec. 2016, theweek.com/articles/669346/all-hail-angry-women-2016. Accessed 9 Jan. 2020.

Lyons, Margaret. "Yes, Of Course That Was Rape on Last Night's *Game of Thrones*." *Vulture*, 21 Apr. 2014, www.vulture.com/2014/04/rape-game-of-thrones-cersei-jaime.html. Accessed 15 Jan. 2020.

Mantoan, Lindsey. "Daenerys Targaryen's Momentous Fate." *CNN*, 6 May 2019, www.cnn.com/2019/05/06/opinions/daenerys-targaryen-leads-jon-snow-credit-opinion-mantoan/index.html?no-st=1557165908. Accessed 13 Jan. 2020.

_____. "For Longtime Fans, the End of *Game of Thrones* Beggars Belief." *CNN*, 13 May 2019, www.cnn.com/opinions/live-news/who-will-win-game-of-thrones/h_27dc2a463fa2104112168a5e6bcc8964. Accessed 13 Jan. 2020.

Mantoan, Lindsey, and Sara Brady, eds. *Vying for the Iron Throne: Essays on Power, Gender, Death and Performance in HBO's Game of Thrones*. Jefferson, NC: McFarland, 2018.

Martin, George R.R. *Fire and Blood*. New York: Bantam Books, 2018.

Miller, Claire Cain. "Women Did Everything Right. Then Work Got 'Greedy.'" *New York Times*, 26 Apr. 2019, www.nytimes.com/2019/04/26/upshot/women-long-hours-greedy-professions.html?fbclid=IwAR0EmLsv5XZPEp_W2WQkMqWUepKsGqvgDGHZ1X3Ix bVzotUiOzbCO0Kf83c. Accessed 26 Apr. 2019.

"Nigeria: 5,000 rescued from Boko Haram." *Al Jazeera*, 26 June 2016, www.aljazeera.com/news/2016/06/nigeria-5000-rescued-boko-haram-borno-160626094621430.html. Accessed 13 Jan. 2020.

Nilsen, Ella. "'Likeability' ratings in a recent New Hampshire poll show just how tough female candidates have it." *Vox*, 23 Jul. 2019, www.vox.com/2019/7/23/20699724/likeability-gender-new-hampshire-poll-warren-harris. Accessed 13 Jan. 2020.

Nordberg, Anna. "In the World of *Game of Thrones*, Mothers Have Power, but They Pay a Terrible Price for It." *Slate*, 10 Apr. 2019, slate.com/culture/2019/04/game-of-thrones-motherhood-cersei-lannister-daenerys-targaryen.html. Accessed 14 Jan. 2020.

O'Keefe, Meghan. "*Game of Thrones*: Is It All Tyrion's Fault?" *Decider.com*, 16 May 2019, decider.com/2019/05/16/game-of-thrones-tyrions-fault/. Accessed 14 Jan. 2020.

Otterson, Joe. "Alan Taylor Breaks Down Timeline in 'Beyond the Wall,'" *Variety*, 21 Aug. 2017, variety.com/2017/tv/news/game-of-thrones-season-7-episode-6-beyond-the-wall-timeline-director-1202534403/. Accessed 14 Jan. 2020.

Reston, Maeve. "Fiona Hill left a legacy for angry women during impeachment hearing," *CNN*, 23 Nov. 2019, www.cnn.com/2019/11/23/politics/fiona-hill-angry-women-impeachment-hearing/index.html. Accessed 9 Jan. 2020.

Rosen, Christopher. "*Game of Thrones* Stars Who Openly Criticized Season 8." *TVGuide*, www.tvguide.com/news/game-of-thrones-stars-criticize-final-season-8/. Accessed 15 Jan. 2020.

Sandwell, Ian. "How Game of Thrones season 8 has totally let Cersei down." *Digital Spy*, 15 May 2019, www.digitalspy.com/tv/ustv/a27453196/game-of-thrones-cersei-death-season-8/. Accessed 14 Jan. 2020.

Sharf, Zack. "Lena Headey Says *Game of Thrones* Cut "Traumatizing' Scene of Cersei's Miscarriage." *Indie Wire*, 20 June 2019, www.indiewire.com/2019/06/lena-headey-game-of-thrones-deleted-scene-cersei-miscarriage-1202151596/. Accessed 15 Jan. 2020.

Tackett, Michael. "Women Line Up to Run for Office, Harnessing Their Outrage at Trump." *New York Times*, 4 Dec. 2017, www.nytimes.com/2017/12/04/us/politics/women-candidates-office.html. Accessed 9 Jan. 2020.

Tassi, Paul. "*Game of Thrones* Season 8 Gave Women Just 22% of All Lines, The Lowest Ever." *Forbes*, 25 May 2019, www.forbes.com/sites/paultassi/2019/05/25/game-of-thrones-season-8-gave-women-just-22-of-all-lines-the-lowest-ever/#7c46cc8c4eab. Accessed 14 Jan. 2020.

Thompson, Courtney. "This Episode Shows *Game of Thrones* Finally Gives A Crap About Women." *Whimn*, 6 May 2019, www.whimn.com.au/play/unwind/this-episode-shows-game-of-thrones-finally-gives-a-crap-about-women/news-story/1fa2a0b48ed4b38bd0d2 4a82eeb3456e. Accessed 14 Jan. 2020.

Tufekci, Zeynep. "The Real Reason Fans Hate the Last Season of *Game of Thrones*." *Scientific American*, 17 May 2019, blogs.scientificamerican.com/observations/the-real-reason-fans-hate-the-last-season-of-game-of-thrones/. Accessed 15 Jan. 2020.

VanDerWerff, Emily. "Why Daenerys Targaryen could be *Game of Thrones*' Ultimate Villain." *Vox*, 26 Apr. 2019, https://www.vox.com/culture/2019/4/26/18516137/game-of-thrones-finale-predictions-dany-villain. Accessed 14 Oct. 2020.

Wired Staff. "*Game of Thrones*' Biggest Losers Were the Fans." *Wired*, 28 May 2019, www.wired.com/story/game-of-thrones-finale-disappointment/. Accessed 18 Jan. 2020.

Yglesias, Matthew. "Daenerys was right: King's Landing had to burn." *Vox*, 26 May 2019, www.vox.com/culture/2019/5/26/18637091/game-of-thrones-targaryen-restoration-daenerys. Accessed 14 Jan. 2020.

The Developing Verbal Power of Daenerys

A Pragmatics Analysis

GRAHAM P. JOHNSON

HBO's television series *Game of Thrones* has proven to be enormously popular around the globe—genuinely becoming an entertainment cultural phenomenon. This medieval-inspired fantasy epic, based upon George R.R. Martin's series of novels, certainly deserves serious study within the academic field of medievalism, both to determine the reasons for its appeal, as well as to evaluate the skill with which it was created or constructed. Already some fine scholarly work has been done, but now that the final, 8th season, has aired more should be done, and indeed deserves to be done. Particularly when it comes to examining the depiction of power within the series, a more detailed, illuminating examination can be made of the dialogue itself using the field of pragmatics—a field within sociolinguistics.

Pragmatics can be brought to bear to examine dialogue from *GoT* to reveal a great deal more about the meaning and sub-text of both key scenes and overlooked scenes from the series. In particular, for analyzing the dialogue, we can use the pragmatics framework provided by H.P. Grice with the Co-operative Principle and Geoffrey Leech with the Politeness Principle, and their ideas about face, FTAs (face-threatening acts), implicatures, and speech acts (an introduction to and an overview of pragmatics can be found below). Because of the enormous amount of *GoT* material to choose from for analysis—this series, after all, which ran from 2011 to 2019, has eight seasons, 73 episodes, totaling 69.8 hours—we must first recognize that, while there are numerous characters involved with different story-lines, of all the different types of characters, the one that arguably warrants the greatest interest is the group that lacks imposing, physical (fighting) power. In other words, if pragmatics can be employed as a useful analytical tool to gain insight about characters through the dialogue alone, then the characters who rely on verbal skill or power, rather than physical (fighting) skill or power, should be the first group to draw attention. Moreover, this group—which includes Daenerys Targaryen, Tyrion Lannister, and Bran Stark—is made up of some of the most essential characters to the entire series. Indeed, these characters, these "underdog" (and physically less imposing) characters, are so essential to George R.R. Martin's original vision, that Bran ends up "winning" the game of thrones, demonstrating that the writers who continued his work past adapting his books (Davis Benioff, D.B. Weiss, as well as Bryan Cogman, Jane Espenson, Dave Hill, Vanessa Taylor), favored these physical underdogs in a fantasy world where, at least superficially, might makes right. Daenerys, Tyrion, and even Bran can have their dialogue analyzed pragmatically for excellent results about not only the characters themselves, but also some of the major themes and issues of *GoT*. Of these underdogs, the two who lend themselves the best to pragmatics analysis are Tyrion and Daenerys. However, due to space constraints, the focus here will be on Daenerys—particularly because her rise and eventual fall are by far the most dramatic in the series, especially when viewed in terms of verbal power. She goes from being a passive, abused sister of Viserys Targaryen, to an imperious and victorious queen with control over dragons and multiple armies. She becomes the most powerful person in *GoT* (even though two of the dragons are killed once she is in Westeros), until her nephew Jon Snow kills her in the final episode. Her one unique physical skill is her imperviousness to extreme heat and fire (which she uses to spectacular results in the series, especially in S1, E10 and S6, E4); otherwise, she lacks physical (fighting) power, and she relies on others for that (dragons, soldiers, etc.).

Of the Daenerys scenes to analyze, the goal here is to trace her developing verbal power as her character grows, or as her character's arc progresses. Because she has so many scenes, not all will be included in this analysis. In fact, to trace her verbal power, some of the most physically dramatic (action) scenes involving Daenerys will not be included in a pragmatics analysis (such as the scene in which she escapes the fighting pits of Meereen). Instead, it is often the "quieter" scenes of conversations—scenes that can be overlooked by the casual fan who notices rather the sex and violence—that reveal the most about her character. It is these scenes that can best be mined for deeper meaning and sub-text using the pragmatics tools of Grice and Leech, combined with close reading. These five scenes for analysis are the following:

- S1, E1, when we first see Daenerys and her brother Viserys.
- S1, E7, when we see a deceptively quiet moment between Daenerys and her now-husband Drogo.

- S3, E7, when Daenerys talks to the Yunkai envoy.
- S5, E1, when Dany talks to her advisors about the Sons of the Harpy.
- S8, E4, when Daenerys talks to Jon about keeping their aunt-nephew relationship secret.

There are, of course, literally dozens of captivating scenes of dialogue to choose from when analyzing Daenerys, but these scenes listed above, taken as a grouping, show her progression well, effectively providing the bones of the pattern established about her character on *GoT*.

Please note that for copyright matters regarding the use of original HBO material in scholarly articles, only the first and fifth scenes (S1, E1 and S8, E4) will be provided in full for the reader. The second, third, and fourth scenes (S1, E7; S3, E7 and S5, E1) will not be, with only shorter quotations used instead of the fuller conversations. However, for all five scenes being analyzed, the time stamp within each episode will be noted, so that readers can find and view each original scene—and readers are encouraged to watch each scene before reading the pragmatics analysis presented here. Readers may also look to online transcriptions of the scripts, at least for seasons one through five, at https://gameofthronesscripts.wordpress.com/.

An Introduction to (and Oversimplified Overview of) Pragmatics

First, I offer an overview of pragmatics to show what pragmatics is and how it can be used to analyze dialogue in a work of fiction, especially how pragmatics can be used to gain insights and identify additional sub-textual meaning. Please note that this necessarily will be an oversimplification of an entire field of linguistics, and note that the type of pragmatics being emphasized here is the one that follows from the work of H.P. Grice and Geoffrey Leech.[1]

To begin, imagine a long-married, heterosexual couple sitting on their living room couch.[2] The wife asks her husband, "Are you cold?" On the surface, this is a simple question. The literal meaning is simple as well. Using the typical linguistic tools available, we can see that this is a question (as indicated by inverting the subject and verb and the question mark at the end), an independent clause, that the wife uses the second person singular pronoun "you," etc. We could even look up the word "cold" in a dictionary to see its range of meanings. So, we can use the tools of grammar, morphology, semantics, lexicography, etc., in order to determine the meaning. However, for anyone who has been in a long-term relationship, we might realize that the wife could be, in fact, asking a loaded question. She might not actually be saying this to her husband to inquire about his body core temperature, and whether it is on the chilly side. Instead, the wife may be using this question indirectly to mean something else, which we might identify using sociolinguistics, which means we should pay attention to the social context, and realize that for a generation that grew up in the 1950s to 1970s U.S., and knowing what we do about human nature as well as language and gender, something else might be going on here. For example, she might actually mean: (a) turn up the thermostat because I am cold; (b) bring me a cup of tea because I am cold; (c) get the blanket for me because I am cold. Or, she might be meaning: (d) you look cold, and I care about how you are feeling, so I wonder if I can do anything to help. Of course, there are dozens of other possibilities, depending upon the background of these two people, their relationship, their history, etc. For instance, they may have had an ongoing conflict about the temperature setting on the thermostat, where she is usually feeling cold if it is set below 74°F, but he is comfortable at 68°F, and he sets it that low because, as he has argued, he is saving them money on the heating bill. They then have had a series of arguments because she is uncomfortably cold much of the time, and the phrase "penny-pinching miser" was used. So, from what we know about relationships and human nature, it would not be difficult to find the sub-text of the wife's question, without a little more background information. In fact, learning to read "between the lines" is an important skill that many of us learn (with varying degrees of success), as we move from adolescence to adulthood.

The next question then is, why does the speaker (wife) not use the direct approach (an imperative verb) to do one of a, b, or c above, by simply telling him, "Get the blanket off the back of the chair and give it to me because I'm cold." The answer to this is that, in order to be polite, and to avoid giving the impression of ordering him about, she is being indirect. "Ordering" someone is potentially a face-threatening act (FTA—see below), or it could be taken as a threat to his status. In other words, here she was being indirect to avoid putting him on the defensive or to avoid seeming insulting. However, depending upon what she means, it is possible that she was being passive-aggressive here, particularly if they had a long-running argument about the thermostat.[3]

Unfortunately for the linguists, who attempt to analyze human language using the scientific method, this is annoying. Back in the 1950s, for instance, they could bring to bear all their linguistic tools to the wife's simple question (grammar, morphology, etc.), but none of the traditional linguistic tools could explain or decipher the actual, sub-textual meaning of the wife's question. Clearly, new areas of linguistics needed to be developed. They quickly realized that the social context should be taken into consideration for analyzing language in certain circumstances, and sociolinguistics was born. Not surprisingly, being professional studiers of language, when developing the field of sociolinguistics, the linguists needed to develop ways of describing and explaining what was happening with language in these social situations: something that was testable, verifiable, repeatedly with the same result. Different branches of sociolinguistics then developed to describe and explain with accuracy and precision, as well as could be hoped when dealing with the messy complexities of human interactions involving language.

H.P. Grice's Co-operative Principle, Geoffrey's Leech's Politeness Principle, and an Introduction to Face, FTAs, and Implicatures

H.P. Grice introduced the concept of the co-operative principle (CP). In 1975, Grice published "Logic and Conversation." To simplify the significance of this work for the purposes of this essay, let us simply say that he created a scheme or methodology to explain how conversations go, when both the speaker and listener are trying to communicate clearly and honestly with each other, being "co-operative" in their conversation. When these rules are being followed, the conversation is going well. When the rules are being broken, then something is going wrong. Perhaps someone is not being clear enough to be understood. Perhaps someone is not telling the truth.

The Co-operative Principle (CP)[4]

I. *Quantity: Give the right amount of information*: i.e.,
   1. Make your contribution as informative as is required.
   2. Do not make your contribution more informative than is required.
II. *Quality: Try to make your contribution one that is true*: i.e.,
   1. Do not say what you believe to be false
   2. Do not say that for which you lack adequate evidence.
III. *Relation: Be relevant*
IV. *Manner: Be perspicuous*: i.e.,
   1. Avoid obscurity of expression.
   2. Avoid ambiguity.
   3. Be brief (avoid unnecessary prolixity).
   4. Be orderly.

In short, Grice argued that, as long as the speaker is following the rules of quantity, quality, relation, and manner, then the conversation is co-operative. When one or more rules are being broken, then the conversation has problems. These problems could be intentional or unintentional by the speaker. For example, the speaker could be accidentally telling the listener something that he or she already knows, thus breaking CP I. Or the speaker could be intentionally telling a lie, thus breaking CP II.

The next important scheme or methodology came from Geoffrey Leech. He (and other linguists) recognized that Grice's work was important and intellectually powerful, but one problem with Grice's ideas is that sometimes people use language indirectly, such as in order to be polite or impolite. For example, with the "Are you cold?" question discussed above, the wife might be breaking CP II 1 "Do not say what you believe to be false" (if she did not actually think her husband was cold), or CP IV 2, "Avoid ambiguity" (not being direct about wanting him to turn up the thermostat). So, Leech came up with his own scheme or methodology, with a list of things people follow in order to be polite to each other in conversations, which he called the politeness principle (PP). In other words, sometimes people will break the CP in order to follow the PP. An obvious example would be telling someone that their shoes look great (to be polite), when in fact the speaker thinks the shoes are not flattering.

The Politeness Principle (PP)[5]

I. *Tact Maxim (being tactful)*
   1. Minimize cost to other.
   2. Maximize benefit to other.
II. *Generosity Maxim (being generous)*
   1. Minimize benefit to self.
   2. Maximize cost to self.
III. *Approbation Maxim (giving praise)*
   1. Minimize dispraise of other.
   2. Maximize praise of other.
IV. *Modesty Maxim (being modest)*
   1. Minimize praise of self.
   2. Maximize dispraise of self.
V. *Agreement Maxim (being in agreement)*
   1. Minimize disagreement between self and other.
   2. Maximize agreement between self and other.
VI. *Sympathy Maxim (being sympathetic)*
   1. Minimize antipathy between self and other.
   2. Maximize sympathy between self and other.

This list of maxims, when followed, shows politeness in conversation. When the maxims are broken (or flouted), the speaker is being somehow impolite.

Not surprisingly, in works of fiction with emotionally charged scenes full of conflict, characters break the CP and PP all the time. Even though the reader or viewer has not studied these CP and PP lists of principles, once one is aware of these rules or maxims, one can quickly identify when a speaker is being un-co-operative or impolite. Using the schemes of Grice and Leech in concert provides a straight-forward way to identify, and especially to explain exactly how, these issues are present in dialogue.

The idea of "face" is fairly simple at its core. It has to do with one's status or esteem. Leech defines "face" as, "the positive self-image or self-esteem that a person enjoys as a reflection of that person's estimation by others" (*Pragmatics of Politeness* 25). So, linguistically, the term means that one can have a positive or negative "face"—self-image or self-esteem—depending upon what that person believes that others think or feel about him/her. This leads to the idea of a "face-threatening act" (FTA), in which someone says something that potentially hurts or lowers the "face" of another. So, being given a compliment (that is genuine or believed to be genuine), will increase the person's "face." If one is insulted that will decrease the person's "face." Of course, how much one's "face" is helped or hurt will depend upon the status of the person giving the compliment or insult; i.e., how much weight their words carry with the listener.

Combining all the above, the result is that we can analyze dialogue, focusing on what a speaker is saying and how it is said, to see if the CP and PP are being followed or not. Then we can identify ways that FTAs are being employed. From this, we can see more analytically exactly what that speaker is doing, and thus gain insights into his or her character. Additionally, how the listener reacts becomes essential—particularly whether or not the listener acknowledges or reacts to any breaking (or flouting) of CP or PP by the speaker, and whether that listener then responds in kind or not, and how exactly.

As an aside, "Implicature" is a somewhat tricky concept at first; one might think that it is a way for linguists to mean "implication" or something that is being implied. However, the definition of implicature is, "Grice's term for an inferred meaning, often with a different (i.e., non-truth-preserving) form from that of the original utterance. In Grice's theory, 'the inferential process by which a hearer derives a conversational implicature is calculable, and the implicature is defeasible (cancellable without a contradiction arising)'" (Archer 486). The key is that implicatures are implied by the speaker, but they can have multiple meanings so that the speaker can say after, "I didn't mean that," thus taking back something insulting. So, it is a useful way to insult someone (impolite), or to suggest something perhaps gently (polite) without committing yourself to actually saying it. This is an important tactic for another reason: you can be indirect, understated. This can be used to reduce the possibility of causing offence or an FTA.[6] All that said, for the sake of this essay, I will employ a less strict, and simpler, definition of "implicature." When analyzing the dialogue involving Daenerys, we will consider what characters are implying and inferring only.

The concepts of positive politeness and negative politeness are useful terms to use in concert with Leech's PP. In short, in the work *Politeness* by Penelope Brown and Stephen Levinson, positive politeness is "boosting the listener/hearer, such as giving a compliment." Negative politeness lowers oneself (the speaker), such as with self-effacement, deference, showing respect for the listener, making an apology.

The last concept to summarize before getting to *GoT* and the Daenerys scenes is speech acts. One of the most important breakthroughs in sociolinguistics was with identifying speech acts, and the different kinds of speech acts, such as ordering, requesting, promising, making an oath, pleading or begging. Again, for the purposes of streamlining the methodology, we will not be using the detailed studies of speech acts from sociolinguistics. Rather, we will be using the broader idea that, in a literary work or television program, a speech act is when a character is performing a type of action through speaking that is beyond normal conversation; normal in this case might be such as one would find when speakers are following the CP. We should not be surprised that in *GoT* we have numerous examples of characters doing the expected when it comes to speech acts: with powerful characters giving orders and commands, sometimes insulting underlings, sometimes threatening them. Less powerful characters (and mentor figures) give advice, suggestions, even warnings to more powerful ones. Characters perform speech acts of vowing, promising, making oaths; characters ask loaded questions, sometimes particularly awkward or rude and insulting questions. We also have characters disagreeing with and contradicting each other, which would be more CP and PP than speech acts as such. An example of a speech act which Daenerys performs several times in *GoT*, but which will not be analyzed here, is her use of speaking the High Valyrian word, "*dracarys*" to order a dragon (Drogon) or dragons to breathe fire.

As a brief addendum, it should be noted that questions can be particularly interesting areas to focus upon for analysis. While in polite conversations, a question may simply be a way to request information from someone, or to show an interest in that person, impertinent questions can be among the most impolite things that people do in a conversation. First, the listener may not want to answer, may not want to divulge the information being requested by the speaker. Providing or admitting information may cause the listener to lose "face" or status, for example. Second, if the listener does not know the answer, then that would reveal gaps in the listener's knowledge, which also may again cause the listener to lose "face." Third, the question itself might be impertinent or aggressive, and the listener is then placed in a predicament: be impolite by not answering a question or offer compromising information. Fourth, the question might be used by the speaker to imply something about the listener. There are, of course, other elements to the minefield that is questions, but these four are the most central to the following analyses.

Scene 1: Daenerys and Viserys Talking in the House of Illyrio in Pentos

This scene is found starting at 33 minutes, 14 seconds of S1, E1. The corresponding scene from Martin's books is found on pp. 28–29 of A Game of Thrones.

Context: Daenerys is bullied and molested by her brother Viserys, and he has made a deal for her to be married to Khal Drogo in exchange, he thinks, for access to Drogo's army of Dothraki. Note: this is the first scene with Daenerys in GoT.

> VISERYS: Daenerys! There's our bride to be. Look—a gift from Illyrio. *[He holds out a dress of gossamer fabric.]* Touch it. Go on. Feel the fabric. Mmm. Isn't he a gracious host?
> DAENERYS: We've been his guests for over a year, and he's never asked us for anything.
> VISERYS: Illyrio is no fool. He knows I won't forget my friends when I come into my throne. You still slouch. Let them see. You have a woman's body now *[as he takes off her dress, touches her chest]*. I need you to be perfect today. Can you do that for me? You don't want to wake the dragon, do you?
> DAENERYS: No.
> VISERYS: When they write the history of my reign, sweet sister, they will say it began today.

A traditional overview and reading of this scene might be as follows: Viserys is eager to marry his sister to Drogo, in essence selling or trading her in exchange for Drogo's military support, as Viserys needs it in his ambition to gain the throne of Westeros. So, having already made the deal, and with Drogo coming to the house to see Daenerys for the first time, he wants to make sure that she looks as attractive a bride-to-be as possible. So, he enters her room, carrying and presenting to her a dress of thin fabric, for her to wear. Daenerys wonders why Illyrio has been helping them so generously, and Viserys says that Illyrio has been doing it for future favors. Viserys then encourages her to stand up straight (i.e., present her chest more), and takes off her dress, molesting her by touching her appraisingly. He then threatens her: that she needs to win over Drogo as best as she can, or she will "wake the dragon"—which is a reference to Viserys losing his temper and abusing her, something that we presume he has done before. She replies that she does not want to wake the dragon, which he takes as an assurance of her complying, and he starts talking about this point in time being the beginning of his rise to the throne.

In short, we see that he demonstrates both the physical and verbal power, and that she has none. We can see that he is controlling, physically and emotionally abusive, and that she is passive, seemingly (and numbly, in line with Emilia Clarke's performance) completely controlled by him as a result of presumably his past pattern of behavior, in that she does not object or fight back. So, he is vile, and she is a victim. Moreover, we see what will turn out to be an issue that runs through much of *GoT*, which is the dysfunctional relationships between brothers and sisters. His use of the phrase, "sweet sister," is loaded and creepy. Indeed, critics can look at the use of this phrase throughout the series and Martin's books, as it seldom is used in a positive context. Instead, the phrase is most-often used by Tyrion to refer to Cersei sarcastically or ironically. The meaning of "sweet" is often the opposite, which ties in with the overall tone of both the series and the books and subversion. That said, when adding the tools of pragmatics to the analysis, a much more detailed micro-interpretation is possible, which supports the close reading above, but also presents nuances of Daenerys's character as well as Viserys's, which suggest elements of the dynamic between them that will be manifested later, when she gains some power and independence from him.

The speech pattern of Viserys here, overall, is to use imperative verbs and follow that up with one or more questions: the imperative verbs are "Look," "Touch," "Go on," "Feel," followed by the question, "Isn't he a gracious host?" He is offering the fabric for her, but clearly he is ordering her. According to the co-operative principle, he is being relevant (CP III) in bringing up the subject of her being a bride soon, and showing her the dress for her to wear. He also tells her its origins, which is as a present, so she knows where it comes from—again, relevant. He is also following CP I and II, in giving her correct information. One might argue that he is also following CP IV, in that he is not being obscure. So, from that perspective, this is superficially starting as a co-operative conversation—even though the imperative verbs already provide a clue that the style in which he talks to her is controlling.

Her reply to his question is the key moment where the conversation turns, albeit subtly at first view. One assumes that he expected her to reply, "Yes, you are right. Illyrio giving me this dress shows that he is a gracious host." She might even have added something about how happy she is to be married, or that she is happy to help him gain this advantage of Drogo's forces. Instead, she makes a statement, in which she wonders why Illyrio has been supporting them. She is implying, that Illyrio wants something. She is being indirect here, carefully polite in the conventional sense (by avoiding being direct), but rather than agreeing by answering Viserys's question (to do so would be following PP V), she wants to know about Illyrio's motives. She is being indirect, in not stating baldly, "I know Illyrio is only helping us because he wants something in return," which would be impolite. But using the politeness principle, one might argue that she is bringing up the obligation that Viserys owes Illyrio, because he has needed Illyrio's help and material support to survive. This would, depending upon one's interpretation of the application of Leech's PP, mean that Daenerys is being impolite, breaking PP I and III. This would also mean that, on a subtle level, she is attacking the "face" or status or self-esteem of Viserys.

He is obviously not pleased with how she responded to his question, because he says, "Illyrio is no fool," and he explains that Illyrio will want favors in return. What is interesting about this, is that he is arguably using an implicature, a face-threatening act (FTA) against her, possibly as a reaction to what she has just raised. By his saying, "no fool," and because she did not directly say what Illyrio's motives are, Viserys is implying that Daenerys *is* a fool for not knowing the motives, which is an insult and would lower her "face." He then supports this interpretation as he explains the Illyrio motives to her.

At this point, Viserys changes the subject to her appearance and criticizes her posture, breaking the PP I and II. The insulting, molesting, and threatening elements of this and what follows are obvious. However, of particular interest is that he asks her two questions, and he does not get an answer to the first. In the scene, there is a pause after he asks the first question, "Can you do that [i.e., be perfect] for me?" She does not answer, breaking the CP completely by not providing any information, and PP by not replying. He is clearly not happy with that, so he adds a second question, in which he threatens her. She does answer that with "No"—one word to answer that she does not want to be abused by him.

So, the pragmatics analysis supports the close reading of the characters and the dynamic between them: Daenerys has neither physical nor verbal power, and she is controlled and abused by her brother. However, pragmatics identifies a sub-text which indicates that there is more to her than simply a passive victim. When she does not answer his first question, and instead changes the subject, two important seeds about her character are quietly planted for the viewer: (1) that she is a thoughtful person, in that she wonders about peoples' motives; (2) that she is subtly willing to hurt the "face" of her brother, both by not being completely controlled by answering his question the way he likely wanted, and more importantly by bringing up the subject of what her brother owes Illyrio as well as their complete reliance upon Illyrio's help.[7]

Scene 2: Daenerys and Drogo Discuss the Dothraki Army

This scene is found starting at 26 minutes, 43 seconds of S1, E7. The corresponding scene from Martin's books is found on pp. 583-4 of A Game of Thrones.

Context: Daenerys and Khal Drogo (now married), in their abode, talking; she stands behind him, and he is sitting, while she is doing his hair.

The close reading of this scene is fairly simple. Daenerys is attempting to convince Drogo to take his army across the sea to Westeros, so that he can become king and she queen. He has no interest in that and rebuffs her. He then says the subject is closed and leaves. The scene offers an interesting view of the developing dynamic between these two characters. The most important is that she is polite, but she is trying to get what she wants, and it is not something that he wants. It is also noteworthy that they are learning each other's languages, with the conversation being in Dothraki, but Daenerys uses the word for "dirts" rather than "lands," and he corrects her. Then he uses the word "chair" rather than "throne," and she corrects him. Because of the horrible way that they were married, and the circumstances surrounding it, as well as the "honeymoon," this scene is important for showing the adaptability of Daenerys, in how she is seemingly making the best of this situation, and not only surviving but attempting to find ways to improve her life.

From the pragmatics perspective, this scene is essential for understanding Daenerys's character, and her growing confidence and even verbal power—even though she is, at this point in *GoT*, still subject to and her life is dictated to by the men. Instead of looking for all the nuances of the CP and PP being followed or not, one can start a pragmatics analysis primarily upon how Daenerys and Drogo contradict each other or disagree, how she maintains the veneer of politeness to avoid giving offense, while trying to persuade him to see her point of view. He opens the scene talking, but the sense for the viewer is that the conversation began before that. Regardless, in the scene, he speaks six times, and she five. The words "no" and "not" appear seven times, which on the surface would suggest a negative conversation with conflict. However, Daenerys uses verbal skills here to get her ideas across effectively, not that she is able to convince Drogo at this point to take his forces across the sea to Westeros, but he only becomes annoyed so that he gets up and leaves, not insulted to the point that he raises his voice, or loses his temper, or becomes threatening. Of course, one could simply argue that this is because Drogo has become so smitten with her that he controls his temper, but that would discount the insights we can gain here about how exactly Daenerys employs verbal skill.

First, he denies that the "stallion" or the Khal of Khals, would even need a throne. She does not address this directly (arguably breaking CP), instead bringing up the prophecy and using the phrase "ends of the earth." Using the term "prophecy" is perfectly following CP because the "stallion" idea is part of the Dothraki prophecy. The next exchanges in the dialogue are about defining exactly what "ends of the earth" means, with Drogo arguing that the world essentially ends at the shore of the sea, and with Daenerys insisting that it includes the lands across the sea, i.e., Westeros. She then offers proof that such lands exist, by saying that she was born there (arguably following CP I, II, III, and IV all at once).

At this point, the conversation is seemingly sidetracked by Drogo correcting her Dothraki, that she means "lands," but she said "dirts." She repeats the word "lands" and says "yes," showing that she accepts his correction and agrees with him (fulfilling PP V: agreement). She provides more information, explaining that there are "thousands of ships" and that these are "[w]ooden horses" for transportation (following CP).

Drogo then breaks both CP and PP by trying to end the conversation, "Let's speak no more," but he uses the word "chair" instead of "throne," so she continues the conversation by correcting him just as he had done about "dirts" and "lands." Now distracted from ending the conversation, he repeats "throne," thus agreeing with her correction (PP V), just as she had done. She explains what a throne is, but he again rejects the idea of thrones being of any importance to a Khal.

The symmetry of the conversation shows that, while not exactly equals—at least Drogo does not seem to think so—she is suggesting that they are. In fact, the most important word in the entire scene is the "or"— when Daenerys says, "A chair for a King to sit upon *or* a Queen." The fact that she does not say "chairs" along with "king and queen" is striking; it means that she is already thinking in terms of being not only a queen, but the queen of Westeros, and that she would willingly take up the position of ruler instead of Drogo. He seems not to notice the significance of what she implies.

That Daenerys and Drogo have this conversation with so many negative words, and contradictions and corrections, yet they avoid FTAs, is remarkable, and the way they both use PP V immediately after having vocabulary corrected, is remarkable. This, combined with the symmetry of the conversation (as well as the on-screen chemistry between Emilia Clarke and Jason Momoa), results in a scene that almost shows them as equals, and it certainly shows that the power of Daenerys is increasing, and that she is both intelligent and clever with her language skills, according to what the CP and PP indicate. The only component arguably missing from her verbal arsenal here, is that she does not explicitly use PP III, in flattering or praising Drogo, which might have been an effective additional tactic. That said, by agreeing that he is the "stallion" at the beginning of the conversation, she is flattering or praising him, and verifying his high status or "face" too.

Scene 3: Daenerys Insults the Yunkai Envoy, Razdal Mo Eraz

This scene is found starting at 21 minutes, 50 seconds of S3, E7. The corresponding scene from Martin's books is found on pp. 578–80 of A Storm of Swords.

Context: Jorah has advised Daenerys to bypass Yunkai, but when she learns that there are 200,000 slaves in the city, she tells him that they have that many reasons to fight the masters' forces to free the slaves. Daenerys has ordered Grey Worm to give the slavers of Yunkai an ultimatum: surrender. An envoy for the city of Yunkai arrives at the camp of Daenerys on a litter carried by slaves, and he tries to get her to leave Yunkai alone, in exchange for ships that she can use to take her forces to Westeros.

In this scene, Daenerys has gone against the advice of Jorah Mormont, and is determined to free the slaves of Yunkai. She is offered the ships she needs to leave Essos and to take her forces to Westeros and claim the Iron Throne, which was her original goal. Instead, she will put that ambition on hold in order to work towards her goal of ending slavery. In the conversation with the Yunkai envoy, she demands that the Yunkai slaves are freed and given reparations, or she will attack the city. He rejects the ultimatum and leaves, forced into leaving his gold behind, gold that she was being offered to leave Yunkai alone. This scene is essential for showing her growing power and confidence, and how that is manifested when talking to this representative of the slave system that she hates. Being a scene of verbal conflict, it has several examples of speech acts, such as insults and threats, and of FTAs.

The envoy offers the ships, and she asks what he wants in return. In this case, the question is relevant and perfectly conventional in this context. His reply begins with following the CP, telling her that she simply has to "make use of these ships" and leave Yunkai alone—which is informative, unambiguous, and he is fulfilling his role as an envoy. However, when he adds the phrase "where you belong," this changes the tone of the conversation, suggesting that she should not even be in Essos; when he adds that the

Yunkai want to "conduct our affairs in peace," he is inadvertently insulting her values, in that for him, "peace" is maintaining the slavery system, which is hardly "peace" for those unfortunate enough to be slaves.

Her reply, that her gift to him is "Your life," meaning that she will not kill him, is clearly a threat. Incredulous, he asks, "My life?" and she replies with clarification: she will not have the slave masters of Yunkai killed if they surrender and free the slaves with reparations. The fact that clarification is needed suggests that she broke CP IV to be dramatic. Also, the suggestion that she could have him killed could be viewed not only as a threatening act but a FTA, in that she is establishing her confidence of physical power over him, and that he lacks the power to stop her.

He, in disbelief, calls her "mad" meaning crazy (but it also captures her emotions towards slavery), which is insulting (arguably breaking PP I and III), and he explains why she cannot defeat the masters of Yunkai—that they have "powerful friends," and adds the threat that these are "[f]riends who would take great pleasure in destroying you" (threat), and he says that they will enslave her army, people, and herself (threat). The interesting part to this is that he does not specify who these friends are (breaking CP I and IV). As long as he actually has these powerful friends, he is not breaking CP II.

When Drogon then acts aggressively towards him, he says to her, "You swore me safe conduct"—which is perfectly true—and reminds her that she made a speech act (promise or vow) spoken or implied because he is an envoy, not to hurt him. He is accurate, following CP and reminding her of PP, and the implication is that if she were to hurt or kill him now, she would be injuring her own "face" or status or honor by breaking her word.

The reply of Daenerys is one of the most important lines that she utters in all of season 3: "I did, but my dragons made no promises, and you threatened their mother." With this, she acknowledges that what he said about "safe conduct" is right, but that she promised, and that her dragons did not—which is humorous in the sense that the dragons do not talk or have the agency of humans in *GoT*. However, this is exactly her point: she cannot control the dragons, and they will protect her if she is threatened, not caring a whit for the conventions of people. In this way, she is able to threaten him, while insisting that she is absolved from breaking her word if the dragons hurt or kill him. This is then doubly threatening to the envoy.

When the envoy tries to leave and take the gold with him, she tells him that the gold is now hers, and she orders (speech act) him to leave. Her argument is that he gave the gold to her already. Of course, she is being dishonest, in that the gold was presented as a gift in exchange for her buying or hiring ships and leaving the area for Westeros. If he had stayed long enough at this stage to point that out, he could have damaged her "face" and perhaps salvaged something from the conversation. Instead, he leaves. If one were to examine this conversation as a verbal contest, she has clearly won and demonstrated her now undeniable verbal power and linguistic skills—impressing her people and disturbing her enemy.

Scene 4: Daenerys in Council in the Pyramid of Meereen

This scene is found starting at 15 minutes, 41 seconds of S5, E1. The corresponding scene from Martin's books is found on pp. 35–8 of A Dance with Dragons.

Context: Daenerys talking to her advisors (Grey Worm, Mossador, Barristan Selmy, Missandei) after an Unsullied soldier, White Rat, was murdered by the Sons of the Harpy. Daenerys is informed that the Sons of the Harpy are responsible; she comments upon this development, and then gives her orders, which her advisors realize will upset the Sons of the Harpy even more, and she lets her advisors know that this is her intention: to prod the S.H. into making a mistake.

This particular scene might seem, upon first glance, an odd choice for analysis. Usually scenes with conflict, where FTAs and implicatures are found, yield strongest results using pragmatics. However, this scene, which is easily overlooked, still presents keen insights about the growing verbal power of Daenerys. It is also an interesting scene dynamically because she is talking to all her advisors in the room at the same time, getting information from them, coming to decisions, and giving orders. She is not merely being commanding, but just as importantly, she is displaying the qualities of a ruler who is attempting to problem-solve and is sending a message to her enemies, in this case the Sons of the Harpy.

The first observation is that all the advisors are using the phrase "your Grace" when speaking to her, using the honorific to show respect and her status as their queen. The second is that she initiates matters to get what information she wants, first asking the question "Sons of the Harpy?" to verify who committed the murder, then, "They never killed before," indicating that she did not realize that the Sons of the Harpy were a deadly threat. She is not so egotistical that she cannot acknowledge when she is wrong, or at least has overlooked a potential threat. Barristan suggests that the escalation was inevitable, because "[c]onquerors always meet with resistance." He uses a gnomic statement, or statement of wisdom that is widely acknowledged to be true, or a general truth. This is usually a safe rhetorical technique, because the speaker is simply repeating wisdom said by others, and thus it should not be taken as personal or as being critical by the listener. But significantly, Daenerys fixes on the word "conquerors" and contradicts

Barristan (PP). She rejects the idea that her forces conquered Meereen; instead, she insists that the freed slaves of Meereen took the city back from the slave-masters. At her use of the word "people," the former slave, Mossador, says that the slave-masters never viewed slaves as people. With this, Barristan (we were always going to have resistance) and Mossador (the masters do not view the former slaves as people) have given Daenerys key information about their situation (CP). So far, this conversation is all about the CP and Daenerys learning and evaluating what has happened and why, overall. Because of her position of power and status in the room, she is not required to follow the PP so closely, especially because she needs to be cognizant of her status and maintaining "face" to hold the position of queen, and to hold their respect. She also has to avoid flouting the PP completely, or of insulting her advisors, which would indicate poor leadership, in that it could weaken her position by eroding their willingness to follow her.

From this point, the conversation shifts as she begins reacting, first by pronouncing that the former masters will learn to see things her way, that the Sons of the Harpy are cowards, and that she will not allow the city to devolve into "chaos." She then wants to know who exactly was murdered, and Grey Worm tells her, at which point she decides to use the burial as a way to send a message to the Sons of the Harpy and the former masters—that this Unsullied soldier will receive a highly honorable burial. Barristan and Mossador give their evaluation of how the Sons of the Harpy will react, and she says that it is part of her strategy to make their enemies more aggressive, daring them to show themselves or make mistakes. She concludes by ordering her advisors to locate the perpetrators. For a speaker and listeners of equal status, ordering others is of course impolite and likely insulting; with the queen and advisors dynamic, it is appropriate.

The way that Daenerys explains the point of the very public burial, using a proverb, "Angry snakes lash out," again demonstrates verbal skill. She is comparing the Sons of the Harpy to snakes, indicating that she will make them lose their temper (and thus clear-headedness), and reveal themselves to her soldiers. When she adds, "Makes chopping off their heads that much easier," she follows the CP in explaining exactly what she means with the metaphor, so that her advisors will understand unequivocally. Additionally, she displays a confidence that they will beat their enemies. Barristan clearly understands and accepts, as he simply says "Your Grace" before leaving the room with the others.

From this, we see that Daenerys follows all four of the CP: she gives the right amount of information (CP I), says what she believes to be true (CP II), stays relevant to the subject at hand (CP III), and is clear to the point of explaining exactly what she means when using a proverb (CP IV). As for the PP, she does not follow it, in making any particular efforts to be polite to her advisors. Neither does she actively insult them. She does contradict ("I did not conquer them") and order, but the first case is a clarification that she deems essential to her narrative (that she freed the slaves, who took back the city), and the second is essential to her job as leader, telling them what they are doing next in response. She also avoids pointing out or, even worse, berating them for not making it clear to her the dangers that the Sons of the Harpy posed (thus avoiding an FTA or damaging Barristan's "face").[8]

This overview of the scene is enough to show how Daenerys's verbal power has evolved dramatically, especially from what we saw in S1, E1 and S1, E7. By S5, E1, she demonstrates several traits that can be viewed through the lens of pragmatics, that in her leadership position, she is following CP and when going against PP, she is doing it within the expected parameters of someone in charge, a queen, who respects her advisors and does not belittle, demean, threaten, or insult them. These are traits of a successful ruler, who listens to her advisors, gains intelligence from them, then makes thoughtful decisions, even if they might go against her counselors' wishes, while making her own wishes clear.

Following Season 5, a great many Daenerys scenes could be cited and examined showing her continuing developing verbal power, should space allow. From the point of view of analyzing her character, some of the most important scenes are in: S6, E4, when she sets the Dothraki temple on fire after a verbal confrontation with the Khals; S6, E6, when she makes a rousing speech to the Dothraki, gaining their support to follow her; S6, E9, when she meets the three envoys of Meereen; S6, E10, when she says her farewell to Daario, who will not be accompanying her forces to Westeros; S7, E2, when Daenerys has councils and conversations at Dragonstone with leaders of Westeros who are against Cersei's rule from King's Landing; S7, E3 & 4, when Daenerys first meets Jon Snow and has several conversations with him about the army of the dead.

That said, we can see her dramatic change for the worse, with her increasing imperiousness and her uncompromising, even murderous change, as the seasons progress, especially as we move into S7. At the end of S7, E4, the Lannister forces are routed (and roasted), leading to S7, E5, where she has the captured Tarly senior and junior (Samwell's father Randyll and brother Dickon) burned alive for refusing to pledge their loyalty to her. It is, in fact, this scene that is clearly the (somewhat heavy-handed by the writers) turning point for her character; she goes against the advice of Tyrion, uses her absolute power supported by the dragons and Dothraki, and changes her role from a savior to destroyer. Her transformation from S1, E1, when she was a passive victim with only subtle verbal skill and little-to-no-power, to an imperious, commanding queen who refuses to listen to counsel and uses murderous violence to solve her problems is remarkable. This, of course, continues most dramatically with the destruction of King's Landing in S8, E5 & 6.

Daenerys's unbridled and unchecked power is not only shown in the extended action sequences with the burning of King's Landing, but in her speech to her army in S8, E6, following her victory. In a dramatic scene, with the still burning and smoking King's Landing in the background, she addresses her forces (at the 13 minute mark of the episode). It is a victory speech, but it is more importantly a call to war against the rest of the world, to conquer all the lands and free all the slaves. Due to copyright concerns and HBO's policies, her speech will not be quoted here, but some of the interesting pragmatics elements can be pointed out, and the significance tied in with major themes and to Daenerys's character. In sum, she thanks her army, officially names Grey Worm as "Queen's Master of War"—i.e., in charge of the army—reminds the Unsullied what was done to them as infants to turn them into slave soldiers, and she calls them "liberators" who freed King's Landing from a "tyrant"—i.e., Cersei. She then pivots to her declaring that they will not stop until they "have liberated all the people of the world!" And she names all the places they will go to war, asking her troops, "Will you break the wheel with me?" The Dothraki cheer and Unsullied thump their spears in agreement, that they will continue to go to war until they have taken over the world. So, we see her now unchecked ambition and power on full display.

Pragmatically, the speech contains several noteworthy elements, and these are more due to speech acts rather than elements of the CP or PP, although some of that is in evidence as well. She begins by seeking agreement or concord with her army (agreement), reminding them of how they are joined together and their accomplishments (compliment and PP). By mentioning that they fulfilled their "promises" to her, she is reminding them of obligation (what is owed). By calling over Grey Worm and publicly naming him as leader of her army, she is preforming a speech act, promoting him with a title in full view and hearing of those he will be commanding (ritual performative). By reminding all the Unsullied of their origins, she is essentially arguing why they must continue fighting, going to war against all oppressors to free everyone else. By ending with the question of if they will follow her, she is putting them under another obligation or promise to go to war against the world, should they agree—and they do (collaborative performative).[9] In several ways, the speech is a masterclass on the kinds of speeches that today we might associate with fascist dictators or similar.

That said, it is worth noting that she is not being completely truthful, arguably breaking the CP II 1 by avoiding the fact that many of the "liberated" people of King's Landing have been killed by her dragon or army, that anyone who has not pledged loyalty has been or will be executed—in essence, that her definition of "liberty" or "liberated" is problematic considering the awful collateral damage and loss of life. However, it is also arguable that Daenerys is breaking CP II 1 because she may, in fact, believe that she has truly liberated everyone, and that those killed were justified collateral damage, so that, according to the CP, "Do not say what you believe to be false," has not been broken or flouted by her in this speech. Indeed, the likelihood that she believes everything in her speech to be true demonstrates how her character has become by this point a murderous zealot and tyrant—as evidenced by her verbal power. She has come to dominate verbally in the public arena.

Interestingly, it is in the more private arena, when it comes to convincing others who disagree with her, that her point of view is the right one, that she increasingly fails. She fails to reach agreement with, among others, Tyrion, Varys, and Sansa, and most importantly, she fails to persuade Jon, which ultimately leads to her death.

Scene 5: Daenerys and Jon Snow Talk of Their Secret

This scene is found starting at 26 minutes, 30 seconds of S8, E4. The corresponding scene is not found in Martin's as yet unfinished work.

Context: Daenerys begs Jon Snow not to tell his sisters (Sansa especially and Arya) the truth about the fact that she and he are aunt and nephew. While the entire conversation could receive a close pragmatics analysis, only the end of the conversation will be examined here to emphasize the most important element of all: that she has no verbal power when talking to Jon Snow. The end of the conversation is:

> Jon: I owe them [Sansa and Arya] the truth.
> Daenerys: Even if the truth destroys us?
> Jon: It won't.
> Daenerys: I've never begged for anything. But I'm begging you, don't do this, please.
> Jon: You are my queen. Nothing will change that. And they are my family. We can't live together.
> Daenerys: We can. I've just told you how.

In the complete conversation, Daenerys begins by expressing her love for Jon; they kiss, but then he turns away. He has revealed to her the truth of their blood connection—that she is his aunt—and she says she wishes she did not know, that she could forget that they are related. The conversation then moves to her frustration brought on by the feast that immediately preceded, at which the people of the North and Wildlings showed true affection for Jon as their leader, but not for her. Jon says that he does not want to be in charge, that she is his queen. He has also told her that Samwell Tarly and Bran Stark already know about the aunt-nephew revelation. She asks him to keep that information quiet, to swear to tell no one, so that nobody else will find out; at which point, the rest of the conversation is included above.

The scene demonstrates first that she loves Jon and wants to be with him, which she thinks is possible as long as no one besides Sam and Bran know the truth. The next key point is that she is unhappy with the idea of Jon being called king, which is a threat to her dream of having the power as queen of the Seven Kingdoms. The scene shows them contradicting each other: Jon saying "It won't" and "We can't live together," while Daenerys says, "We can." It also shows her performing the speech acts of begging and pleading with Jon, which does not sway him from wanting to tell the truth to his family. Jon tries to calm her worries about not being viewed as the legitimate queen of Westeros, because she knows that tradition would have Jon as the rightful ruler of Westeros when his true lineage is known. He seems to think that calling her "my queen" and insisting that he would not take power will solve the problem. They are both being honest, truthful, and direct with each other, with little ambiguity, thus following the CPs. They are also not trying to be rude to each other, even though PPs are being broken with the lack of agreement, contradictions, and arguably with Jon breaking PP VI in lacking sympathy for her point of view. In some ways, the very direct CPs (perhaps too-direct) results in brevity that removes sympathizing with each other from the conversation.

The fact that she cannot persuade Jon illustrates the fatal flaw in her verbal power: she exercises no power over him. While Jon has his loyalties divided, and is upset by this, he sides with his adopted family (the Starks) and his values (I cannot be the lover of my own aunt) over his romantic love for her. We see the same thing playing out in S8, E6 when he murders her. He is upset doing it, but he believes that he is putting the good of the Seven Kingdoms over his love for her. At this point, one might well question just what kind of love Jon has had for Daenerys anyway? She herself seems to have recognized this, certainly by S8, E2 when she and Sansa are talking. While Sansa suggests that Daenerys is manipulating Jon, Daenerys says that the opposite is true: that because she loves Jon, she has been doing what he wants, taking her forces North to fight the dead, at great cost.

In fact, not only does Daenerys lack the power to persuade Jon to do what she wants, she even loses "face" by begging, pleading, and being refused. The end of the scene demonstrates more clearly than anything else in Season 8, how Daenerys will lose her power and eventually be killed. In short, she has become too imperious and unyielding in political and military matters (for example in S7, E5 with killing the Tarlys), and she has become too ineffectual in personal matters, especially with Jon—a combination that ends up being deadly for her.

Thus, it seems that employing a combination of close reading and pragmatics on even a small number of carefully selected scenes can yield surprisingly solid results, in this case providing insights into the major character of Daenerys, her developing verbal power, and identifying some of the essential sub-texts in the dynamics she has with other important characters in *GoT*, as well as revealing central themes and issues for the series. The hope is that further studies will be done using pragmatics for literary analysis, and that, even though pragmatics was originally designed by sociolinguists for analyzing real-life conversations, rather than dialogue from works of fiction, a modified pragmatics framework relying on H.P. Grice's CP and Geoffrey Leech's PP in particular, has the power to provide insights into works of fiction, insights that may even suggest the skill with which dramatic dialogue from fiction has been constructed—thus not only providing literary analysis of a work, but also revealing some of the writing skill of the authors.

Notes

1. *The Oxford Handbook of Pragmatics* from 2017 is 711 pages long, which shows how much the field has developed from its core beginnings in the mid-1970s with the work of H.P. Grice. For the sake of streamlining this overview, and for the sake of using a more wieldy form of pragmatics for literary analysis, this author will only be using what he terms "classic pragmatics"—a combination of the work of Grice and Leech, which was introduced to him by Tom Shippey in a graduate seminar at SLU. Shippey's work using pragmatics for literary analysis can best be read in his articles, "Principles of Conversation in Beowulfian Speech" and "Speech and the Unspoken in *Hamðismál*." This author also recommends the work of Eric Bryan for pragmatics analysis of Old Norse sagas.

2. While this example of a heterosexual couple is a bit reductive and based on not only gender but marital stereotypes—such as those involving human males generally feeling warmer and females colder, and the ongoing battles over thermostats—the reasons for presenting it this way will become evident over the course of this essay. On a more serious note, this scenario can actually be rather significant when it comes to office settings and business attire and comfort.

3. For those interested in the study of gender and language, the work of Deborah Tannen, such as *You Don't Understand*, is an excellent starting point. From there, *Language and Gender* edited by Jennifer Coates and Pia Pichler, as well as *Language and Gender* edited by Penelope Eckert and Sally McConnell-Ginet are recommended. Indeed, sociolinguistic analyses of gendered language on *GoT* (outside the scope of this essay) will without doubt yield excellent results and insights. Insightful scholarship has already been produced and will not doubt continue analyzing gender roles and power, using cultural studies, but this is different than linguistic-focused analyses.

4. From Geoffrey Leech's *Principles of Pragmatics* (1983), p. 8. Adapted from H.P. Grice's "Logic and Conversation" (1975) by Leech.

5. From Geoffrey Leech's *Principles of Pragmatics* (1983), p. 132.

6. For those interested in more details concerning politeness and impoliteness, see the

work of Jonathan Culpepper, perhaps starting with *Impoliteness: Using Language to Cause Offence*.

7. Further analysis could be made by comparing the television series scene to that from pp. 28–9 of Martin's *A Game of Thrones*. Martin's version is much longer, with not only dialogue but also narration and description as well as some of the thoughts of Daenerys.

8. It should be noted that the dynamic between Daenerys and Barristan is essential, and that when she loses him as her trusted advisor, this damages her ability to rule much more than the casual viewer might realize. For some of the key scenes involving these two, see S3, E3; S4, E4; S5, E2.

9. See Jonathan Culpepper and Michael Haugh's section "Traditional speech act theory" from *Pragmatics and the English Language*, p. 157 in particular, for an overview of speech acts and terms such as *ritual performative* and *collaborative performative*.

Works Cited

Archer, Dawn, and Peter Grundy, eds. *The Pragmatics Reader*. London: Routledge, 2011.
Brown, Penelope, and Stephen C. Levinson. *Politeness: Some Universals in Language Usage*. Cambridge: Cambridge University Press, 1987.
Coates, Jennifer, and Pia Pichler. *Language and Gender: A Reader*. 2nd ed. Hoboken: Wiley-Blackwell, 2011.
Culpepper, Jonathan. *Impoliteness: Using Language to Cause Offense*. Cambridge: Cambridge University Press, 2011.
Culpepper, Jonathan, and Michael Haugh. *Pragmatics and the English Language*. London: Palgrave Macmillan, 2014.
Eckert, Penelope, and Sally McConnell-Ginet. *Language and Gender*. 2nd ed. Cambridge: Cambridge University Press, 2013.
"Game of Thrones." *IMDB*, imdb.com. 31 May 2020, https://www.imdb.com/title/tt0944947/?ref_=nv_sr_srsg_0.
Game of Thrones. Seasons 1–7. DVD set. HBO, 2017.
Game of Thrones. Season 8. HBO, 2019.
Game of Thrones: Transcript Database. https://gameofthronesscripts.wordpress.com/, 2020.
Grice, H.P. "Logic and Conversation." *Syntax and Semantics*, Vol. 3. *Speech Acts*, edited by P. Cole and J.L. Morgan. New York: Academic Press, 1975, pp. 41–58.
Huang, Yan, ed. *The Oxford Handbook of Pragmatics*. New York: Oxford University Press, 2017.
Leech, Geoffrey. *Principles of Pragmatics*. London: Longman, 1983.
_____. *The Pragmatics of Politeness*. New York: Oxford University Press, 2014.
Martin, George R.R. *A Game of Thrones*. 1996. New York: Bantam, 2011.
_____. *A Storm of Swords*. 2000. New York: Bantam, 2011.
_____. *A Dance with Dragons*. 2011. New York: Bantam, 2013.
Shippey, T.A. "Principles of Conversation in Beowulfian Speech" in *Techniques of Description: Spoken and Written Discourse*, edited by John M. Sinclair et al. A Festschrift for Malcolm Coulthard. London: Routledge, 1993, pp. 109–26.
_____. "Speech and the Unspoken in *Hamðismál*" in *Prosody and Poetics in the Early Middle Ages: Essays in Honour of C.B. Hieatt*, edited by M.J. Toswell. Toronto: University of Toronto Press, 1995, pp. 180–96.
Tannen, Deborah. *You Just Don't Understand: Women and Men in Conversation*. New York: William Morrow, 2007.

"Who has a better story than Bran the Broken?"

The Power of Disability Narratives

Jan Doolittle Wilson

On May 19, 2019, over nineteen-million viewers watched the series finale of the HBO television phenomenon *Game of Thrones* to discover who would finally win the battle for the Iron Throne, a contest that had formed the narrative backbone of the show's eight seasons. The victor, as it turned out, was not the valiant but reluctant hero Jon Snow nor the magnetic and power-hungry Daenerys Targaryen but an enigmatic, wheelchair-using young man named Brandon Stark. In making a case for why Bran should sit the Iron Throne, Tyrion Lannister—a character with dwarfism who would soon assume the second most powerful position in the kingdom as Bran's chief advisor—declared: "There's nothing in the world more powerful than a good story.... No enemy can defeat it. And who has a better story than Bran the Broken?" (S8, E6).

For those who had watched *Game of Thrones* from its initial launch in the spring of 2011, and particularly for those who were familiar with the sprawling *A Song of Ice and Fire* book series on which the show was based, Bran and Tyrion's ascension to the highest seats of power in the fictional kingdom of Westeros should have come as little to no surprise. Long recognized and even awarded for its disability representation, *Game of Thrones* includes numerous characters with a wide range of disabilities, most of whom are multilayered and complexly drawn. Neither tragic nor inspiring, neither wholly evil nor wholly good, they are active agents in asserting their own identities and condemning the unaccommodating attitudes and environments that cast them out. By making disabled characters the protagonists and the antiheroes of the narrative, the show centralizes disability experiences and offers a powerful critique of the social meanings and stigmas that surround them. Yet, the show often relies on some well-worn disability tropes and privileges the disability experiences of white, straight, cisgender men. And with very few exceptions, nondisabled people comprise the show's creators, writers, producers, directors, and actors.

With its massive audience and reputation as one of the most "disability friendly" shows in history, *Game of Thrones* is an important and useful vehicle for addressing questions of disability representation in popular media. What makes a particular representation of disability "good" or "bad"? Are these categories discrete and self-evident? What constitutes "authentic" disability representation? Who gets to decide? Are disability tropes always wholly negative or can they be useful mechanisms for analyzing and critiquing popular understandings of disability and the treatment of disabled people in specific historical and cultural locations? Does more authentic disability representation depend merely on increasing the number and variety of disabled characters in popular media, or does it require deeper structural changes that allow people with disabilities to participate fully in the creation, production, and performance of the stories that we tell?

Perhaps most importantly, *Game of Thrones* is a useful tool for examining the potentially subversive power of disability narratives. Historically, those with the most power and privilege have been the creators, controllers, and subjects of our stories, and the narratives of inclusion and exclusion that they have constructed teach us whose lives and experiences matter and whose do not. Challenging these stories—and the systems of power that they represent—requires that we pull back the curtain and expose their creators; that we stretch their narrative boundaries and train their spotlights on the lives and experiences of those who have been the least valued; and that we demand much greater inclusion and diversity in the processes that determine how and by whom these stories are told. *Game of Thrones*, while flawed and limited in many ways, is an important contribution to this challenge. By putting disabled characters like Tyrion and Bran at the center of the narrative and telling its story from their points of view, *Game of Thrones* prompts its audience to reconsider and perhaps even to push back against stories that pathologize, exclude, and invalidate disabled lives. If we continue to demand a richer and fuller disability representation at all levels of the creative process, we will be better positioned to produce additional narratives that offer a much more complete and diverse picture of lived disability experiences that, in turn, will help to foster a society in which all forms of human variation are accommodated and valued.

Disability Representation in Popular Culture

Disabled people[1] currently comprise fifteen percent of the global population, by far the world's largest minority group ("World Report on Disability"). In the United States, more than one in four people live with a disability (CDC). Spanning every epoch, culture, and demographic, disability is an intrinsic, natural, and constant part of human history. Some people experience disability from birth while others acquire disability suddenly and without warning. Some experience temporary disabilities throughout their lives, and some slide gradually toward disability as they age. Nearly everyone experiences disability on some level via their relationships with disabled family members, friends, and co-workers. Disability, then, is a universal human experience, although one's experience of disability is highly variable depending on type of disability and one's gender, race, age, ethnicity, sexuality, geographic location, and a host of other factors (Garland-Thomson 5). It is a dynamic form of embodiment and an identity used both to justify discrimination and marginalization of disabled people and one claimed by disabled people themselves as a form of positive self-actualization. Disability identity is and has been a source of community and the basis for collective movements for disability justice.

Disability is "everywhere," as historian Douglas Baynton has observed, yet "curiously absent" or woefully misrepresented in the stories that we create (52). On television, the number of regular characters with disabilities on original scripted series reached only 2.1 percent during the 2018–2019 television season (Ellis 7). In the 100 highest-grossing movies of 2018, only 1.6 percent of speaking characters were portrayed as having some form of disability. The vast majority of disabled characters in media are white, cisgender, heterosexual men. Over seventy percent of characters in the top 100 movies of 2018 were male, while less than a third of characters with disabilities were women. Nearly three-quarters of disabled characters were white, while only 36.9 percent were from underrepresented racial or ethnic groups. Just two characters with a disability were from the LGB community, and no characters were transgender (Smith 5). When television shows and movies feature characters with disabilities, disabled actors are rarely hired to portray them; in fact, more than ninety-five percent of characters with disabilities on television are played by nondisabled actors (Woodburn and Kopic 1).

When disabled people do appear in popular media, they are rarely central to the narrative but serve instead to advance, foil, or add comic relief to the journey of the story's protagonist. Typically, disabled characters fit within a narrow range of constantly recycled disability tropes. The most ubiquitous tropes connect disability to violence and criminality (the "evil cripple"); portray disability as a tragic or pitiable condition best met through miraculous cure or a merciful death (the "tragic cripple"); link disability to the possession of extraordinary or supernatural abilities (the "supercrip" or the "mystic cripple"); or use disability to inspire nondisabled audiences to lead more authentic lives and to measure their own experiences more favorably by comparison ("inspiration porn") (Barnes; Young).

A tremendous disparity exists, then, between the reality of disability and the depiction of disability in the stories that we tell. This disparity has significant consequences for disabled viewers, who are left "without role models to whom they can relate, which can lead to outright rejection of their disabled identity in a futile effort to fit with the nondisabled ideal they see on TV" (Landre). This was certainly the case for Judith Heumann, an international disability rights activist, who rarely, if ever, saw disabled characters in the television shows and movies that she devoured as a child growing up in Brooklyn during the 1950s. Such characters, when they did appear, were nearly always portrayed as villains, objects of pity, or one-off characters whose disability was miraculously cured at the end of the story. Without anyone in media about whom she could say, "That person's like me—they understand my life, joys, sorrow, and complexities," she "felt invisible" (Heumann). Keah Brown, a journalist and contributing writer for online magazines, was similarly unable to locate herself in the romantic comedies that she enjoyed watching as a young girl. Within this genre, blackness is typically marginalized and stereotyped, she notes, while disability is either wholly absent or used as a form of comic relief. "How are we, black girls with disabilities, supposed to see ourselves as worthy of romantic love, worthy of the chance to feel at home in our bodies and personalities," Brown asks, "if the only representation we receive is that of a plot device or a joke? We have no choice but to see ourselves in the able-bodied, often white women who acquire lead roles" (Brown).

Media serve not only as a tool of self-actualization but "a lens through which we view the world" and a primary means by which we encounter individuals and groups whose identities and experiences differ from our own (Woodburn and Kopic 3). For those whose interactions with disabled people are infrequent, narrow, or perfunctory, media representations are particularly powerful in creating knowledge and shaping attitudes about disability. Media messages are not absorbed uncritically, of course. But they "are key to the setting of agendas and focusing public interest on particular subjects," write media scholars Catherine Happer and Greg Philo, "which operates to limit the range of arguments and perspectives that inform public debate" (321). The disparity between media representations of disability and actual lived disability experiences, therefore, helps to produce and perpetuate public misperceptions of disability that, in turn, contribute to the stigma surrounding disability and systemic discrimination against disabled people.

In some cases, however, media have the potential to disrupt dominant understandings of disability and to serve as a catalyst for social change. This potential is particularly evident in the fantasy genre, where audiences often encounter fantastical subjects who serve as metaphors for disability or, less commonly, live with actual disabled bodies or minds. Particularly when their depictions are nuanced and complex, these subjects give audiences the opportunity to engage with disabled individuals in ways not always possible in the real world and encourages them to question their society's negative misperceptions and fears surrounding disability. Fictional depictions of disability have the greatest "subversive power," argues Mia Harrison, when they grant the most stigmatized and marginalized characters the agency to reject their society's perception of them; when they present disability as the product of disabling environments and attitudes; and when they depict disability not as a feature of a handful of freakish outsiders but as a common, natural part of the human experience ("George R.R. Martin and the Two Dwarfs" 115).

Game of Thrones' *Subversion of Dominant Disability Narratives*

The *Game of Thrones* television series fulfills and sometimes exceeds the subversive potential of the fantasy genre. Like the books on which it is based, *Game of Thrones* often challenges dominant narratives about disability and gives its audience "moments of stunning insight" (Wong) into disability issues and experiences in several different ways. First, the show depicts disabled characters with a frequency, range, and complexity unequaled in other fantasy stories. It features a plethora of named, recurring characters who represent a variety of physical and, less frequently, mental disabilities. Some disabilities are congenital while others are incurred through illnesses or injuries. There are characters with paralyzed and amputated limbs, blindness, facial disfigurements, scarred and twisted bodies, mutilated genitals, and minds affected by trauma and abuse. Characters with disabilities rarely fit wholly or neatly into identifiable disability media tropes but exhibit a complex range of human emotions and behaviors. Second, as "freaks and outsiders," disabled characters in *Game of Thrones* have "situated knowledges," or particular perspectives and ways of seeing the world, that are different from those in more dominant social locations. From their position as outsiders, they directly experience cruel and prejudicial treatment and are able to see more clearly than those at the center the forms of privilege bestowed on the so-called able-bodied. Hence, they are uniquely positioned to offer critiques of the society in which they occupy marginal locations. By placing characters with disabilities at the center of the narrative, *Game of Thrones* invites the audience to see the world from their point of view. Third, while disabled characters suffer from the cruelty of disability stigma, they do not lack agency and are sometimes able to use their bravery, cleverness, and wit to discover forms of survival and empowerment. Finally, disabled characters offer a social model of disability by demonstrating that they are disabled not primarily by any condition of their bodies or minds but more from disabling attitudes and practices.

Complex Depiction of Disabled Characters

More than any other disabled character in *Game of Thrones*, Tyrion Lannister forcefully transgresses the "strict disability tropes of the fantasy genre" and provides important insights into several aspects of lived disability experiences (Harrison, "George R.R. Martin and the Two Dwarfs" 118). Tyrion is a dwarf and the story's central protagonist; he therefore challenges typical depictions of a literary hero and disrupts a highly ubiquitous fantasy trope in which dwarfs are positioned as otherworldly curiosities who invite the audience's ableist gaze through their bizarre costumes and crude, comical behaviors. Unlike the earth-dwelling miners of Germanic and Scandinavian folklore; the cheerful, singing, childlike dwarfs of Disney and Baum; and the solid, ax-wielding, bellicose dwarves of Lewis and Tolkien, Tyrion is not an archetype but a fully fleshed-out, multilayered character. He is neither saint nor sinner but a very human person who strives to make the right choices yet sometimes succumbs to his baser desires. He is highly critical of the environments and attitudes that marginalize and abuse him but is vulnerable at times to internalized oppression, which causes him to doubt whether he is worthy of love. Tyrion is played by Peter Dinklage, an actor with achondroplasia, whose eight seasons on *Game of Thrones* won him critical acclaim and multiple acting awards. Dinklage was George R.R. Martin's first and only choice to play Tyrion, but Dinklage, well aware of the stereotypical portrait of fantasy dwarfs, was initially reluctant to accept the offer. (In fact, Dinklage had appeared just a few years earlier in a film installment of the popular *Chronicles of Narnia* fantasy series in which he played a dwarf named Trumpkin.) As he explained in an interview with the *New York Times* following *Game of Thrones*' successful first season: "Dwarves in these genres always have this look. My guard was up. Not even my guard—my metal fence, my barbed wire was up. Even 'Lord of the Rings' had dwarf-tossing jokes in it. It's like, *Really*?" Dinklage ultimately decided to take on the role after receiving assurances from showrunners David Benioff and Daniel Weiss that Tyrion was a richly drawn character who complicated the tropes of the fantasy genre. "He's somebody who turns that on its head," Dinklage stated. "No beard, no pointy shoes, a romantic, real human being" (Kois).

While it is notable that *Game of Thrones* places a character with dwarfism at the center of the narrative, it is equally notable that some of the show's most important characters become disabled at some point in their story arc. In the show's very first episode, young Brandon (Bran) Stark is paralyzed after being pushed out of a high tower window by Jaime Lannister. Paralysis does not end Bran's story arc, however; it launches it (and, not unproblematically, becomes central to it, as I will discuss later). Bran's would-be assassin, the dashing but deeply flawed Jaime Lannister, occupies an even greater place within the story and eventually grows into one of the show's primary heroes; yet he, too, becomes suddenly disabled in Season Three when his sword hand is viciously lopped off by the member of a rival family. Hence, *Game of Thrones* subverts an unspoken rule of the fantasy genre that the heroes of the narrative will survive and emerge relatively unscathed at the end of the story (Kornhaber). And, by representing disability as a common human experience that can happen to anyone at any time, *Game of Thrones* demonstrates the impermanency of "ablebodiedness" and reveals as extremely porous the border between ability and disability.

Disability as a Social Location for the Production of Subjugated Knowledges

Importantly, *Game of Thrones* recognizes that disability is not simply an embodied state but a social location from which particular forms of knowledge are created. Hence, disabled characters are in a unique position to offer critiques of the society in which they hold marginal positions and to create new meanings about disability. When Tyrion notes that he has a "'tender spot in my heart for cripples and bastards and broken things,'" he is acknowledging his membership in a group of outsiders who experience the disabling environments and attitudes of the world that they inhabit (Martin, *A Game of Thrones* 206). From the moment of his birth, Tyrion is a target of stigma and hatred and a scapegoat for his society's misfortunes. His mother, Joanna, died giving birth to him, a tragedy for which his father, Tywin, and his sister, Cersei, hold Tyrion personally responsible. Soon after he was born, news spread throughout the kingdom about Lord Tywin's monstrous son, who was rumored to have an enormous head, an evil eye, sharp claws, a curly swine's tail, and the private parts of both a girl and a boy (Martin, *A Storm of Swords* 434). Prince Oberyn Martell recalled his disappointment on finally getting a glimpse of Tyrion during a visit to Casterly Rock, the Lannister family home, when he was a boy. Instead of a monster, Oberyn saw only a baby with a slightly larger than average head, short, stunted legs, and "a tiny pink cock" between his legs. When he remarked to Cersei that Tyrion "seemed a poor sort of monster," she replied, "He killed my mother.... Everyone says he's like to die soon. He shouldn't even have lived this long" (Martin, *A Storm of Swords* 435). Tyrion's heroic and central role in saving King's Landing from Stannis Baratheon's siege during Season Three receives no public recognition or official reward; in fact, he is demoted from his position as the king's acting hand and forced into an arranged marriage in order to fortify his family's political stronghold. When Tyrion attempts to claim his rights to Casterly Rock, Tywin notes that while "[m]en's laws give you the right to bear my name and display my colors since I cannot prove that you are not mine," the laws of "neither gods nor men shall ever compel me to let you turn Casterly Rock into your whorehouse" (Martin, *A Storm of Swords* 53).

From his position as a "monstrous" outsider, Tyrion is able to offer scathing, powerful indictments of the cruel and prejudicial attitudes that have mistreated and marginalized him his entire life. In Season Four, Tyrion is falsely charged with the killing of his nephew, the sadistic King Joffrey, and stands trial in a criminal court presided over by his father, who views Tyrion's probable conviction as a convenient means of ridding himself of a despised son. During the trial, Tyrion is stung by the false testimonies of those he had considered his friends and by the betrayal of the woman he loves. For him, the trial seems to illustrate starkly what he had always feared—as a dwarf, he was expendable, valueless, incapable of being truly loved. Despite all of his cleverness, bravery, generosity, and tremendous capacity for love, he would never be anything but a monster and a freak. Turning to his father, Tyrion suddenly shouts that he wishes to confess, not to the crime of killing Joffrey of which he is innocent, but to the "more monstrous crime" of being a dwarf. When Tywin replies that he is "not on trial for being a dwarf," Tyrion remarks, "That is where you err, my lord. I have been on trial for being a dwarf my entire life." Addressing the spectators crowding the throne room, Tyrion angrily yells that he did not kill Joffrey but "now I wish I had.... I wish I had enough poison for you all. You make me sorry that I am not the monster you would have me be" (Martin, *A Storm of Swords* 791–792).

In addition to characters with congenital disabilities, characters with acquired disabilities occupy equally important social locations from which they are able to offer critical insights about disability. As border crossers who have experienced both the privileges of ability and the social stigma attached to disability, these characters are uniquely positioned to create knowledge about the transformative nature of disablement, particularly how the experience of *becoming* disabled affects one's identity and public perception. Too often in film and television, characters who acquire disability recover swiftly (and often miraculously) or adapt fairly unproblematically after an intense but brief period of struggle. On *Game of Thrones*, disability brings challenges that are not "heroically" surmounted within a single episode but rather continue to cause varying levels of discomfort and even trauma. As characters struggle to come to terms with a change in form and function, they gain a valuable disability view of the world through which they are sometimes able to construct a new, fulfilling identity; better relate to other disabled people; and criticize the injustice of unaccommodating attitudes and environments. Unlike many characters with acquired disabilities in popular media, characters on *Thrones* do not suddenly transform into better people or become one-dimensional saints or heroes once they are disabled but instead retain many of the flaws and weaknesses that make them fully human.

Bran Stark, for example, is a character who is suddenly disabled and who struggles initially to come to terms with his new reality. When Bran realizes that his fall from the tower window has left him paralyzed and unable to move around without the assistance of Hodor, the family's hulking servant, he tells his brother Robb that he wishes he were dead (S1, E3). His dream of one day becoming a knight and joining the prestigious Kingsguard dashed in an instant, Bran spends the early days following his injury mourning what he has lost. Lying in bed day after day listening to the bustling sounds of the world outside of his window, he longs for things "to be the way it had been before" when he could run, climb, and ride his pony. In his dreams, he can fly, but when he awakens, he is still "broken and the world was changed" (Martin, *A Game of Thrones* 201). Bran chafes against the way that he is infantilized by the attitudes of his family and is embarrassed that he has to be carried around in Hodor's arms "like a baby." But with some adaptations, such as a special saddle for his horse and a wicker basket strapped to Hodor's back (which Bran considers less "shameful" than being carried), Bran is able to leave the confines of the castle and find a familiar freedom and pleasure in interacting with his environment. Such interactions, however, bring a level of public scrutiny and ridicule that Bran had never previously experienced as an "able-bodied" child of privilege and wealth. Over time, such stigma only strengthens Bran's resolve. When Bran encounters a group of riders, who stare and guffaw when they witness the strange sight of Bran bouncing against Hodor's back in his wicker basket, for example, he refuses to retreat to the safety of the castle. "Let them mock," Bran thought to himself. "No one mocked him in his bedchamber, but he would not live his life in bed" (Martin, *A Game of Thrones* 477–478).

Once paralyzed, Bran does not suddenly transform into a saccharine, Dickensian trope of the pitiful child "cripple," however, but remains as morally ambiguous as any other character in the series (Massie and Mayer 53–54). Eventually, he learns that he can achieve freedom of mobility by inhabiting the bodies of other beings, first animals like his direwolf and, eventually, his faithful companion, Hodor, who appears at this point in the story to have an unspecified cognitive disability. Using Hodor as a resource to recapture his strength and mobility is a violative, abusive act that causes Hodor extreme discomfort and mental anguish. Slipping into Hodor's skin, Bran feels Hodor's terror and resistance, but shoves and squirms his way in, regardless (Martin, *A Storm of Swords* 633). While becoming disabled shifts his identity and his relationship to the world he inhabits, then, it does not necessarily create in Bran a minority identity through which he relates to and unites with other disabled people to protest systemic discrimination. In fact, Bran "becomes the abuser of the more disabled" and thus avoids "the hero/victim dichotomy of disability fantasies and becomes simply another flawed opportunist of the epic's world" (Massie and Mayer 20).

Bran's disability experiences provide an interesting comparison to Jaime Lannister, another central character with an acquired disability. As one of the most skilled and respected swordsmen in the Kingdom of Westeros, Jaime previously served in the Kingsguard of Aerys Targaryen, known as the "Mad King." When rebel forces led by Jamie's father, Tywin Lannister, invaded King's Landing, Aerys ordered Jaime to kill Tywin and to burn the entire city and its inhabitants with wildfire. Refusing to carry out this command, Jaime broke his sacred oath to protect his king and killed Aerys by stabbing him in the back, an act that saved tens of thousands of lives but earned him the loathsome nickname "Kingslayer." After Jaime is disabled, he initially faces an identity crisis so severe that he briefly loses the will to live. He had lost his sword hand, "and without it he was nothing.... It was his right hand that made him a knight; his right arm that made him a man" (Martin, *A Storm of Swords* 344). Over the course of the series, Jaime constructs a new identity from a shift in his social location. Throughout his life, his nobility, wealth, beauty, and strength had allowed him to move relatively effortlessly throughout his world, buoyed by a trove of privileges of which he remained blissfully unaware. When he loses his hand, he moves from the very center of his society's masculine ideal to somewhere outside of it. From this more liminal position, Jaime is able to see what had previously been invisible—the social system that rewards and punishes individuals and groups based on their level of adherence to normative bodily standards and, importantly, the injustice of this system. As he weeps from the pain of his severed hand, he hears his captors laughing at him. "Now I know how Tyrion has felt, all those times they laughed at him," he thinks (Martin, *A Storm of Swords* 342).

Jaime's disability, then, causes him to forge a new identity and to see his world from a different perspective. Amputation of his hand does not transform Jaime into a completely different person, however. In fact, he remains a complicated character who retains many of the virtues and weaknesses he possessed before his injury. His loyalty to his family, difficulty standing up to his father, desire for Cersei, love for Tyrion, and commitment to the Kingsguard remain unchanged. Jaime flings a child out of a window to cover up his incestuous and adulterous affair and strangles his own cousin in order to escape imprisonment, but he risks himself to save Brienne from rape and Tyrion from execution. He seems to take a malicious delight in his reputation as the Kingslayer while privately experiencing intense shame over the betrayal of his oath. He claims on multiple occasions that he cares for no one but himself and his family, but he eventually defies Cersei by traveling to Winterfell to help defeat the army of the dead. Burdened by the weight of his reputation and many misdeeds, he continues to make poor choices and struggles to locate his own goodness despite Brienne and Tyrion's faith in him. "If it weren't for you, I never would have survived my childhood," Tyrion tells Jaime during a tender moment between the brothers that would prove to be their last. "You were the only one that didn't treat me like a monster" (S8, E5). When Danaerys Targaryen wants to execute Jaime for killing her father, Brienne vouches for him, claiming that Jaime is an honorable man who protected her from assault and upheld his oath to return Sansa Stark to her family (S8, E2). Ultimately, Jaime cannot resist the pull of his desire for Cersei; he abandons Brienne and the Northern army to join Cersei in King's Landing and arrives just in time to die in her arms as the Red Keep crumbles on top of them.

Disabled Characters as Active Agents

Disabled characters on *Game of Thrones* certainly experience the cruelty of prejudice and discrimination but they do not lack agency. Tyrion, for example, often pushes back against those who treat him as a "monster"—as his speech during his trial demonstrates—and at other times, he cleverly weaponizes perceptions of his monstrosity to escape punishment, to threaten his enemies, and to amass personal power. Most importantly, his "transgressive reappropriation" of the invectives hurled against him serves as a means by which he is able to offer a searing critique of how badly he and other marginalized individuals are treated.

Tyrion regularly deploys his gift for wit and sarcasm to deflect prejudicial attitudes and to defuse the power of ableist slurs, a practice he often advises others to follow. Jon Snow, for example, is the presumed "illegitimate" son of Lord Eddard Stark and thus holds a marginal position within Westerosi society and within the Stark family. Jon is offended when Tyrion calls him a bastard, but Tyrion replies: "Let me give you some counsel, bastard.... Never forget what you are, for surely the world will not.... Armor yourself in it, and it will never be used to hurt you" (Martin, *A Game of Thrones* 47). Similarly, Tyrion has no reservations about calling Bran Stark a "cripple," a label that Bran initially rejects. When Bran retorts "I'm *not* a cripple!" Tyrion sarcastically responds, "Then I am not a dwarf.... My father will rejoice to hear it!" (Martin, *A Game of Thrones* 205). Later, when Bran is ultimately named king by the lords and ladies of Westeros, Tyrion hails him "Bran the Broken." Through his use of language, Tyrion imparts an important lesson. Having been called objectifying and demeaning names such as "Imp," "halfman," "little man," "demon monkey," "freak," and "monster" his entire life, Tyrion learned early on to embrace his dwarf identity and even to reclaim and deploy derogatory labels with an obvious ironic pride.

Tyrion's ability to exercise agency is bolstered exponentially by his class privileges. Like most other disabled characters on *Game of Thrones*, such as Bran and Jaime, Tyrion is a person of wealth and nobility. Thus, while he is devalued and even mocked for his disability, he avoids the sort of poverty and social ostracism experienced by most disabled people who do not share his advantages, a point that the narrative makes explicit on a few occasions. "Had I been born a peasant," Tyrion acknowledges, "they might have left me out to die, or sold me to some slaver's grotesquerie. Alas I was born a Lannister of Casterly Rock, and the grotesqueries are all the poorer" (Martin, *A Game of Thrones* 103). Indeed, only Tyrion's noble parentage spared him from infanticide or abandonment at birth, as his father never permits him to forget. And due to his family's wealth and status, Tyrion is able to cheat death, torture, and capture on multiple occasions by bribing his enemies and by exploiting the fear and respect that his father commands throughout the kingdom of Westeros. During Season One, Tyrion avoids imprisonment and execution at the hands of Catelyn Stark and Lysa Arryn in no small part due to his ability to bribe his jailer, Mord, with the promise of gold (S1, E6). When he is later ambushed by the hill tribes of the Vale, he manages to evade capture by telling the tribesmen that if they escort him safely through the mountains to the Lannister soldier camp, his father will reward them with riches and weapons. Through promises of wealth, he also manages to win the protection and loyalty of the roguish sell sword Bronn, who saves his life on numerous occasions (S1, E8).

Male disabled characters on *Game of Thrones* exercise agency most clearly in how they claim masculinity through the performance of their sexuality. Because disability is usually associated with dependency and helplessness, it appears to be inherently incompatible with the key attributes of hegemonic manhood, most especially virility. Yet, on *Game of Thrones*, male characters such as Grey Worm and Samwell (Sam) Tarly are granted a sexuality usually denied disabled men both in fiction and in the real world. Sam is a fat man with very few traditionally masculine skills, but he manages to attract a woman named Gilly with whom he has his first sexual experience and eventually a committed relationship. By the series end, Gilly is pregnant with Sam's child. At the beginning of his narrative arc, Grey Worm is a warrior-eunuch whose castration and slave status place him far outside of society's masculine ideals. Eventually, Grey Worm shares a deeply intimate, passionate relationship with a woman named Missandei; their ability to achieve mutual sexual satisfaction through cunnilingus challenges conventional, androcentric understandings of sex and, importantly, centers female sexual pleasure. By depicting male characters with disabilities in loving and sexually intimate relationships, then, *Game of Thrones* calls into question popular perceptions of disabled people as inherently asexual and destabilizes the foundation of dominant, heteronormative masculinity (Wade).

Because disability is thought to call one's masculinity into question, some male characters feel compelled to prove their manhood through exaggerated or aggressive displays of traditional masculine qualities and sexual behaviors. Jaime is missing a hand, but he refuses to relinquish his position in the Kingsguard or his role as Cersei's lover. When he returns to King's Landing following his capture, Cersei is repulsed by his stump and initially rebuffs his sexual advances. Hurt and angered by her coldness, Jaime grabs hold of her and, ignoring her protestations, forces himself on her in an act that signals his determination to reclaim his manhood through the forceful assertion of his sexual domination over another (Martin, *A Storm of Swords* 700–701). In his marriage to Sansa Stark, Tyrion, by contrast, explicitly rejects the sort of sexual control that Jaime exerts over Cersei. Hoping to secure the Northern kingdom that Sansa is set to inherit, Tywin forces Tyrion to marry Sansa and commands him to cement his claim to the Stark lands by impregnating his new bride. "Get her with child," Tywin tells him, "and the prize is all but won" (Martin, *A Storm of Swords* 362). Tyrion desires Sansa but wants her to come to him willingly and without the "revulsion in her eyes whenever she looked on his body" (Martin, *A Storm of Swords* 354). On his wedding night, therefore, Tyrion promises Sansa that he will not touch her until she wants him to (Martin, *A Storm of Swords* 326).

For Tyrion, conspicuous displays of his virility serve to underscore his manhood and to challenge his society's ableist assumptions that disability and sexuality are mutually exclusive. Tyrion's reputation for sleeping with prostitutes, for example, is legendary; in fact, when we first meet Tyrion in Season One, he is in a "whorehouse" thoroughly enjoying the company of a red-headed courtesan named Ros. Throughout the first three seasons, Tyrion maintains a highly active and satisfying sexual relationship with Shae, a prostitute with whom he falls deeply in love. For Tyrion, having sex with prostitutes functions not only as a tool of resistance to ableist norms but to his father's control. At the age of thirteen, Tyrion had met, instantly loved, and hastily married a crofter's daughter named Tysha. Furious that a Lannister had wed a commoner, Tywin instructed Jaime to tell Tyrion that Tysha was a prostitute hired to give Tyrion his first sexual experience. Not satisfied merely to have the marriage annulled, Tywin decided to punish Tyrion for his transgression by forcing him to watch while a garrison of Lannister soldiers raped Tysha. He then commanded Tyrion to "take her one last time, after the rest were done" so that Tyrion would remember that his bride was nothing but a "whore" (Martin, *A Clash of Kings* 483). By so publicly preferring the company of prostitutes, then, Tyrion undermines Tywin's efforts to safeguard the family's standing and reputation and thus exercises some measure of resistance to his father's power and authority.

Tyrion's sexual behavior is not only a form of agency and resistance, however, but an indication that he has internalized to some extent his society's ableist assumptions. Tyrion has sex with prostitutes in part because he believes that no woman would want to sleep with him unless she is paid to do so, a belief that his sexless marriage with Sansa seems to confirm. Lying next to Shae in a post-coital bliss, Tyrion has to remind himself that he is a dwarf and that the woman with whom he has just had sex is a prostitute: "Will you never learn, dwarf? She's a whore, damn you, it's your coin she loves, not your cock. Remember Tysha?" (Martin, *A Clash of Kings* 51). Just when Tyrion dares to believe that Shae's affection for him is real, she testifies against him at his trial for Joffrey's murder, humiliating him with false descriptions of how he forced her to engage in indecent sex acts to satisfy his deviant predilections. For Tywin's role in engineering Shae's betrayal, for his deception regarding Tysha (whom Tyrion learns in the book version was not in fact a prostitute), and for his inability to love and accept his youngest son, Tyrion commits the ultimate act of defiance to his father's authority. He sneaks into the tower where Tywin is sitting on the privy and kills him by shooting a crossbow bolt into his belly.

The Social Model of Disability

By continually emphasizing the disabling impact of stigma and inaccessible environments, *Game of Thrones* embraces a social model of disability. Such a model rejects a medicalized view that locates the "problem" of disability in individual bodies and minds and seeks to "fix" disability through the cure, prevention, containment, or eradication of disabled people. The social model, instead, recognizes that while physical and mental disabilities can be challenging and painful, people are disabled primarily by environments, policies, and attitudes that fail to accommodate and include the vast array of human particularities. Disability, then, is not an individual problem best solved through medical intervention, normalization, or personal effort but a natural and common human variation that deserves accommodation through social change and political transformation (Kafer 6).

The cruel treatment to which disabled characters on *Game of Thrones* are subjected provides a useful illustration of the social model of disability, particularly the disabling impact of social stigma. In a world in which women's value is tied rigidly to their beauty and their adherence to traditional feminine behaviors, Brienne of Tarth's appearance and interest in traditionally masculine activities like sword fighting render her socially disabled. Described in the books as tall, muscular, flat-chested, and ungainly, Brienne has broad, coarse features, crooked teeth, freckled skin, and dirty, tangled hair. On seeing Brienne for the first time, Catelyn Stark is filled with pity, as she wonders privately whether there exists "any creature on earth as unfortunate as an ugly woman?" (Martin, *A Clash of Kings* 259). In Season Five, Brienne reveals to her squire, Podrick, something of the pain she experienced growing up as a young girl who was unable to fit her society's expectations of women of noble birth. To find a suitable marriage partner for her, Brienne's father had arranged a ball to which dozens of young lords of Tarth were invited. Brienne's initial delight with the young men's attentions to her soon turned to anguish when she realized that it had all been a game at her expense. Behind her back, they shared jokes about her size and mocked her appearance, Brienne recalled. "And I realized I was the ugliest girl alive" (S5, E3). Samwell Tarly is similarly disabled by his inability to fit his society's model of manhood. When he first arrives at the Wall as the newest recruit of the Night's Watch, he is a timid and highly sensitive young man who is terrified of nearly everything and, to the astonishment of his new brothers, admits freely to his own cowardice. Jon Snow describes him as the "fattest boy he had ever seen" with a "great round moon of a face, and plump sweaty fingers" (Martin, *A Game of Thrones* 218). The eldest son of Lord Randyll Tarly, Sam had grown into a corpulent and awkward boy who loved kittens, rich foods, and velvet clothing, and who preferred music and books to hunting and swordplay. Despite his father's efforts to "toughen him up," Sam only grew fatter and more frightened, which in turn fueled his father's resentment and loathing. Finally, on the morning of Sam's fifteenth name day, Lord Tarly told his son that he must either renounce his birthright and travel north to join the Night's Watch or suffer a fatal "accident" during a hunting expedition the very next day. "Nothing would please me more," his father added, "than to hunt you down like the pig you are" (Martin, *A Game of Thrones* 226).

As several characters in *Game of Thrones* demonstrate, bodily differences are not inherently disabling; they become disabling only in a society that refuses to accept and validate them. Brienne's tallness and unattractiveness, Sam's timidity and fatness, and Tyrion's ugliness (in the book version) and short stature are disabling because they deviate from normative standards of beauty, gender, and ability. While Jaime and Bran face many challenges due to their injuries, they are disabled primarily by a society that scorns and devalues "damaged" and "broken" men. But within environments that accommodate and even embrace their bodily and behavioral particularities, their social disablements disappear and they begin to flourish. As Tyrion notes when he shares his special saddle design that will enable Bran to ride a horse, "[Y]ou must shape the horse to the rider.... With the right horse and the right saddle, even a cripple can ride" (Martin, *A Game of Thrones* 205). Tyrion manages to find a niche within a society that values traditional manly strength and skill by sharpening his mind and his powers of observation. It is his mental acuity that leads to his appointment as acting hand of the king, a position from which he is able to use his intelligence to make successful political and military maneuvers that earn him the respect of the royal troops and the gratitude (albeit temporarily) of the people of King's Landing. Eventually, Tyrion becomes a trusted advisor to Queen Daenerys Targaryen, whose assassination he engineers from inside a jail cell, and cleverly manipulates the rulers of the Seven Kingdoms into choosing Bran Stark as the next occupant of the Iron Throne. When King Bran chooses Tyrion as his hand, Tyrion becomes the second most powerful person in Westeros. On joining the Night's Watch, Sam enters a community of misfits who for various reasons have all faced rejection and stigma for failing to live up to societal norms. Within this community, Sam's social disability is greatly muted; as his confidence grows under the protection, encouragement, and friendship of Jon Snow and the other members of the Night's Watch, it all but disappears. Ultimately, Sam becomes a brave, if still unskilled, combatant, a wise counselor, a devoted partner and father, and Grand Maester of the Kingdom of Westeros. Brienne eventually finds a productive use for her swordsmanship when she is welcomed by King Renly Baratheon as the first and only female member of his newly formed Kingsguard. Mockery and rejection due to her unfeminine appearance and pursuits gradually turn to respect as she bests some of the most skilled male warriors in the kingdom and nobly defends those she has sworn to protect. And in what is arguably one of the series' most sincere and moving moments, Brienne finally realizes her lifelong dream when she is knighted by Jaime Lannister, becoming Ser Brienne of Tarth and ultimately joining the prestigious Kingsguard (S8, E2). Bran begins the series as a "broken" boy who no longer has the military future to which he has long aspired. Over the course of the show's eight seasons, he plays a key role in uncovering the mysteries of the White Walkers and their army of undead wights, knowledge that the army of the living uses in the final season to defeat the Walkers and thus prevent the destruction of all human life. Bran ultimately ascends to the throne at the end of the series, not because he has proven his bravery in battle, as in the tradition of previous kings, but because he is the repository of his society's historical memory and "the keeper of all our stories," as Tyrion notes (S8, E6). In this new Kingdom of Westeros where wisdom is valued over might, "Bran the Broken" is able to occupy the most powerful and prestigious position.

Game of Thrones' *Perpetuation of Dominant Disability Narratives*

Undeniably, then, *Game of Thrones* portrays disabled characters with a richness and complexity rarely seen in media in general and fantasy in particular. Yet, in several ways, the show does not fully transcend some of the most egregious problems with disability representation typical in popular culture and thus perpetuates media's narrow and inaccurate depiction of disabled lives. First, *Game of Thrones* frequently dips into some ubiquitous and tired tropes that solidly connect disability to stereotypical behaviors, traits, or abilities. Second, the show tends to use disability as a narrative device to advance the plot or development of a nondisabled character. Third, the series leaves mostly unexplored the relationship between disability and multiple, other, intersecting identities. Finally, the show relies almost entirely on nondisabled actors and creators to portray the lives and experiences of disabled people. While all of these factors are problematic in and of themselves, as the following discussion will outline, they also provide important starting points for thinking more deeply about the potentially generative work of disability tropes and metaphors and raise important questions about what constitutes authentic disability representations—questions whose answers are far from axiomatic or uncontested.

Disability Tropes

Several characters in *Game of Thrones* exhibit traits consistent with stereotypical representations of disability commonly depicted in popular media. Bran Stark's character arc, for example, plays into the supercrip trope by which characters develop some sort of compensatory, mystical superpower as a result of their disability. Following his spinal-cord injury, Bran gains the power to see past and future events and the ability to inhabit and control the bodies of animals. As his powers grow stronger, Bran becomes more detached from human emotions and relationships until he is no longer Brandon Stark but the Three-Eyed Raven, living mostly in the past with little need for typical human wants and desires. The narrative does not allow Bran simply to be a "regular" person who has a disability, one who rediscovers joy and meaning in life with a paralyzed body; on the contrary, his character arc indicates that his life as a disabled person has to take on some sort of special purpose in order to be meaningful. By developing magical, exceptional abilities, he can transcend the "deficits" of his impairment and demonstrate that his life still has value. The tragedy of disability, Bran's narrative seems to suggest, need not be tragic as long as it results in something extraordinary. Hence, by attempting to make disability more palatable, the supercrip trope indicates that "plain old ordinary" disability is inherently undesirable and unworthy of recognition. Furthermore, it perpetuates the damaging myth that disability is an individual "problem" that can and should be overcome rather than a human variation deserving accommodation and acceptance through the removal of environmental and attitudinal barriers. By emphasizing "prodigious achievement," which "is praiseworthy in anyone, disabled or not," writes Joseph Shapiro, the supercrip trope "does not reflect the day to day reality of most disabled people, who struggle constantly with smaller challenges, such as finding a bus with a wheelchair lift to go downtown or fighting beliefs that people with disabilities cannot work, be educated, or enjoy life as well as anyone else" (17).

At times, Bran seems to fit into a common media trope by which disabled characters are defined almost completely by their disabilities. When Tyrion asserts that Bran is the most suitable choice for the next ruler of the Seven Kingdoms, he does so by referencing the disability that sparked Bran's supernatural abilities. Bran survived a fall from a tower, Tyrion says, and learned to fly when he could no longer walk, transforming from a crippled boy into the Three-Eyed Raven (S8, E6). Tyrion goes on to point out that because Bran cannot have children and thus cannot produce heirs to the throne, he is the perfect sovereign for the new system of government in Westeros by which rulers will be chosen for their abilities, not granted succession due to their birthright (S8, E6). With this statement, Tyrion is tapping into the widespread but inaccurate assumption that people with disabilities are unable to reproduce either because they are uninterested in or incapable of having sex or because their disability automatically makes their reproduction impossible or morally repugnant. Historically, the erasure or invalidation of disabled people's sexuality and reproduction has made it very difficult for people with disabilities to access sexual and reproductive health information and services and has made them vulnerable to discriminatory policies, involuntary sterilization, and sexual abuse. Despite *Game of Thrones*' nuanced portrayal of disabled people's sexuality elsewhere in the story, Tyrion's justification for why Bran is the most suitable occupant of the Iron Throne helps to perpetuate misperceptions about disability and sexuality and reduces the complexity of disabled lives to a single identity.

Similarly, the character arcs of Sandor Clegane and Theon Greyjoy seem to be rooted primarily in their disability identities. As a child, Clegane is disfigured when his brother, Gregor, pushes his face into a burning brazier as punishment for taking one of his toys, a vicious act that leaves Clegane physically and emotionally scarred and forever triggered by the sight of fire. Known as the Hound for the viciousness of his appearance and demeanor, he is a bitter and angry man who has little regard for human life and seems motivated solely by his desire for vengeance against his brother (who is called "the Mountain" for his enormous size and strength). Attempting to dissuade Arya Stark from continuing her quest to kill Cersei, the Hound tells Arya that the only thing that he has ever cared about is revenge and that she should not waste her life following the same path (S8, E5). Ultimately, the Hound's pursuit of retribution leads to his own destruction; the long-awaited confrontation between the Hound and the Mountain (referred to as "Cleganebowl" by *Game of Thrones* fans) takes place in the penultimate episode of the show's final season. After a protracted struggle during which he is unable to kill his brother in hand-to-hand combat, the Hound grabs hold of Gregor and hurls them both over the side of a crumbling tower and into the fiery ruins of King's Landing below.

A ward of the Stark family in retaliation for his father's treason, Theon Greyjoy grows into an unpleasant young man whose boastfulness and sexual conquests serve as a mask for his insecurity and sense of inferiority. Theon betrays the Starks and commits several murders in his campaign to seize control of the North. He is eventually captured by Ramsay Bolton and subjected to extensive physical and psychological torture, which shatters his sense of self and eventually transforms him into "Reek," Ramsay's utterly dejected and servile captive. Following his escape from Ramsay, Theon spends the rest of the series haunted and broken. Deeply ashamed of his past wrongs and suffering from the effects of complex trauma, Theon ultimately finds redemption when he rescues Sansa Stark from the Boltons and sacrifices his own life to defend Bran from the Night King (S8, E3).

While the Hound and Theon gain complexity and depth as their story arcs develop, both expressing empathy and remorse for past actions, their characters remain anchored to their disabilities and the trauma they experience as a result of them. In Theon's case, *Game of Thrones* seems to play into popular stereotypes of sexuality, disability, and masculinity that it elsewhere disrupts. Once he is castrated, Theon is no longer considered a man, a belief that the show leaves unchallenged by Theon's internalization of it. No longer "fit" to inherit his father's land and titles, he concedes his birthright to his sister, Yara, whose "dominant personality and sexual relationships with women," writes Mia Harrison, "afford her an identity of masculinity that Theon no longer possesses" (Harrison, "Power and Punishment" 39). Still, within the context of other traumatized characters like Lord Varys and Sansa and Arya Stark, the Hound and Theon help to illustrate the range of reactions that people subjected to serious emotional and mental abuse exhibit. Such characters, therefore, provide a useful lens through which to identify the characteristics of trauma and the various mechanisms that individuals use to survive it (Cole 87).

While *Game of Thrones* sometimes offers a nuanced portrait of complex trauma, its depiction of other mental health issues is much more problematic. Nowhere is this more evident than in the character arc of Daenerys Targaryen. Daughter of "Mad" King Aerys, Daenerys, or "Dany," is descended from a noble house whose members commonly intermarry in order to preserve the "purity" of the family bloodline. Their propensity for incest results in a strong genetic disposition toward mental instability, leading to a common saying in the kingdom that "[e]very time a new Targaryen is born, ... the gods toss the coin in the air and the world holds its breath to see how it will land" (Martin, *A Storm of Swords* 811). Beginning the series as a timid girl who eventually discovers her own strength and power, Daenerys becomes a liberator of slaves and amasses an enormous army of devotees who support her campaign to seize the Iron Throne and bring about a better world order. Although she is one of the primary and most popular heroes throughout most of the series with a tremendous capacity for empathy and mercy, she exhibits early signs of ruthlessness and megalomania when she crucifies the slave masters of Meereen and burns alive those who resist her rule. Ultimately, Dany succumbs to the "Targaryen madness" in the penultimate episode of the show's final season when she disregards the surrender of the Lannister troops defending King's Landing and razes the city with dragonfire, killing tens of thousands of innocent civilians.

Daenerys's character arc, particularly in the show's final season, plays into some of the worst and most damaging stereotypes of mental illness. Suggesting that biology is destiny, it perpetuates the myth that those with a family history of mental illness are genetically predetermined to develop a neurological disorder that will dictate their future choices and actions. More damaging, it connects people with mental disabilities to criminality and violence. While having a mental health condition does not make a person more likely to be violent or dangerous (in fact, having a mental health condition greatly increases a person's chances of being the victim of violence), this connection remains pervasive in popular media and contributes to the misperception, stigma, and shame surrounding mental disabilities. Finally, Dany's character arc contributes to the "scary powerful woman goes crazy" trope by which a woman's power is so threatening that it has to be pathologized and contained (VanArendonk). During Season Seven, Dany explains to Jon Snow why she is destined to take the Iron Throne. Unwavering faith in her abilities and destiny, she tells him, had allowed her to survive the many brutalities—including exile, rape, defilement, and multiple assassination attempts—she had endured throughout her life. As the woman who had brought forth dragons and convinced the Dothraki to cross the narrow sea, "I was born to rule the Seven Kingdoms," she declares, "and I will" (S7, E3). Naked ambition and confidence in one's abilities are qualities applauded and even expected in men who attempt to seize authority and power, but in women, such qualities are potentially disruptive to traditional gender roles and therefore dangerous. Historically, women who have displayed such qualities have been accused of witchcraft, diagnosed with hysteria, confined to mental institutions, "corrected" with unnecessary surgical interventions, and treated with psychotropic drugs. The current, real-world sociopolitical landscape is replete with illustrations of talented, creative women whose ambitions are met with derision, whose legitimate anger over discriminatory treatment is dismissed as hysterical, and whose efforts to compete equally in male-dominated spaces that were not created for them lead to frustration and self-doubt. Dany's experiences have a very strong corollary in these real-world examples. She is abused, infantilized, disregarded, underestimated, doubted, and held back even by her closest advisors. In a conversation with Tyrion before the battle of King's Landing, Lord Varys, a member of Dany's small council, expresses doubts about Dany's ability to rule effectively and speculates that because Jon Snow is a man, he is more rational and even tempered and thus better suited to the Iron Throne. When Tyrion responds that Jon could check Dany's impulsivity if they were appointed co-rulers of the kingdom, Varys quickly objects that Jon would be too easily swayed by Dany's domineering nature (S8, E4). Instead of complexly exploring how Dany's history of trauma and abuse, as well as the discriminatory treatment she faces as a woman trying to seize traditionally male power, affects her mental health and how others perceive her, the showrunners chose instead to depict Dany as an overbearing, increasingly unhinged woman who—unlike her male counterpart—is unable to control her irrational "womanly" impulses and thus ends up committing a sudden and uncharacteristic act of mass genocide (VanArendonk).

Disability as Narrative Prosthesis

At times, disability in *Game of Thrones* serves as a narrative prosthesis, or a plot device that is not intended to communicate any meaningful knowledge about disability per se but rather meant to support an aspect of the central storyline or to serve as a metaphor for complex social issues (Mitchell and Snyder 4–10). Arya Stark, for example, is temporarily blinded as punishment for refusing to carry out an assassination order and spends a couple of episodes at the start of Season Six dressed in rags and begging for charity from passersby on the streets of Braavos. In a bit of a supercrip scenario, blindness heightens her powers of perception, which become instrumental in her defeat of her nemesis, the Waif, and in the successful completion of her training as an assassin at the House of Black and White (S6, E8). Shireen Baratheon's facial disfigurement is another type of narrative prosthesis. Scarred by greyscale disease when she was a baby, Shireen is an innocent and sweet but lonely little girl whose parents keep her mostly hidden from public view. She remains a fairly one-dimensional character who functions primarily to inject pathos into the narrative and to signal something about the more important characters with whom she interacts. Her father, Stannis, ultimately sacrifices Shireen to his own ambitions when he agrees to have her burned at the stake in a tribute to the Lord of Light to ensure victory in battle, a terrible and costly choice that results in the defeat of his campaign and the loss of his own life (S5, E9; S5, E10). Shireen's death, then, is not really about Shireen but a plot point meant to illustrate her father's misguided faith in religious prophecy and the tragedy of his single-minded pursuit to rule the Seven Kingdoms.

Hodor, the Stark family's loyal servant, is perhaps the most obvious and egregious example of disability as narrative prosthesis in *Game of Thrones*. Nearly seven feet tall, Hodor is portrayed as a gentle giant, a great lumbering man with an apparent intellectual disability rendered innocent and docile and sometimes comical for his single-word vocabulary (the only word he is capable of uttering is his own name). Throughout most of the story, Hodor functions as Bran's literal prosthesis (Harrison, "Power and Punishment" 33). Bran uses Hodor's body first as a means of transportation and eventually as a site of possession and control. Typically, those with warging powers can only take possession of the bodies of animals, but Bran is able to warg into Hodor presumably because Bran's abilities are extraordinarily powerful and because Hodor's mind is exceptionally weak. Bran wargs into Hodor on multiple occasions, at times using Hodor's body to regain freedom of movement and at other times to harness Hodor's strength and size to defend himself and his friends from danger. Such violations of his bodily autonomy terrify and traumatize Hodor, but Bran continues to employ him as a useful resource with ultimately tragic consequences. In Season Six, Bran wargs into Hodor while he is psychically observing a younger version of Hodor in the past. Because Bran's mind is connecting the past and the present, the younger Hodor—who at that point was a cognitively typical boy called Wylis—can hear and see the older version of himself being clawed and torn apart by wights as he steadfastly holds a door to ward off an attack by the army of the undead. So traumatized by witnessing his violent, future demise, young Wylis has a seizure and begins repeating the phrase "hold the door" over and over until it blends into the single word "Hodor," the only word that he will be able to say from that point on (S6, E5). Tragically, Hodor is stripped of his own autonomy and becomes the agent of someone else's destiny. His sole purpose is to wait for that fateful day in the future when he will hold the door and save Bran by sacrificing himself. As in the case of Arya's blindness and Shireen's facial disfigurement, Hodor's neurological condition does not communicate any meaningful knowledge about disability but serves merely as a plot point for other more "important" aspects of the story. Typically one-dimensional and simplistic in their depictions of disability, narrative prostheses, then, have the tendency to promote disability stereotypes and to trivialize lived disability experiences.

Despite its reputation for positive disability representation, *Game of Thrones* perpetuates some of the most damaging disability stereotypes common in popular media. Yet, the existence of stereotypes should not lead scholars or viewers to dismiss a particular cultural production, particularly ones like *Game of Thrones* that draw in an enormous audience (Schalk 84). Disability stereotypes and metaphors, in fact, can serve a useful, generative function. For example, they present a "representational conundrum" helpful for thinking about the differences between representations of disability in narrative and the material reality of lived, disability experiences (Sandahl 135). Narratives that present disability as an individual tragedy, for example, can generate useful conversations about the joy and positivity of many disabled lives and the disabling impact of environments, policies, and attitudes. Disability's representation as magical and powerful can help to highlight the precarity and disfranchisement of disabled people. Thinking of disability representation in this way allows us to move beyond the sometimes reductive project of merely identifying and judging stereotypes and toward the more productive task of using disability tropes in popular media to analyze shifting meanings of disability and the complexity and materiality of disabled experiences within specific historical and social locations (Sandahl 135). To what extent, for example, does *Game of Thrones* tell us about George R.R. Martin's and the showrunners' engagement with contemporary disability issues? What can we learn about these issues by comparing and contrasting the narrative's disability representation with actual disabled experiences? How can the show's depiction of mental illness, for example, start important conversations about popular misconceptions of mental health conditions, and how can such conversations improve the status of people who live with these conditions? What does a comparison of *Game of Thrones* with other fantasy or literary narratives from different time periods and/or cultures tell us about shifting views of disability across time and place? In short, what are the values of stereotypes as narrative devices, and how "[m]ight we harness a stereotype's power and instant recognizability to purposeful ends"? (Sandahl 133–134).

Lack of Intersectionality

Game of Thrones also offers an opportunity to think more deeply and critically about the voids of intersectional diversity in media depictions of disability. Aside from a few notable exceptions, all of the most important disabled characters in *Game of Thrones* are white, heterosexual, cisgender, wealthy men. The lack of intersectionality in *Game of Thrones*' depictions of disability is due perhaps to a couple of factors. Because white, heterosexual, cisgender, wealthy men occupy the very center of systems of power and privilege, their disablement is presumably more significant and compelling from a narrative standpoint. Additionally, women, people of color, and/or poor people are already outsiders and therefore do not need the added "layer" of disability to emphasize their marginalized status; they are, in many ways, already disabled by their gender, race, or class.

Yet with few exceptions, the socially disabling impact of gender, race, sexuality, and class is not given the often rich and complex treatment afforded the impact of physical and mental disabilities on white, heteronormative, male characters in *Game of Thrones*. While a few notable characters of color fill important places in the books and the show, for example, none are leading characters with fully developed personalities and storylines. More troubling, characters of color tend to be "Otherized," presented as exotic, uncivilized, and subjugated. Based on the historical Huns and Mongols, the Dothraki are nomadic warriors who slaughter and rape their way through the eastern continent. The slaves of Essos are all brown-skinned people who appear passively to accept their status until they are liberated by the "white savior" Daenerys Targaryen. While the inhabitants of the southern kingdom of Dorne, who seem to be inspired by real-world

Spanish and Middle Eastern cultures, are a prosperous, tolerant people, their place in the narrative is marginal and underdeveloped. Often, people of color in *Game of Thrones* exist in the story primarily to advance the plots of the leading, white characters—primarily Daenerys Targaryen—and are depicted as disturbingly expendable in service of these plots. Khal Drogo has to die—in a "mercy killing" dangerously meant to suggest that once he loses many of his cognitive abilities, his life is no longer worth living—so that Daenerys can transition from a devoted wife into a heroic leader of the Dothraki warriors and a liberator of colonized peoples (S1, E10). In the show's final season, the only named black female character, Missandei, is killed off in order to provide a justification for Daenerys to sack and burn the city of King's Landing (S8, E4).

Women in *Game of Thrones* are the ultimate outsiders. They experience social disablement due to their lack of access to traditional forms of power and privilege and their vulnerability to sexual violence and oppression. Yet, the depiction of women's disablement in the show and, less frequently, in the books is fraught with troubling implications. Not only is there an alarming number of sexual assaults on female characters, sexual violence against women is sometimes romanticized, trivialized, or used as a plot device to advance the story arc of a male character. In the show's very first episode, Daenerys Targaryen is sold into an arranged marriage by her sadistic brother, Viserys, and then raped by her new husband, Khal Drogo, on her wedding night (S1, E1). Subsequent sexual encounters show Daenerys weeping with pain and despair while Khal Drogo penetrates her roughly from behind. In time, however, she grows to love her rapist and even takes pleasure in sexually satisfying him. Early in Season Four, Cersei resists Jaime's sexual advances by beating on his chest and verbally objecting a total of twelve times; the scene ends with Cersei crying and protesting that "it isn't right" while Jaime grunts "I don't care" as he forces himself inside of her (S4, E3). In an astonishing statement in response to viewer outrage, the episode's director denied that this was an act of rape because "it becomes consensual by the end" and "because anything for them ultimately results in a turn-on, especially a power struggle" (Marcotte). Such an interpretation not only romanticizes sexual violence by depicting rape as a form of titillation, it perpetuates one of the most "pernicious lies of rape culture"—that when a woman says no, she actually means yes (Lyons). In the books, a character named Lollys Stokeworth is viciously raped a "half a hundred times" and impregnated as a result. The narrative does not permit readers to view this trauma from Lollys's point of view but instead treats her rape as a form of comic relief, as her father searches futilely for an eligible suitor on which to unload his "ruined" daughter (Frankel 13).

As Lollys's storyline illustrates, *Game of Thrones* tends to highlight how sexual violence against women affects the male characters of the story. The savage rape and murder of Elia Martell is the motivating force that drives her brother, Oberyn, to seek out and attempt to kill her abuser, Gregor Clegane. The gang rape of Tysha is important to the story only for its harrowing impact on Tyrion and its effect on his relationship with Tywin. During the rape of Sansa Stark by Ramsay Bolton, the camera lingers on the tear-streaked face of Theon Greyjoy, who has been ordered by Ramsay to watch the assault, thus highlighting his pain instead of Sansa's (S5, E6). And when Brienne is nearly raped by her captors, leading Jaime to rescue her and getting his hand cut off as a result, the books and the show emphasize Jaime's trauma while almost completely ignoring hers (Frankel 14). By failing to center women's experiences in its depictions of the rape and sexual assault of female characters, *Game of Thrones* trivializes sexual violence and inadequately portrays how women complexly experience its disabling effects.

Cripping Up

Finally, *Game of Thrones* contributes to a long tradition in which the stories of people with disabilities have been told by people without them and thus raises important questions about what constitutes positive and authentic disability representation in media. With only one notable exception, the show's disabled characters are played by nondisabled actors, a widespread practice known as "cripping up" that has become a focal point of analysis and criticism within disability studies and activism (Fox and Sandahl 122). Julianne Vallera, for example, writes that cripping up "is part of a larger pattern" of the entertainment industry's discrimination against actors with disabilities, who "need opportunities and resources to succeed," and contributes to ableist attitudes and practices by sending a message to audiences that disabled actors are not capable of taking on these roles (Vallera). For Rachel Handler, disabled actors' lived experiences of disability bring an authenticity to their portrayals of disabled characters that the portrayals by nondisabled actors do not (Handler). Others, like Regan Linton, recognize that disabled actors are able to help transform perceptions of disability not only when they play disabled characters but when they "play across disability," that is, when they portray characters not specifically written as disabled. Disabled actors in these sorts of roles can perform a type of "subversive advocacy" by bringing creativity and fresh interpretations to established works (such as the depiction of Ado Annie in the current Broadway production of *Oklahoma* by Ali Stroker, a wheelchair-using actress). By showing disabled people engaging in regular, even mundane, activities unrelated to their disability, such roles can also help to "normalize" disability experiences (Holicky).

The inclusion of disabled people in popular media is vitally important to changing how we understand and treat disability in the real world. Consistent engagement with actual disabled people on the screen (especially when this engagement is limited in real life) forces audiences to confront their fear of and unease with disability and, hopefully, leads to a greater recognition of disability as a common, natural human variation (Calla and Rucker 4). But better and more authentic representations of disability in media depend not only on creating greater and more subversive roles for disabled actors but on more extensive, structural changes that work to break down barriers to the full inclusion of disabled people in every aspect of the creative process. "[W]hether in books, comics, TV, or films," as Vilissa Thompson argues, "we need actually disabled people consulted, writing, producing, directing, and casted to tell our experience the way it should be… 'Nothing about us without us' is the mantra proudly proclaimed in our community about ensuring that we are at the forefront in the way disability is understood" (Thompson).

Conclusion

With its enormous popularity and unprecedented inclusion of complexly depicted disabled characters, *Game of Thrones* is uniquely and powerfully positioned to illuminate disability issues and experiences. Through characters like Tyrion, Bran, Jaime, and Brienne, *Game of Thrones* presents disability as the product of discriminatory environments and attitudes and as a common, natural part of the human experience. By placing characters with disabilities at the center of the narrative, thereby inviting viewers to see the world from their point of view, *Game of Thrones* encourages its audience to question society's negative perceptions and fears surrounding disability. The show's tendency to play into well-worn disability stereotypes presents an opportunity to analyze the usefulness of tropes for understanding the social meanings of disability in different times and places and for exploring actual, lived disability experiences. These tropes also provide a way to think more productively about what constitutes "authentic" disability representation in popular media and who has the authority to decide what this looks like. Ultimately, *Game of Thrones* makes clear that authentic disability representation cannot be achieved only through the multiplication of disabled characters on screen, even when they are complexly depicted. Instead, real change will come from the much harder work of "spend[ing] uncomfortable time with representational conundrums" (Sandahl 132) and breaking down attitudinal and institutional barriers that have so far prevented disabled creators, writers, and actors from occupying central stage in the telling of their own stories.

Tyrion was correct—nothing is more powerful than a good story. Bran the Broken's story was so powerful not merely because it served as a unifying force for a previously fractured kingdom but because it firmly positioned a disabled life at the center of the narrative, thereby insisting on the value of this life and irrevocably transforming the narrative itself. Likewise, in the real world, when stories about disability center and complexly depict disabled lives and experiences, they have the potential to challenge and subvert dominant discourses about disability and to contribute to a society in which disability is recognized and accepted as a valuable human variation. As feminist writer and scholar Sara Ahmed reminds us, when we insist that "we matter, we are transforming what matters" (Ahmed).

Note

1. Throughout this essay, I tend to use identity-first language instead of people-first language (e.g., disabled people, rather than people with disabilities). There is considerable debate and disagreement within the disability community over the use of such language, and I acknowledge and respect different perspectives.

Works Cited

Ahmed, Sara. "Selfcare as Warfare." *feministkilljoys*, 25 Aug. 2014, https://feministkilljoys.com/2014/08/25/selfcare-as-warfare/comment-page-1/.

Barnes, Colin. "Disabling Imagery and the Media: An Exploration of the Principles for Media Representations of Disabled People." The British Council of Organisations of Disabled People, 1992, disability-studies.leeds.ac.uk/wp-content/uploads/sites/40/library/Barnes-disabling-imagery.pdf.

Baynton, Douglas. "Disability and the Justification of Inequality in American History" in *The New Disability History: American Perspectives*, edited by Paul Longmore and Lauri Umansky. New York: New York University Press, 2001, pp. 33–57.

Brown, Keah. "Love, Disability, and Movies." *Catapult*, 27 Apr. 2016, catapult.co/stories/love-disability-and-movies.

Calla, Deborah, and Allen Rucker. "Employing Writers With Disabilities: A Best Practices Guide." Media Access Awards, 2019, pp. 1–10, www.wga.org/uploadedfiles/the-guild/inclusion-and-equity/maa_best_practices_for_hiring_disabled_writers.pdf.

"CDC: 1 in 4 Adults Live with a Disability." Centers for Disease Control press release, 16 Aug. 2018, cdc.gov/media/releases/2018/po816-disability.html.

Cole, Myke. "Art Imitates War: Post-Traumatic Stress Disorder in *A Song of Ice and Fire*" in *Beyond the Wall: Exploring George R.R. Martin's A Song of Ice and Fire*, edited by James Lowder. Dallas: BenBella Books, 2012, 73–88.

Ellis, Sarah Kate. "Where We Are on TV, 2018–2019." GLAAD Media Institute, pp. 1–34, glaad.org/files/WWAT/WWAT_GLAAD_2018-2019.pdf. Accessed 20 Sept. 2019.

Fox, Ann, and Carrie Sandahl. "Beyond 'Cripping Up': An Introduction." *Journal of Literary & Cultural Disability Studies* 12:2, 2018, pp. 121–127.

Frankel, Valerie Estelle. *Women in Game of Thrones: Power, Conformity and Resistance*. Jefferson, NC: McFarland, 2013.

Garland-Thomson, Rosemarie. "Integrating Disability, Transforming Feminist Theory." *NWSA Journal* 14:3, Autumn 2002, pp. 1–32.

Handler, Rachel. "Stop Excluding Actors with Disabilities." *Backstage*, 9 Feb. 2016, www.backstage.com/magazine/article/stop-excluding-actors-disabilities-7387/.

Happer, Catherine, and Greg Philo. "The Role of the Media in the Construction of Public Belief and Social Change." *Journal of Social and Political Psychology* 1:1, 2013, pp. 321–336, doi:10.5964/jspp.v1i1.96.

Harrison, Mia. "George R.R. Martin and the Two Dwarfs" in *The Routledge Companion to Disability and Media*, edited by Katie Ellis, et al. London: Routledge, 2020, pp. 113–121.

_____. "Power and Punishment in *Game of Thrones*" in *The Image of Disability: Essays on Media Representations*, edited by JL Schatz and Amber E. George. Jefferson, NC: McFarland, 2018.

Heumann, Judith, et al. "Road Map for Inclusion: Changing the Face of Disability in Media." Ford Foundation, 26 Mar. 2019, www.fordfoundation.org/media/4276/judyheumann_report_2019_final.pdf.

Holicky, Richard. "The Transformation of Regan Linton." *New Mobility*, 1 May 2015, www.newmobility.com/2015/05/regan-linton/.

Kafer, Alison. *Feminist, Queer, Crip*. Bloomington: Indiana University Press, 2013.

Kois, Dan. "Peter Dinklage was Smart to Say No." *New York Times*, 29 Mar. 2012, www.nytimes.com/2012/04/01/magazine/peter-dinklage-was-smart-to-say-no.html.

Kornhaber, Spencer. "The Ethics of Hodor." *The Atlantic*, 27 May 2016, www.theatlantic.com/entertainment/archive/2016/05/the-ethics-of-hodor/484643/.

Landre, Anna. "Represent Disability in Media." *The Hoya*, 12 Apr. 2019, thehoya.com/represent-disability-media/.

Lyons, Margaret. "Yes, Of Course That Was Rape on Last Night's *Game of Thrones*." *Vulture*, 21 Apr. 2014, www.vulture.com/2014/04/rape-game-of-thrones-cersei-jaime.html.

Marcotte, Amanda. "The Director of Sunday's *Game of Thrones* Doesn't Think That Was Rape." *Slate*, 21 Apr. 2014, slate.com/human-interest/2014/04/game-of-thrones-rape-director-alex-graves-says-the-sex-becomes-consensual.html.

Martin, George R.R. *A Clash of Kings*. New York: Bantam Books, 2011.

_____. *A Game of Thrones*. New York: Bantam Books, 2011.

_____. *A Storm of Swords*. New York: Bantam Books, 2011.

Massie, Pascal J., and Lauryn S. Mayer. "Bringing Elsewhere Home: A Song of Ice and Fire's Ethics of Disability" in *Studies in Medievalism XXIII: Ethics and Medievalism*, New ed., edited by Karl Fugelso. Suffolk: Boydell and Brewer, 2014, pp. 45–60. *JSTOR*, www.jstor.org/stable/10.7722/j.ctt5vj7s0.9.

Mitchell, David T., and Sharon L. Snyder. *Narrative Prosthesis: Disability and the Dependencies of Discourse*. Ann Arbor: University of Michigan Press, 2000.

Sandahl, Carrie. "Using Our Words: Exploring Representational Conundrums in Disability Drama and Performance." *Journal of Literary & Cultural Disability Studies*, 12:2, 2018, pp. 129–144.

Schalk, Sami. "Reevaluating the Supercrip." *Journal of Literary & Cultural Disability Studies*, 10:1, 2016, pp. 71–86.

Shapiro, Joseph. *No Pity: People with Disabilities Forging a New Civil Rights Movement*. New York: Times Books, 1993.

Smith, Stacy, et al. "Inequality in 1,200 Popular Films: Examining Portrayals of Gender, Race/Ethnicity, LGBTQ & Disability from 2007 to 2018." Annenberg Foundation and USC Annenberg, September 2019, pp. 1–36, assets.uscannenberg.org/docs/aii-inequality-report-2019-09-03.pdf.

Thompson, Vilissa. "'Nothing About Us Without Us'—Disability Representation in Media." Center for Disability Rights, cdrnys.org/blog/disability-dialogue/nothing-about-us-without-us-disability-representation-in-media/. Accessed 25 Oct. 2019.

Vallera, Julianne. "Casting Disabled Actors Is About More Than Just Inclusion." *The Mighty*, 3 Mar. 2019, themighty.com/2019/03/cripping-up-movies-tv-disability-unemployment/.

VanArendonk, Kathryn. "*Game of Thrones* Finally Got Its Mad Queen." *Vulture*, 13 May 2019, www.vulture.com/2019/05/game-of-thrones-daenerys-mad-queen-trope.html.

Wade, Holly Anne. "Discrimination, Sexuality and People with Significant Disabilities: Issues of Access and The Right to Sexual Expression in the United States." *Disability Studies Quarterly*, 22:4, 2002, dsq-sds.org/article/view/369/485.

Woodburn, Danny, and Kristina Kopic. "The Ruderman White Paper on Employment of Actors with Disabilities in Television." Ruderman Family Foundation, Jul. 2016, pp. 1–38, rudermanfoundation.org/wp-content/uploads/2016/07/TV-White-Paper_7-1-003.pdf.

Wong, Alice. "Unbroken and Unbowed: Revisiting Disability Representation on *Game of Thrones*." *bitchmedia*, 29 May 2019, www.bitchmedia.org/article/game-of-thrones-disability-roundtable.

"World Report on Disability." World Health Organization, www.who.int/disabilities/world_report/2011/report/en/. Accessed 21 Sept. 2019.

Young, Stella. "I'm Not Your Inspiration, Thank You Very Much." TEDxSydney, Apr. 2014, www.ted.com/talks/stella_young_i_m_not_your_inspiration_thank_you_very_much?language=en.

Magic's Failure to Reanimate Fantasy

Jason M. Embry

Joan W. Scott argues in her 2001 article, "Fantasy Echo: History and the Construction of Identity," that "fantasy is the means by which real relations of identity between past and present are discovered and/or forged" (287). To be clear, Scott employs the word fantasy to suggest that the writing of history employs creative and empathetic storytelling as much as textual support "to achieve a coherent aim, that of writing oneself or one's group into history" (287). Scott uses the fantasy echo, or "retrospective identifications [...] and repetitions of imagined resemblances," (287) to critique how our methods for writing history have a certain confirmation bias that must be acknowledged so that it can be transcended. In other words:

> Fantasy can account for the ways subjects are formed, internalizing and resisting social norms, taking on the terms of identity that endow them with agency[...]. And it can be used to study the ways in which history—a fantasized narrative that imposed sequential order on otherwise chaotic and contingent occurrences—contributes to the articulation of political identity [289–90].

If historical narratives subconsciously write the story of how people see themselves as political entities, regardless of historical truth, then writing history might be more related to writing fantasy than many would realize. Like history, literature writes the stories of how people know themselves and provides a space for readers to experiment with and understand themselves in relation to others. And like historians, writers fall prey to the fantasy echo of genre. James Gifford, in *A Modernist Fantasy*, argues that "the establishment of a canon is likewise an apt reflection of the works that are most intelligible to the prevailing critical paradigms that seek to analyze literary history" (14). For this reason, many popular fantasy series involve world-building that echoes the places, people, and cultures of our past histories and our past fantasies. Subsequently, readers identify with these familiar tropes, characters, and settings that reaffirm or challenge their understanding of themselves, their history, and genre conventions. Of course, not all contemporary fantasies employ these historical settings, but by and large, the more popular ones seem to lean on history for their world-building models. While the fantasy echo is still prevalent in the affirmation of genre fidelity, some scholars note that within fantasy there does exist a "fuzzy set" that "[allows] strong texts to differ from each other while at the same time exerting a deep influence on the process of categorization and stabilization that is implicit in genre" (Gifford 32). So while some critics see fantasy as "a reactionary or conservative process of normalization that reinscribes systems of domination, at best understood as repressive desublimation" (Gifford 35), other critics, Gifford included, see fantasy, and magic in particular, "as a radical potential, the opportunity to see the world as being less than it ought to be or that a great possibility has failed" (Gifford 92). Fantasy, like history, has the privilege, and burden, of reinscribing or subverting the status quo.

David Benioff's and D.B. Weiss's HBO television series, *Game of Thrones* (*GoT*), based on George R.R. Martin's epic fantasy book series *A Song of Ice and Fire* begins with both possibilities. This series sets the primary action in a medieval-inspired world and tells the story about a kingdom in political turmoil at the same moment that magic slowly returns after having disappeared for generations. The cultural influence of medieval romances and histories on modern and contemporary fantasy are undeniable and one important aspect of the medieval romance is magic. Fredric Jameson argues, in *Archaeologies of the Future*, that, "the charm of the world of magic [...] persists in medieval romance, of which the Arthurian cycle is the fundamental expression" (71) and that "Medieval culture-material then offers [...] the omnipresence of the binary opposition between good and evil and the sense of radical otherness" (60). The reappearance of magic signals a key component of the world-building in the series—a tension between good and evil that manifests as a tension between lost and established histories. The reappearance of the lost allows for a radical reinterpretation of the world of the text. This reinterpretation manifests in two important ways. First, there is a political tension between the old monarchy and the new monarchy. The current King and his line struggle to remain in power as others, domestic and foreign, threaten their reign. Some seek to maintain their control and uphold the status quo, others seek to revolt and bring about a new order, and still others desire to return to an older world order lost in the past. The challengers represent a subversion of the established power and authority. Second, there is tension between the natural and the extranatural, the human and the magical respectively. The reappearance of magic suggests a radical return of the ancient extranatural power structures long buried within Westeros and a re-identification with deeper and older traditions. However, as would-be king slaughters would-be king, dragons and people are reanimated by magic, and hope or fear is inspired by these events, the television series ultimately refuses to allow a radical subversion of these power structures in Westeros. Instead, by the end of the series, the old line of monarchs die, magic is subjugated to the mundane political game of thrones, and a kind of fantasy echo of Westeros is established by the new King. The end of the television series, in effect, refuses the magical subversion the show had so painstakingly crafted and forces magic's fealty, not its opposition, to history. The choice to allow magic to return, only to lose again, signals a contempt for the transformative power of magic and a belief only in the perpetual power of politics. The conclusion of the series illustrates the preference of the fantasy echo over transformative magic in determining the identity of the agents of the text as well as the identity of the Seven Kingdoms. Magic fails when pitted against the material logic of established history.

This conclusion is disappointing because of the potential that the reemergence of magic in the series seems to represent. Since J.R.R. Tolkien's *The Lord of the Rings*, many of the most-read epic fantasy tomes have involved systems of magic, totems of magic, practitioners of magic, and heroes battling bad magic with good magic. Fantasy has been defined as a "form of popular escapist literature" that employs devices like wizards, magic, young heroes, and dragons with "stylistic playfulness, self-reflexiveness, and a subversive treatment of established orders of society and thought" (Attebery). In fact, in the popular imagination, the most common identifier of fantasy story-telling, aside perhaps from maps, has been magic. *GoT* is a fantasy series, and as such, in order to align with the genre designation, certain conventions are expected. John Lanchester, in his review of the series for the *London Review of Books*, suggests the fact that "people are willing to read fantasy novels in practice emphasizes the parallel fact that, most of the time, they aren't willing to read them in principle. They're only willing to read the freak mega-sellers: fantasy itself is off limits to large sections of the general reading public" (Lanchester). Precisely because Martin has said that his ambition was "to create an imaginary world with the atmosphere of the Wars of the Roses" (Lanchester), many readers and viewers see this series primarily as a historical, and therefore political, story with a little magic thrown in instead of the other way around. However, fantasy provides unique opportunities for storytelling because it is primarily "composed of narratives in which an 'extranatural power' plays a fundamental role and that aim is to create an illusion of reality" (Eilers 318). Like the fable or the fairytale before, fantasy transports modern human drama to another world to celebrate "human creative power and freedom" released from "material and historical restraints" (Jameson 66). Consequently, the addition of magic could be read as "a figure for the enlargement of human power and their passage to the limit, their actualization of everything latent and virtual in the stunted human organism of the present" (Jameson 66). A story about kings and queens, like *GoT*, would clearly fit into this category of successful drama, but kings and queens with fantasy motifs, like heroic figures, quests, clashing cultures of warriors, and magic, make for excellent storytelling. Add these to a drama that seems intent upon defeating an existing, forgotten, or imminent evil, and quite a compelling world has been created. *GoT* possesses all of these motifs, coupled with the allure of people struggling to maintain or acquire more power. Much of the run of the series benefits from its simulation of our historic past and the power structures listed in our history books. Scott's fantasy echo aligns with the dissonance inherent in speculative fiction. Viewers understand themselves in relation to their perceived identity within the real world and therefore align themselves with the establishment, the revolutionary, or the agent of chaos.

But it is still a fantasy, and so it must employ those motifs that signal difference from our past and make this place, other than in name, different from our history. This can be a central challenge for modern fantasy—walking the line between history and the extranatural. John Grant, in his article, "Gulliver Unravels: Generic Fantasy and the Loss of Subversion," argues that in order for a fiction to be fantasy, "it must take risks by exploring precisely those dangerous territories where no one has ever ventured before. […] It must meddle with our thinking, it must delight in being controversial" (22). Based on this argument, without the engagement with the extranatural, *GoT* would be considered generic fantasy. Furthermore, the inclusion of the extranatural means that the story pushes against natural history, providing an alternative to the biased fantasy echo enshrined in historical record. Instead, these texts might slide into the generic fantasy camp. Grant explains:

> Some devotees of generic fantasy are not just frightened of the dangers of real fantasy: they are actually angered by it, and vociferously so, presumably because it represents a threat to what they have come to perceive as the genuine form of the two confusingly named literatures. Rootstock fantasy, they seem to be saying, is neither Gulliver nor Gormenghast but only the derivative stuff that can exist only within the walled frontiers of a pseudo-Tolkienesque and ultimately hack Fantasyland [25].

Many might compare *GoT* to *The Lord of the Rings* (*LotR*) because both have commandeered such a huge swathe of the public media consciousness for the last 20 years (and longer in the case of *LotR*). The only competition to these might be Marvel Cinematic Universe and Star Wars.

The comparison between *GoT* and *LotR* bears consideration as both Westeros and Middle Earth are worlds with lost magic. Elves exist in Middle Earth, but they have largely removed themselves from the world of Men as they prepare to leave Middle Earth for good. It seems important to note that the Elves embody memory of Middle Earth, so their abandonment of Middle Earth begins a new memory, and therefore a new identity for its inhabitants. Also, there are wizards, like Gandalf and Saruman, but they and their council have also been removed from central power. The Shire, Rohan, and Gondor are all separate and self-consumed with their normal day-to-day events. The only thing that forces the story along in Middle Earth is the discovery of the One Ring and the stirrings in Mordor for its power. Similarly, the Westerosi drama is two-fold: the death of the king and the threat from beyond the Wall, Westeros's Mordor. This loss of magic and the re-emergence of its importance in both Westeros and Middle Earth allow viewers to understand the quotidian world and experience the reemergence of the fantastic along with the characters who have grown comfortable with their world's established natural history and the identities that comport with it. Both of these media giants succeed because the entrance into the tale is easy for the average viewer, but the stakes change as the tale is told; the viewers realize that more is going on than first appeared and that there are forgotten histories that conflict with the established ones. Greg Betchel explains this response slightly differently: "the construction of a Tolkienian secondary world can enact a sophisticated naiveté in which everyday, primary 'reality' is both enriched and challenged by the translocation of the everyday into the realm of the 'marvelous'"(162–3).

For years, since the slow extinction of the dragons raised by the Targaryen rulers, magic has disappeared, and with this disappearance, the people of Westeros no longer believe in their "marvelous" extranatural history. Even the religion of the realm is a religion of social history, not extranatural power, and it has replaced the old gods across the kingdom, save for the kingdom of the North where they are still quietly observed. The newer religion, the Faith of the Seven, worships one god with seven distinct faces—the Mother, the Father, the Maiden, the Crone, the Warrior, the Smith, and the Stranger. This faith echoes the values the people of Westeros and illustrates how they wish to behave toward one another. The adherence to this Faith, at least in the first half of the series, seems to be mostly situational. These faces represent the social codes within the political world of Westeros. The Mother stands for mercy; the Father stands for justice; the Maiden for courage; the Crone for wisdom; the Warrior for protection; the Smith for strength; and the Stranger for the unknown. However, the Seven never actually manifest in the story. The values each of the Seven represent direct the characters' behavior within the series, but never threaten to actually appear in Westeros as divinity or an extranatural presence. However, even within the natural codes for social behavior, the Stranger exists and arguably becomes more important within their world, not for its divinity, but for its vestigial representation of forces outside of the historical and political realm, nodding to the Many-Faced God worshipped in Essos. Imbedded within this mundane religion is the seed for a return of the extranatural. Antithetically, the Old Gods still worshipped by the Kingdom in the North have a much more immediate impact on the world. These old gods were found in nature—rocks, streams, and trees. Because these Gods were embodied in nature, the mystery surrounding them was heightened and the concern about weather, winter in particular, was always present. This concern was further symbolized by the Wall that separated the Seven Kingdoms from the Wildlings who lived beyond it and were outside of the rule of the King of the Seven Kingdoms. They lived free and among things long-thought disappeared like giants, wargs, and White Walkers. Since this time, the Wall has been guarded by the Night's Watch, a band of soldiers charged with the defense of the Realm. They must take an ascetic oath that commits them to forsaking land, love, family, and glory, essentially eschewing the political life of Westeros, for the remainder of their lives so that they can protect the Realm from threats beyond the Wall. This order once included warriors, knights, and royalty, but at the time of the first episode, the ranks of the Night's Watch are populated primarily by murderers, rapers, thieves, and scoundrels. People choose this service in order to avoid death sentences for crimes, not to defend the Seven Kingdoms from extranatural threats. Few people believe in these threats any longer and this loss of magic in Westeros consequently diminishes the station and service of those committed to the Night's Watch. Tyrion Lannister jokes that "the Night's Watch exists to protect the Realm from storybook 'grumkins and snarks and all the other monsters your wet nurse warned you about'" (S1, E2).

Ultimately, this statement provides an important lesson about history and identity. Disruption from within and without compete in the series and provide several layers of narrative webbing that threaten the stability of identity within the Seven Kingdoms and those groups that populate it. Alyssa Rosenberg observes that "magic in Westeros effectively functions as a reminder of the dangerousness of assuming that certain challenges to your stability have vanished from the earth, and of assuming that new and hugely disruptive forces can't suddenly emerge to create enormous technological asymmetries. […] A disbelief in magic is a belief in the relative stability of your political and economic system" (Rosenberg). The series leans into these asymmetries as the supernatural occurrences, at first, slowly begin to overshadow the squabbles of ambitious men and women. All the political schemes will ever amount to is control over the Seven Kingdoms; the stakes beyond the Wall involve power over life and death. For this reason, much of the narrative's structural value resides in the extranatural subversions to the natural, established history. Yuko Ashitagawa argues in "Can Fantasy be More Real than Reality? The Fantastic, the Realistic, and Textuality in Literary Criticism" that "the supernatural element is something that intervenes and disrupts the 'system of pre-established rules.' The supernatural is justified because of this intervention; it cannot exist without the pre-established system" (36). This disruption elevates this series from the simple Wars of the Roses facsimile to a story that can effectively interrogate the fantasy echo of history using the genre convention of magic available to fantasy to rewrite and transform the world. Ashitagawa continues: "the fantastic is constituted as the 'other' side of the real or the realistic, but flips over to be the 'most real.' Thus, while the notion of fantasy or the fantastic entails otherness and impossibility, fantastic narratives are often assumed to allow access to something primordial" (30). Because the series introduces the fantastic elements slowly, the revision of the fantasy echo of human historical record is attacked, called into question, and threatened to be overturned. As the fantastic, or extranatural, elements amplify and contextualize the political, the series appears to tell a much larger and much deeper story about humanity and how it writes itself.

In first episode of Benioff's and Weiss's *GoT*, "The Long Road," the television audience is introduced to the medieval world of Westeros—a collection of former kingdoms subjugated hundreds of years before by a family of dragon masters, the Targaryens, from across the Narrow Sea. The episode takes place 15 years after Robert's Rebellion, a war that eventually unseated the Targaryens and killed the dragons, all but wiping magic from the land and placing Robert Baratheon upon the Iron Throne. The main storyline follows King Robert as he rides the long road to the capital of the northern kingdom, Winterfell, which is governed by his childhood friend Eddard "Ned" Stark, to ask that he come south to the capital with the King to serve as the Hand of the King after the untimely death of the previous Hand and their mentor, Jon Arryn. Natural history is invoked as old friends bond over their past and prepare for the future history of the Seven Kingdoms. If this trip to Winterfell was the only event of the first episode, the story would be compelling, but not necessarily fantastic. However, the first episode *begins* with a scene in which a mysterious murder in the woods beyond the Wall occurs. Human body parts are positioned in a creepy pattern in the snow and a young child with bright blue eyes stands nearby, unharmed; the audience is left with a clear sense of foreboding. This scene shifts quickly to Winterfell where Ned and Catelyn are preparing for the arrival of the king. These two scenes, one extranatural and the other political, foreshadow the tension between natural and extranatural history, between the political story and the magical tale. The bookending with magic as a frame by which to read the human action of the series suggests that humans are busy with their small-minded pursuit of power and wealth while larger forces *work their magic* to fundamentally reshape the human world and its self-centered view. Therefore, as the series proceeds, this world becomes larger and more magical in response to the growing awareness of larger, extranatural concerns.

One way that the series responds to these extranatural concerns is by considering magic as harbinger of hope. In Westeros, a Red Priestess of R'Hllor, Melisandre, conjures a shadow to kill a political adversary for the general whom she serves, promising him that he is the prophesied return of Azor Ahai. Magic does not reappear in Westeros through a large event like the birth of dragons in Essos; instead, the reappearance of magic in Westeros is found through the narratives brought to Westeros by a native of Essos, the Red Priestess and advisor to King Stannis Baratheon, the older brother of the previous King of the Seven Kingdom, Robert Baratheon. Politics dominates King Stannis' storyline in that he believes himself to be the next in the line to the throne because he knows none of Robert's children were fathered by him. Because there is no lawful heir, he has chosen to fight for his right to sit on the Iron Throne. Nothing about his story is anything other than human, self-involved, and political, with the exception of his advisor who further confirms his beliefs by telling him that the god she worships, the Lord of Light, has foretold his rise to power and that she can help him in his quest.

While Melisandre is clearly motivated by her faith in the Lord of Light and the prophesy of his power and will made manifest in Westeros, Stannis is primarily interested in the political ramifications of this magic. Initially, he sees faith in the Lord of Light as an opportunity to achieve his goal of winning the Iron Throne. Magic, in this case, serves the political aims of a political agent of the narrative. It is a tool wielded according to the political goals of Stannis: first the murder of his brother and then the elimination of Robb Stark. While these acts of magic lead to his victories in the short-term, Stannis's final act, the sacrifice of his only daughter, work against his interests because many in his own army abandon him. The sacrifices made in the shadows to the Lord of Light lead to minor victories, but the public sacrifice leads to his ruin. Eventually, he is punished for his use of the power of a god other than the more socially-acceptable Seven of Westeros. In his defiance of natural history, he eventually loses the faith of his followers and eventually his life. In this way, "magic still was janky, dangerous, and rare. Melisandre, the red-haired priestess of the Lord of Light, embodied this theme. [...] Hers was magic that often had to apologize for itself" (Kornhaber). Stannis operates from the viewpoint of the political, but does not understand how the magical impacts it. Ironically, he tells Jon Snow that people only follow those they fear (S5, E2). What he does not understand is that the political people of Westeros need to understand the choices; they cannot understand the political when it is mixed with the magical. This old knowledge is unstable and reacts to the established knowledge of history. Consequently, the final sacrifice of Stannis's daughter leads directly to his own death and the realization that he is not the Prince-Who-Was-Promised as prophesied by the faith of the Lord of Light. In this case, extranatural hope appears to fail in the face of the politics of Westeros.

This Prince-Who-Was-Promised, signaled by a comet that was spotted in the sky at the beginning of the story, and in the title sequence for the series, figures into the narrative in other ways and with other characters. For example, Jon Snow is painted, like his father Ned, as an honorable man, highly principled and deeply loyal. He differs from Stannis in that he does not want political power and consequently will not sacrifice his principles. These are great qualities for a hero in a world that seems to be on the verge of political upheaval, but are they good qualities when faced with a revision of history. Jon's plotline illustrates magic as extranatural identity. He cannot escape the fantasy echo of his father and the story that is told about them both, yet the one thing that seems to be understood by many, other than the importance of the throne, is that Winter is coming. This Long Winter is historical, but its distance makes it extranatural. While Melisandre represents lost knowledge, Jon represents lost nature itself. The Long Winter represents dread with no solution, like the politics of today or global climate change. The people in the text are resigned to its inevitability, are powerless to stop it, yet believe that it will never really come. The Long Winter has happened before in the history of Westeros; unfortunately, like magic, this event is in the past and most of the people in Westeros are focused on the present. The kingdom of the North, led by the Starks, feels this history more deeply, even if they are still resigned to it, because of their proximity to both the grumkins, snarks, direwolves, giants, and wargs that are believed to live just beyond the Wall and the cold that winter will bring. The winter, like the magic that has been lost, will come from outside of the Seven Kingdoms. Jon has grown up believing that threats from beyond the wall are to be taken seriously, so he joins the Night's Watch. As an honorable man, he sees protecting the realm as his duty; as a bastard, he can see going to the Wall as his only option. Once he joins, he is made privy to extranatural events, like the one the opens the series, as well as the existence of the Night King and his army of White Walkers.

Jon's storyline in *GoT* tries to create a balance between the political and the magical. On the one hand, Jon struggles throughout the series to accept leadership. He has been raised to live an honorable life and this quality stands out against those men who have been conscripted or sentenced to live out the remainder of their lives in the service of the Night's Watch. Both his free choice to join and his desire to serve others pull the less directed, more impressionable men, into his orbit and he wins the allegiance of a few new men he trains to fight. Jon appears trapped by his fantasy echo. He is the bastard of a Lord, but he is raised as a full member of the family. He is noble, and his admittance to the Night's Watch does not diminish this echo. In fact, because he believes himself to be honorable, he cannot act otherwise. His own self-identification, against the natural history of the Seven Kingdoms, suggests he is beholden to a deeper, more honorable, extranatural echo. When he is eventually awarded the position of Lord Commander of the Night's Watch, he is given the opportunity to subvert generations of attitudes toward the Wildlings who live beyond the Wall. Jon must decide whether to allow the Wildlings refuge on his side of the Wall as they retreat from the magical forces brewing further north—the Night King and his growing army the reanimated dead. The existential threat posed by magic on the Seven Kingdoms becomes overwhelmingly clear, hurling Jon into a position in which he must now navigate not only the politics of the Night's Watch but those of all Westeros, natural and extranatural, in order to save humanity itself from extinction.

This magical threat, from this point forward in the series, overpowers the political story of *GoT*, but the people of Westeros cannot see this threat clearly because they have forgotten the magical and only operate within the political. The use of magic in this part of the story, for a time, becomes central to the entire series because it threatens the established historical record and political conventions. Magic appears to overwrite the importance of the political machinations in the southern lands because these machinations and schemes will not matter if the Night King rides into Westeros. Jon's extranatural identity, his honor, allow him to rewrite the identities of the men of the Night's Watch as well as the Wildlings. If Stannis's stubbornness is born from established history, Jon's honor is born from an older historical record—one that is just and fair. The extranatural nature of his identity is confirmed when it is finally revealed through Bran's greensight that Jon is not the illegitimate son of Ned, but the legitimate son of Ned's sister, Lyanna Stark and Rhaegar Targaryen. His blood is the blood of the dragon riders as well as those who keep the old ways in the North. He embodies the old power and the old faith. Unfortunately, the men of the Night's Watch cannot allow this older historical record to reassert itself and they murder him for betraying their understanding of their Oath. Outside of speculative fiction, this murder would certainly signal the end of Lord

Commander Jon Snow's political career, but inside a fantasy series, one in which the Red Priestess moves, this event only marks the end of his first chapter and the beginning of his second, magical, one. Melisandre, reeling from her misplaced fealty toward Stannis, returns to Castle Black to find Jon dead. She realizes that the Prince-Who-Was-Promised is Jon and raises him from the dead, like Thoros of Myr had been doing for Beric Dondarrion across the Riverlands, in the name of R'Hllor.

These two figures, Melisandre and Jon, represent an alternative to traditional political power. Melisandre illustrates extranatural hope and Jon illustrates extranatural identity. A third figure in this series, Daenerys Targaryen, illustrates extranatural agency. It is easy to regard Daenerys as the catalyst for the magical return to Westeros. Once her dragons hatch in Essos in the final episode of the first season, the series seems to more fully develop the magical veins deep in the crust of the world. Situated adjacent to the narratives on either side of the Wall, Daenerys rises from a powerless exiled princess in a port city in Essos to become the Mother of Dragons and Khaleesi of the Dothraki by the season's end. In this instance, what lies beyond the Seven Kingdoms is the fantastic rebirth of magic in the form of dragons. The birth of three dragons to the last known heir to the Targaryen line 15 years after that line has been deposed signals a political rise as well as magical one. Through her story, the audience understands that magic never entirely disappears in either Westeros or Essos. There are witches in Khal Drogo's khalasar who raise him from almost death to almost life in exchange for Daenerys's unborn child. In the city of Qarth, Daenerys encounters the warlocks in the House of the Undying and they prophesy her three betrayals. These events, while small in immediate political scope, do exist and propel her toward her political story. It is only once these dragons are hatched that magic moves closer to the center of the action and plot of the political stories. Without these hatched dragons, Daenerys would have been killed by Khal Drogo's bloodriders. But because these dragons did hatch and she survives their birthing flame, the remnants of the khalasar follow her, acknowledging her extranatural agency. In this moment, extranatural history is finally made manifest; Daenerys embodies the extranatural. She is impervious to fire, unlike the White Walkers who are descending on the Wall, and she commands the only dragons in existence. Jameson notes, "as a living being the dragon is also able to incarnate sheer otherness, so that its symbolic capacities well exceed those of inanimate machinery" (63–4). And as these dragons mature, Daenerys is able to parlay their destructive force and the mythology that she is a "Mother of Dragons," added to her "Stormborn" title, into being followed and feared. And these two manifestations of the extranatural, the time before history, award her with legions of warriors and devotees. Through this magical power she develops a political desire to free the slaves of Slaver's Bay from bondage. She fights to liberate these cities, which she believes will lead her to her true purpose—freeing the Seven Kingdoms from the tyranny of the Usurper, King Robert Baratheon and those who bear his name. Daenerys's extranatural agency promises to correct the political history of Essos and Westeros. Missandei, her attendant, announces her by listing political honorifics regarding her lineage, her accomplishments, and her right to rule (S7, E3). She is able to accomplish everything of importance *because* of her magical embodiment and her dragon children. The extranatural political focus of Daenerys's story arc in Essos guarantees a proper challenge to the natural history of Westeros.

Finally, Bran Stark, the younger (legitimate) son of Ned Stark, represents a fourth alternative natural history—magic as history. Bran's journey is perhaps the most traditional in fantasy, other than Daenerys's, because he begins the series as a young adventuring son of a Lord, who, because of his adventuring, discovers a secret that literally cripples him. The established natural history the Baratheons destroys him so that he is able to pursue the extranatural history beyond the Wall. His story, not remotely political, becomes strictly magical. He and his band of caretakers eventually flee Winterfell for their lives and embark on a quest to find the Three-Eyed Raven, a magical figure known only through Bran's dreams, who had called him to fulfill his destiny as the next Three-Eyed Raven. Even before his dreams, his caretaker, Old Nan, has been telling him stories about a more magical time in Westeros, a time of uncertainty and fear:

> Thousands of years ago there came a night that lasted a generation[…]. In that darkness, the White Walkers came for the first time. They swept through cities and kingdoms, riding their dead horses, hunting with their packs of pale spiders big as hounds [S1, E3].

Bran is, perhaps, the most prepared to handle the magical incursion from beyond the wall because he has been told stories about it his entire life—and as a youth he has not yet outgrown those stories. And without magic, his story might have ended in the first episode when he is crippled by a fall from one of Winterfell's towers. If he had not fallen, his story would have been quite naturally different—bound up in the political war that Robb embarks upon after their father's beheading. Instead of this political story, Bran embarks on a magical story that sweeps along him and his friends, Meera and Jojen Reed, and Hodor. In this journey, Jojen's magical greensight guides them toward the Three-Eyed Raven's tree and Hodor provides the brawn that pulls Bran's crippled body along the way. Hodor's second function is that he affords Bran the opportunity to "warg," or possess—like the Night King with his undead army—an incredibly strong body in moments of danger. Everything about Bran's story breaks the historical mold of the gallant knight. He is not physically able, except through his magic and the aid of his friends, to complete his heroic quest. He is singularly focused on meeting the Three-Eyed Raven, learning to control his greensight and warging abilities, and defeating the Night King. It is unnecessary to recount all of the events of the story that pertain to Bran, except to say that his story is the most magical of any character in the series, yet his story is the most frustrating. Its development across the run is uneven, leaving him out of several episodes at a time and dramatizing the journey to the Three-Eyed Raven slowly, withholding the purpose of the meeting for several seasons. This moment in the series sets up the acquiescence of magic to history because the Three-Eyed Raven's extranatural magic is historical. He is the chronicler of Westeros. He sees across time but does nothing to interfere. He simply knows.

The Night King is clearly the most magical character in the series, being transformed from human to the immortal puppeteer of the undead *by* magic. He, like the winter that signals his return, represents an elemental force, beyond the scale of politics and history. The motivations of the Night King are lost to history; they are prehistoric; they are as primal as death itself. What is known is that thousands of years before, at the height of the war between the First Men and the Children of the Forest, the Children pierced the heart of a man with a knife made of dragonglass and created the Night King. His only mission at that time was to defeat the First Men as they began to draw their own historical record. Between that time and the present time of the series, Bran the Builder (different Bran, but current Bran's namesake) built the Wall to separate the Seven Kingdoms from the Night King and his fledgling undead forces. The Wall has stood and defended the Seven Kingdoms for thousands of years, until Daenerys's dragons are born. And seven seasons later, one of these dragons, killed and under the control of the Night King, is used to tear down the Wall and provide a path toward the fulfillment of the Night King's purpose.

The Night King's role in the series, then, is the ultimate evil, promising that binary that has been represented, weakly, by the political forces of the human history. The Night King is the force that threatens not only the sovereignty of the Seven Kingdoms, but its history. Each character represents radical departures from human history. Melisandre is the spark of hope that will allow for change; Jon Snow is the transformation of Westerosi self-image; Daenerys is the power of magic and magical creatures that wages war on the political; and Bran Stark is the true history of the world. But the Night King threatens the political world of Westeros in the series through authoritarianism. His extranatural threat is the result of too much, too fast. If magic in *GoT* had any radical redemptive power over the fantasy echo of natural history, the Night King is magic unchecked and hell-bent on destroying all history, natural *and* extranatural. He is the magical response to the political Westeros. So while he embodies extranatural power, he also embodies the loss of all hope, identity, agency, and history. Nothing can grow in a world ruled by the Night King. All of the subjects are literal extensions of himself. He signals the end all of history, not the transformation of it. Daenerys's campaign in the cities of Slaver's Bay may resemble the Night King's campaign against humanity, but her goal is not to destroy history, but to transform it. The Night King also resembles the Three-eyed Raven's knowledge of the past, present, and future, except for the fact that Bran does not act. He could manipulate, and perhaps even control, using his knowledge and warging power, but he appears content to let things happen as they always have, passively observing and rarely interfering. Bran does not act against the political machinery with his magical knowledge because he knows it is pointless. Daenerys acts against the political machinery with her magical dragons and fails because of political alliances. For the entire series, the Night King acts with magic against the political machinery of Westeros, attempting the radical version of the other character's goals. In this way, *GoT* represents raw magic as utterly destructive, but extranatural humanity as potentially restorative.

Ironically, the Night King's raw magical erasure of history is foiled, not by the Red Priestess who stands for hope, not by the man of the Night's Watch who stands as the new identity of Westeros, not by the Three-Eyed Raven, who stands for deep history, and not by the Mother of Dragons who stands for transformative action, but by the assassin who stands for vengeance. Arya is nothing but an agent of revenge since the beheading of her father, Ned Stark, in the final episode of the first season. Of all of these motives—hope, identity, agency, and history—revenge is the most human extranatural act in the entire series.

Considering Arya Stark at this moment seems to do her character a disservice. She is one of the most important characters in the series, but her quest is smaller and more personal than the others discussed above. She is also the character who makes the clearest case for the failure of magic to transform history. From her first moment in the series, she defies the historical role that has been thrust upon her, that of a Lady of Winterfell. Instead of keeping to her lessons on needlepoint, she favors archery and sword fighting. It is this defiance of echo that makes Arya stand out and ultimately survive the trials that she faces throughout the series. She escapes Sansa's fate in King's Landing when she is forced to masquerade as a boy headed to the Night's Watch. She humanizes the Hound, Sandor Clegane, when she travels with him in the Riverlands. She wins the favor of Jaqen H'ghar, a Faceless Man, who sends her to seek the House of Black and White. She defeats Littlefinger when she anticipates his double-cross. And she defeats the Night King just as he believes he has once and for all destroyed history, embodied in Bran. She proves herself to be intelligent, resilient, and independent. She suffers and is made stronger, wiser, and more self-reliant. But she also achieves these ends with extranatural training, but without becoming extranatural embodied. During her training in Braavos, she learns "valar morghulis" (all men must die) and "valar dohaeris" (all men must serve), the dicta by which the Faceless Men live. Her training at the House of Black and White was meant to strip her of her identity, teach her to assume the faces of the dead, and devote her to Death, yet she resists these lessons. She retains herself. She is transformed, not by extranatural powers but by her own human will. So while the other figures of extranatural transformation struggle and fail, the human, rejecting the extranatural lessons, defeats magic's raw power and ends the march of the army of White Walkers.

The abruptness of the Night King's defeat signals the total dismantlement of the magical subversion of human history. Melisandre, seeing the Night King and his army of the dead all collapse at once, likewise wanders into the snow, and literally fades away. Daenerys attacks King's Landing and lays it to waste with her magical dragon, only to be betrayed by her lover, Jon, who no longer sees honor in her quest to reclaim the Iron Throne. With her death, the last dragon flies away, leaving only the magic of Bran, the Three-Eyed Raven in Westeros. At first Bran's survival appears to be a victory for magic over the political, especially as he is chosen to be the new king of the Seven Kingdoms. But this victory for magic is turned into a political victory as Tyrion argues for Bran's ascendance:

> What unites people? Armies? Gold? Flags? Stories. There's nothing in the world more powerful than a good story[…]. He is our memory, the keeper of all our stories[…]. Who better to lead us into the future? [S8, E6].

Stories are powerful, but Tyrion Lannister's speech reduces the magic that has made this story so powerful to mere rhetoric. This speech convinced the disparate leaders of a shell-shocked Westeros to elect a boy, a boy who had never been interested in ruling and has no experience in doing so, to sit on the new throne of the remaining kingdoms of Westeros … because he knows the history. This decision is, on some level, a great inoculation against the forgetfulness of Westeros. They will no longer forget that magic is real and can be a threat. But how is magic a threat now that the Night King has been defeated, the Lord of Light has retreated, and the last dragon has flown away? There are no more magical threats. The only magic that remains is Bran's and he seems uninterested in using it. In fact, the only time he seemed interested in acting was when he was young and able-bodied. In "Winter is Coming" (S1, E1) Bran practices archery at Winterfell with Jon as his instructor and his father and mother looking on from a balcony. It is clear he looks up to his brother, Robb, his half-brother Jon, and his father Ned. They are all capable fighters. But during this scene, Bran is upstaged by his sister, Arya, as she hits the target at nearly double his distance. It is this scene that sets these characters in stone. Ned and Catelyn Stark sit above and removed from their children. Jon instructs and encourages. Robb looks on, doing little. Arya exhibits the most skill. And Bran, incapable of completing this task, runs after those who can. Bran likely would have grown up to be like Robb and Jon had the events at the end of the episode not occurred. Bran's magic, during the series, had the most potential, if he used it to move backward in time to build the Wall as Bran the Builder or become the Night King. We know that these choices were possible because we see that he can observe the past. He witnesses Jon's birth and discovers his true lineage in "Winds of Winter" (S6, E10). He can see even the most intimate moments in Westeros. But witnessing is not his only power; in "The Door" (S6, E5) Bran wargs into Hodor while observing Wylis the day that he succumbs to a seizure and becomes Hodor. Bran causes this seizure by controlling Hodor in the present while observing his past as Wylis, fusing the two moments together and destroying the mind of his giant friend and protector. Perhaps it is this moment that compels Bran to only use his power to observe and never interfere; but because of this moment, his power is significantly reduced. Bran knows what will happen because it has always happened. Foresight is powerful if it motivates an agent, but foresight that precipitates no altered action is impotent.

So in the end, Bran's impotent magic is the only remaining magic in Westeros, and politics can return to the center of the story. Tyrion turns Bran's magic into myth, like the histories that Tyrion was so fond of reading in the beginning of the series. He is often ridiculed for his interest in histories because histories were the preference of the soft in Westeros while the hard chose knighthood and battle skills. This choice mirrors Bran's turn from battle to history. Tyrion argues that story is important because it chronicles the events of the past, and it is through this common cultural memory that we become better. But even while Bran and Tyrion both chose cultural consciousness over cultural conquest, the day-to-day practice of being Westerosi remains the same. In this case, James Gifford would classify *GoT* as a materialist fantasy whose "fulfillment of desire only functions to create more obedient subjects ever-more deeply bound by ideology to an exploitative series of relations" (41) rather than a fantasy whose magic "presuppose forms of subjectivity […] set on changing the world by acting upon it" (85). As in our world, history teaches nothing; people continue to make the same mistakes over and over again. Westeros is not redeemed by magic; it is enslaved to politics. Jonathan Chau and Chris Vanderwees argue that *GoT* "not only provides a mechanism for wish fulfilment, but it perhaps also functions as a text for thinking about resistance or political dissensus, or for imagining political alternatives" (3). This possibility was available when magic reappears as an agent of transformation in Westeros. Magic provided an alternative to the system of governance that had grown stagnant in Westeros for generations. This potential inspired the faith of the Red Priestess who hoped that a savior would return. Potential drove the young Northern bastard to fight for what he believed was fair and honorable. Potential stirred an exiled princess and her magical dragons to free thousands of slaves from bondage. And potential reinvigorated a crippled Lord to seek a myth beyond the Wall. Yet all of this potential yielded no systemic change in the political world of Westeros. Jameson explains that "the invocation of magic by modern fantasy cannot recapture fascination, but is condemned by its form to retrace the history of magic's decay and fall, its disappearance [becoming] little more than nostalgia" (71). The final scene shows a distracted Bran passing through the chamber where the King's Council is meeting, as it had for all of the king's before him. This council, led by Tyrion, the rhetorician, begins by talking about roads. Tyrion, the champion of stories and Bran the Broken, the keeper of the most complete index of Westeros, does not free the impoverished as he witnessed Daenerys do in Essos. He does what Varys would have counseled him to do—remain consistent and predicable to the fantasy echo of Westeros for the good of the Seven Kingdoms. Robert Baratheon, the drunk, womanizing, war-monger, and Aerys Targaryen, the Mad King, were both ill-suited to run the Westeros. Bran, through inaction, and Tyrion, through good-heartedness, will be better than their predecessors, but they will not transform Westeros. This conclusion ignores one of the most compelling powers of fantasy and the presence of magic—its potential to offer more than amplification of political drama. Magic can transform a story, if it is allowed to do more than make events bigger and brighter. Instead, in this fantasy epic magic matches the course of the White Walkers. It wanders through the early seasons as a political agent. It finds new life and purpose in the middle seasons. Then when that magic is defeated in the final season, the story falls lifeless to the floor and Tyrion lights the match to ensure that it cannot come back to life.

Many viewers were upset with the ending of HBO's *Game of Thrones*. Many felt dissatisfied with the direction certain characters took in the final episodes and with the resolution of several narrative arcs. Amidst a myriad complaints and fan-crafted alternative endings ultimately what emerged about the way the show concluded was the question "What was the point?" And this applies acutely to the role of magic in the series: what was the point of all the fantastic elements of the show if in the end nothing really changed because of its presence? Many wanted Daenerys and her magical dragons, or the magically resurrected Jon Snow, to provide a paradigmatic shift for Westeros. Some wanted Bran to actually *do* something spectacular with his all-seeing power that prevents history from repeating itself. These desires mirror the desires of viewers who might want to escape the horrors of the real world and root for a magical wish-fulfilling transformation in Westeros. This is not merely escapist, rather it is the expression of hope—the yearning for something extraordinary to change the world for the better. When that extraordinary element is so tangibly present in the form of magic, as it is in *Game of Thrones*, the yearning is that much stronger, and even anticipated. When it doesn't happen, when it is all pointless, the feeling of disappointment is equally tangible. Therefore, I will end with this: *Game of Thrones* seems to suggest that while fantasy can offer transformation by introducing extranatural magic, by granting heroic quests, by deposing evil kings, it can also fail to deliver a transformation by subjugating magic to history, by demoralizing heroes, and by ordaining disinterested kings. The television series built and enthralled its viewership on promises of gritty realism and magical transformation. It delivered only one of these at the conclusion—the one we already live with every day. The story is thus deeply realistic, in part because the hope that magic offers fails to supply a new world, and in part because the reality of stagnant political exercises succeeds in reminding us that there is no transformation. Perhaps that is the greatest fantasy of all.

Works Cited

Ashitagawa, Yuko. "Can Fantasy Be More Real than Reality? The Fantastic, the Realistic, and Textuality in Literary Criticism." *Pennsylvania Literary Journal*. 29–51.

Attebery, Brian. *Strategies of Fantasy*. Bloomington: Indiana University Press, 1992.

Betchel, Greg. "'There and Back Again': Progress in the Discourse of Todorovian, Tolkienian and Mystic Fantasy Theory." *English Studies in Canada*. Vol. 30, no. 4, December 2004, pp. 139–66.

Benioff, David, and D.B. Weiss. *Game of Thrones*. HBO, 2011–2019.

Chau, Jonathan, and Chris Vanderwees. "Introduction—High Fantasy, Political Dreams, and the Mainstream: Reflections on *Game of Thrones*." *Canadian Review of American Studies*. Vol. 49, no. 1, 2019. pp. 1–6.

Eilers, Michelle L. "On the Origins of Modern Fantasy." *Extrapolation*. Vol. 41, no. 4. 2000, pp. 319–37.

Gifford, James. *A Modernist Fantasy: Modernism, Anarchism, and the Radical Fantastic*. Victoria: ELS Editions, 2018.

Grant, John. "Gulliver Unravels: Generic Fantasy and the Loss of Subversion." *Extrapolation* vol. 41, no. 1. 2000, pp. 21–7.

Jameson, Fredric. *Archaeologies of the Future: The Desire Call Utopia and Other Science Ficitons*. London: Verso, 2005.

Kornhaber, Spencer. "What Melisandre's Magic Reveals about *Game of Thrones*." *The Atlantic*,

29 Apr. 2019, www.theatlantic.com/entertainment/archive/2019/04/game-thrones-melisandre-and-end-magic/588292/.

Lanchester, John. "When did you get hooked?" *London Review of Books*. Vol. 35, no. 7. 11 Apr. 2017. www.lrb.co.uk/the-paper/v35/n07/john-lanchester/when-did-you-get-hooked.

Rosenberg, Alyssa. "How Magic Works in *Game of Thrones*." *ThinkProgress*, 3 Apr. 2013, thinkprogress.org/how-magic-works-in-game-of-thrones-d184448ca841/.

Scott, Joan W. "Fantasy Echo: History and the Construction of Identity." *Critical Inquiry*. Vol. 27. Winter 2001, pp. 284–304.

A Brief Conclusion on the Conclusion

A. Keith Kelly

Game of Thrones (both in its literary and screen versions) explores deeply the ways in which power and influence can be exercised, abused, gained, taken away, or even given up, and to what lengths people will go to possess it. Sometimes it resides in unexpected sources, or is wielded in completely unanticipated ways. Power can be overt and undeniable—as demonstrated in the first episode of Season Two when Cersei Lannister points out to Littlefinger at the tip of her Queensguard's dagger that "power is power." Or it can be subtle—Littlefinger's assertion earlier in the same scene that "knowledge is power" proves quite prescient after all, since it is the walking repository of knowledge, Bran Stark, who wears the crown in the end. However, while the subject of power certainly resonates deeply, much of the success that *Game of Thrones* enjoyed over nearly a decade can be attributed to the ways in which George R.R. Martin, David Benioff and D.B. Weiss capitalized on, and subverted, the expectations of the audience. Many of those expectations centered upon the shifting loci of power, but at the same time those expectations were unceasingly influenced by the genre of epic fantasy in which the story resides. This method kept audiences of the show fascinated for years, as everyone waited to see who would triumph in the end and who would fall in some gruesome or unexpected manner, and who would eventually attain the titular symbol of power—the Iron Throne.

Ultimately, however, that which made *Game of Thrones* so captivating also contributed to its disappointing—and by many, reviled—conclusion. Like a Greek tragedy, the very traits that made the HBO series truly heroic in its appeal became the instruments of its demise. Where Benioff and Weiss failed was that they stuck diligently to their practice of delivering the unexpected, of subverting the hopes and predictions of a massive and devoted audience, to their last breath. And in so doing they defied the definitive expectation of the heroic epic fantasy—a triumphant ending (though I would note that triumphant doesn't necessarily mean happily ever after). So many of the anticipated, longed for, even feared events were left to wither on the vine. There was no scorching clash between two powerful women—Cersei with her wildfire and Daenerys with her dragon fire. No, Cersei ended up buried under a pile of rubble clinging to her brother, Jaime, and crying pathetically (in a similar manner to what was essentially the unsatisfactory conclusion to Brienne of Tarth's arc when she was left pining in Winterfell). And with respect to Jaime, he did not complete his arc of redemption in a way that fans expected or wanted either; it was instead buried under the aforementioned pile of rubble with Cersei. Neither did Daenerys triumph, bringing her complicated brand of liberation and subjugation to Westeros. Rather she apparently succumbed to her genetic predilections and went mad only to be slain by the hand of the man she loved. And that man, Jon Snow, who in spite of being lauded for his leadership and dedication to honor for years then wandered off into the frozen woods of the far north. Even Drogon's glorious melting of the Iron Throne proved insignificant (and in fact ignored) as there was no dissolution of the Seven Kingdoms in a "nobody wins" scenario. Dragons, magic, honor, redemption, even ruthlessness all prove ineffectual and almost purposeless. Rather, in what (I presume) can only have been an attempt to subvert everyone's expectations and undermine any suggestion of a heroic ending, Benioff and Weiss chose a path of complete mediocrity. Perhaps it was their goal to avoid taking sides in the Daenerys vs. Jon battle for the throne, knowing that awarding the prize to one would disappoint the fans of the other. Perhaps they didn't want to go so far as award the throne to Cersei, the wicked queen, or plunge it all into eternal winter by having the Night King triumph. Maybe the disbanding of the Seven Kingdoms altogether (as seemingly presaged by the melting of the throne) struck them as too simple. Regardless of the reasons behind all the conclusions that the writers did *not* choose, the conclusion they did craft ended up disappointing everyone equally—and quite remarkably.

At the end of the series, faced with such an unsatisfying ending, many were left wondering what was the point? What was the point of dethroning Cersei, the powerful woman who had held onto power for the better part of the show? What was the point of Daenerys's journey, her many accomplishments and subsequent elevation to near-mythic greatness? What was the point of Jon Snow's rise—through both disaster and victory and even death—from obscure bastard son to legitimate heir and prophesied savior? What was the point of the Night King's war against the Seven Kingdoms if it did not bring about either sweeping unity or ultimate devastation? What was the point of magic, dragons, the Iron Throne itself? There apparently was no ultimate political, philosophical, environmental or moral/ethical significance to the conclusion we got. And it was not just the metanarrative that left audiences wondering why. Many of the fascinating character arcs likewise ended in complete disappointment. Daenerys (as Mother of Dragons and Breaker of Chains) did not overthrow a system dominated by violence, abuse and oppressive patriarchy and usher in an era of female-centered power. Cersei likewise failed to prove that a queen could rule well or even successfully for long. Grey Worm, as a representative of both people of color and those freed from enslavement, ended up seeming like an ineffectual protestor embroiled in petulant negotiations. Jaime demonstrated that a path of redemption, however compelling and moving, eventually fails to produce the results that many in the audience desired, and returns simply to where it began. Even the success of Tyrion Lannister, one of the most beloved and complex characters of the entire series, rings hollow in the end—though arguably the conclusion to his arc makes some sort of sense and might seem a victory for him.

Game of Thrones offered audiences no good-triumphs-over-evil conclusion, as one might expect in a traditional fantasy. Neither did it make impactful messages made about gender, other than the fact that all the powerful women were disposed of, save for Sansa Stark who was essentially exiled to her own petty kingdom far removed from the center of real power. People of color in the show either died in a rash cavalry charge, died in chains or sailed back to where they came from. While violence seemed to dominate the ending, it was a "good story" that settled the issue of rulership, though in a way that seemed implausible to many. And while one might argue that disabled people such as Bran and Tyrion triumphed, what were they left to rule "over but" arguments about rebuilding brothels. How disappointing ... or then again, maybe it is simply realistic.

What makes the conclusion of *Game of Thrones* truly a tragedy is that Benioff and Weiss had so many options to craft a compelling and triumphant ending while still holding true to their pattern of shocking and thrilling their audience. I won't spin out my own script for the final few episodes of the show here—I am sure many readers of this volume have already conceived of their own, and the internet is overpopulated with such anyway. But I will conclude by suggesting that sometimes satisfying expectations is not a bad thing, and in fact often serves to give audiences the longed-for sense of validation of the investment they have made in a story. While disappointment, shock, anger and grief are all parts of reality and undeniably contributed to the historically great success of *Game of Thrones*, in the end most people do look for a satisfying ending that leaves room for hope, or at the very least offers excitement and pleasure. And genre *does* matter.

Conclusion

Game of Thrones is not Orwell's *1984*. It was never presented as a dystopian tale with the ever-grim reality of a boot stamping on the face of humanity forever being a distinct possibility—though had the Night King won and turned the world to ice I think most viewers would have been happier than they were with the ending they got. But in an epic fantasy the audience expects, dare I say demands, a conclusion that is in some way triumphant—if not triumphant, at least one that is compelling and not so laden with mediocrity and disappointment that it can best be described as simply boring. But perhaps in the end that was the point. Maybe this is indeed, more than anything, a story about reality, and not fantasy after all. In that case, it is not Benioff and Weiss who got it all wrong, but me.

About the Contributors

Sylwia **Borowska-Szerszun** holds a Ph.D. in literary studies. She is an assistant professor at the University of Białystok, Poland, where she teaches courses in English literature and literary theory. She is the author of *Enter the Carnival: Carnivalesque Semiotics in Early Tudor Moral Interludes* (2016). Her research focuses on medievalism and Gothicism in fantasy literature.

Jason M. **Embry** is an assistant professor of English at Georgia Gwinnett College northeast of Atlanta, where he teaches first-year writing and American literature. His research interests include utopian/dystopian studies, new wave science fiction, science fantasy by Michael Moorcock and Gene Wolfe, and the formation and development of the new weird in relation to the Anthropocene.

Andrew **Howe** is a professor of history at La Sierra University, where he teaches courses in American history, popular culture, and film/television studies. His scholarship includes book chapters on the intersection of the postmodern and the classical in *The Three Burials of Melquiades Estrada*, villain typologies in *Star Trek: Voyager*, and the role played by religion in *Game of Thrones*.

Graham P. **Johnson** is an associate professor of English at Reinhardt University. His areas of interest include Old English, Middle English, and Old Norse language and literature, paremiology (the study of proverbs), pragmatics, and medievalism. He has been trained under the guidance of many talented medievalists, including Dr. Tom Shippey, Dr. Paul Acker, and Dr. Gernot Wieland.

A. Keith **Kelly** is a professor of English at Georgia Gwinnett College, where he teaches medieval literature, linguistics and writing. He has published on an array of subjects, including literary pragmatics, Old Norse saga, the works of J.R.R. Tolkien and the adaptation and reception of the Middle Ages in film and television. He is also a published poet and author of short fiction.

Lindsey **Mantoan** is an assistant professor of theatre at Linfield University. She is the author of *War as Performance: Conflict in Iraq and Political Theatricality* (2018) and coeditor of *The Methuen Drama Book of Trans Plays* (2021), *Vying for the Iron Throne* (2018), and *Performance in a Militarized Culture* (2017). She is an occasional contributor to CNN.com.

Robert Allen **Rouse** teaches medieval literature, spatial studies, and ecocritical studies at the University of British Columbia, Vancouver. He has published widely

About the Contributors

on medieval romance, sexuality, nationalism, geocritical hermeneutics, Arthurian literature, manuscript medievalisms, and the late-medieval English geographical maginary, and is coeditor (with Siân Echard) of the *Encyclopedia of Literature in Medieval Britain* (2017).

Daniel **Vollaro** is an associate professor of English at Georgia Gwinnett College, a writer, and a teacher of writing. His creative nonfiction has been published in *Adbusters, Boomer Café, Litro, Michigan Quarterly Review, Missouri Review, Rise Up Review*, and *The Smart Set*. He writes about literature, popular culture, nature, environmentalism, and politics.

Jan Doolittle **Wilson** is the Wellspring Associate Professor of Gender Studies and History, Director of the Women's and Gender Studies Program, and Director of Graduate Studies at the University of Tulsa. A disability scholar and activist, she is working on her second book, which explores the powerful prism of disability and how it can be used for change.

Index

ambition 24, 79, 93, 116, 121, 126, 151–2, 163, 166
America 2, 13–20, 25, 27–9, 35, 43, 45, 69, 91, 99, 104, 106–7, 158, 178, 185
anger 53, 87–101, 103–7, 149, 151, 183
army of the dead 97, 125, 128, 141, 171, 175
Arya Stark 28, 43, 46, 50–1, 56, 59, 61–5, 71–2, 77, 81–2, 87–90, 92, 98, 102, 104, 127, 149, 150–3, 174, 176
Asia 29, 33, 69; *see also* Mongols
audience 1, 3–5, 13–6, 20–3, 30, 39, 46, 49–50, 53–6, 59, 64, 74, 83, 87, 92–6, 98–109, 132, 135–6, 149, 153, 157, 167, 171, 177, 181–4
authority 24, 26, 51, 59, 65, 79, 88, 92, 144, 151, 157, 162

Balon Greyjoy 71, 77
Barristan Selmy 79, 81, 123–5, 130
battle 2, 20, 37, 46, 48, 69, 70–1, 75–6, 82, 92, 97, 106, 131, 147, 151–2, 176, 182; *see also* war
bend the knee 23, 26, 97
Benioff, David 7–13, 48, 68, 72, 74, 99–102, 109, 137, 162, 167, 178, 181–4; *see also* Weiss, D.B.; the writers
Bran Stark 18–9, 27, 43, 62, 77, 79, 83, 92, 102–4, 109, 128, 131–2, 137, 139–42, 14–9, 152–3, 157–8, 170, 172–8, 181, 183; *see also* Three-Eyed Raven
Brienne of Tarth 50–2, 59, 60–3, 65, 67, 69, 71, 81–3, 86, 102–3, 141, 145–7, 156–7, 182
Brotherhood Without the Banners 26, 82

Casterly Rock 72, 95–6, 138, 142
Catelyn Stark 71, 83, 142, 145, 167, 176
Cersei Lannister 14, 18, 42, 46, 50, 53–4, 63–5, 70, 73, 80–4, 88, 90–8, 100–2, 104, 107, 117, 125–6, 137–8, 141, 143, 149, 155, 181–3
children 16, 22, 36–8, 40, 49, 62, 72–6, 85, 91, 93–4, 97, 100, 104, 106, 134, 139–41, 143, 148–9, 167–8, 171–2, 176
chivalry 52, 60–1, 74, 78–81, 83, 88

Daario Naharis 37–8, 78, 82, 125
Daenerys Targaryen 20–4, 29, 34–40, 50, 54–6, 63–70, 74–9, 81–2, 84, 88, 92–110, 115–131, 146, 150–1, 154–5, 171–8, 182–3; *see also khaleesi*
death 3, 36, 40, 43, 47, 49, 61, 73, 75, 79, 81, 85–6, 92, 96–7, 99–103, 106–7, 127, 134, 142, 152, 165–7, 169, 171, 173, 175, 182
Dorne 40–2, 47, 72, 74–5, 154
Dothraki 26, 33–7, 46, 52, 55, 68–9, 75–6, 80, 84, 97, 116, 119–20, 125–6, 151, 154–5, 171; *see also* people of color
dragons 2, 4, 14, 18, 21–4, 32, 37–8, 40, 46, 63–4, 88, 92, 95–7, 106, 109, 115–7, 122, 125–6, 151, 163, 165, 167–8, 170–8, 182–3; *see also* Drogon
Drogon 21, 23–4, 73, 98, 115, 122, 182; *see also* dragons

Essos 30, 33–5, 37, 39, 41, 48–9, 51, 76, 83, 121, 154, 166, 168, 171–2, 177
Euron Greyjoy 42, 71–2, 94–7, 100–1, 103
Europe 22, 25–6, 33–4, 39–40, 47, 69, 74, 89
evil 3–4, 48, 58, 60, 64, 98, 100, 131, 134, 137, 162, 164, 173, 178, 183

family 3, 22–3, 28, 37, 42, 52, 64, 70–1, 76, 79, 98, 127–8, 133, 137, 138–42, 144, 149–50, 152, 166–7, 170; *see also* House
fans *see* audience
fantasy 2–4, 13, 18, 22, 27, 30–5, 38–44, 46–9, 55, 67, 69, 105, 108–9, 135–7, 147, 154, 161–4, 167, 169–72, 174, 176–85; *see also* genre
fear 33–5, 44, 51, 56, 58, 64–5, 67, 71, 87, 90, 92, 98, 135, 142, 157, 163, 169, 172
female characters 21, 50–1, 56, 65, 68, 70, 82, 89–90, 99–100, 103, 105, 155–6
femininity 52, 57–61, 63–4, 145; *see also* gender; masculinity
final episode 1, 20–1, 27, 102, 109, 171, 174; *see also* Season 8
First Men 42, 79, 173
foresight *see* prophecy
Frey, House 71, 80

gender 5, 26, 30, 48–52, 57–9, 61–2, 64–5, 68–71, 73–6, 81–5, 88–9, 91, 94, 107, 111, 129,

133, 146, 151, 154, 183; *see also* femininity; masculinity
Gendry 61, 72, 82
genre 2–5, 30–2, 54, 69, 93, 134–7, 161–3, 167, 181, 183; *see also* fantasy
gods 9, 42, 138, 150, 165, 166; *see also* Old Gods
Gregor Clegane 70, 79, 84, 149
Grey Worm 37, 40, 76–7, 97, 121, 123–4, 126, 183; *see also* people of color

Hand of the King 74, 95, 167
HBO 1, 5, 7, 13–8, 20, 28–31, 33, 35, 38–43, 46–8, 51–2, 54, 56, 60, 66–71, 85–6, 105–6, 108, 110, 126, 130–1, 162, 177–8, 181
heroic 3–5, 21, 52, 61, 79, 89–90, 98, 106, 131, 136, 138, 140, 155, 164, 169, 173, 178, 181–2; *see also* chivalry
historical 14, 23, 27, 38, 43–4, 48, 69, 81, 132, 147, 154, 161–4, 166–7, 169–70, 173–4
Hodor 139–40, 152–3, 159, 172, 176
honor 18, 25, 36, 42–3, 52, 56, 61, 66, 68, 77–81, 85, 122, 124, 141, 169–70, 175, 177, 182; *see also* chivalry; heroic
hope 2, 4, 21, 72, 94, 105, 129, 163, 168–9, 171, 173–4, 178, 183
the Hound *see* Sandor Clegane
House 10, 72, 77, 82, 89, 92, 105, 116, 152, 171, 174–5; *see also* family

identity 31–7, 41–2, 45–7, 52, 61, 77, 80, 82, 85, 133–4, 139–42, 149, 158, 161, 163–6, 170–1, 174–5
Iron Islands 60, 62, 65, 71, 77, 88, 103
Iron Throne 1–2, 12, 22, 24, 35, 42, 47–8, 85–6, 93–5, 99, 106, 121, 131, 146, 149–51, 167, 168, 175, 181–3, 185; *see also* king; queen

Jaime Lannister 23, 46, 51–4, 67, 73–4, 80, 82–4, 86, 93–4, 96, 100, 102, 137, 140–7, 155–7, 182–3
Joffrey Baratheon 4, 53, 71, 73, 79, 81–2, 84, 138, 144
Jon Snow 21, 23–7, 43, 45, 59, 68, 80–1, 88, 93, 95–9, 102–4, 106, 109–10, 125, 127–9, 131, 142, 145–6, 151, 169–71, 173, 175–6, 178, 182
Jorah Mormont 35–7, 79, 97, 121
justice 4, 16–8, 71, 80, 93, 98, 133, 165

Khal Drogo 35–7, 54–5, 69, 75, 84, 109, 116–21, 155, 171; *see also* people of color
khaleesi 36–7, 55; *see also* Daenerys Targaryen
king 27, 79, 83, 88, 104, 119–20, 128, 138, 140, 142, 146, 162–3, 165, 167, 175, 177; *see also* queen
King's Landing 13–4, 19–20, 23, 25, 62–3, 68, 71, 79, 82–3, 94–8, 101–7, 125–6, 138, 140–1, 143, 146, 149–51, 155, 174

Kingsguard 62, 73, 79, 83, 103, 139–41, 143, 146–7
knight 35, 41, 51, 60, 62, 80, 83, 103, 139–40, 173; *see also* chivalry

language 98, 111–3, 119, 121, 129, 142, 158, 160, 185
Lannister, House 4, 14, 46, 72, 74, 80, 92, 125, 138, 142, 150
leadership 2, 18, 25–7, 43, 63–4, 70, 76, 103–4, 106, 124–5, 170, 175, 182
literary 1, 5, 33–5, 41, 50–1, 115, 129, 136, 154, 161, 163, 181, 185–6
Littlefinger 18, 71, 73, 80, 87, 92, 102, 175, 181
Lord of Light 152, 168–9, 175
Lord of the Rings 4, 136, 163–4; *see also* Tolkien, J.R.R.
loyalty 4, 38, 60, 71, 125, 127, 141–2

The Mad King 23, 73, 140, 177
magic 5, 14, 36, 148, 153, 161–79, 182–3
Mance Rayder 26, 45, 76; *see also* Wildlings
marriage 34–6, 80, 138, 143–5, 155
Martin, George R.R. 1, 7, 9, 13, 31–3, 39–42, 44–8, 50, 53, 56, 60, 64–70, 73–4, 79–81, 84–6, 94, 99, 105–6, 108–9, 116–7, 119, 121, 123, 127, 130, 135–6, 138–46, 150, 154, 158–9, 162–3, 181; *see also* *A Song of Ice and Fire*
Marxist 15–6, 23
masculinity 4, 35, 51, 56, 59–61, 63, 65–6, 68–71, 73–5, 79–85, 140, 143, 145, 150; *see also* femininity; gender
medieval 25, 30–5, 39–41, 43–4, 47, 52, 65, 68, 70, 72, 74, 76, 88, 108, 162, 167, 185–6
Meereen 21–3, 37–8, 66, 78, 109, 123–5, 150
Melisandre 72, 82, 88, 168–9, 171, 173, 175, 178; *see also* Lord of Light
military 19, 51, 60, 70, 72, 81, 93, 96, 98, 106, 116, 129, 146–7
misogyny 4, 64, 93, 98, 102
Missandei 40, 97, 103, 123, 143, 155, 172; *see also* people of color
Mongols 25, 35, 69; *see also* Asia
morality 3, 14, 17–8, 21, 23, 26, 36, 38, 49, 52, 60, 91–2, 94, 105, 183
the Mountain *see* Gregor Clegane
murder 23, 57–8, 72–3, 81, 123, 128, 144, 149, 156, 167–8, 170

Ned Stark 3–4, 18–9, 43, 68, 71, 73, 79–81, 100, 167, 169, 170, 172, 174, 176
Night King 61, 77, 81, 97, 104, 149, 169, 170, 172–6, 182, 184; *see also* White Walkers
Night's Watch 18, 25, 27, 42–3, 45, 80–2, 145–6, 166, 169, 170, 174; *see also* The Wall
The North 25, 27, 42–5, 65, 88, 94, 97, 102–4, 127, 149, 165–6, 169–70

Oberyn Martell 41–2, 138, 156
Old Gods 42, 166; *see also* gods

Index

Olenna Tyrell 71, 73
otherness 31, 40–2, 46, 52, 58, 67, 154, 162, 167, 171
outsider 38, 40, 135, 137–8, 154–5

patriarchy 4, 57, 68–75, 78, 80–8, 91–2, 100–1, 105, 183
people of color 98, 103, 154, 155, 183
politics 2, 5, 13–4, 16, 18–31, 33–4, 38–9, 41–6, 48, 49, 54, 62, 67, 68, 70–4, 76, 80, 87–94, 96, 98, 101, 104–5, 107, 128, 138, 145, 161–3, 165–78, 183, 186
pregnancy 3, 94
Prince-Who-Was-Promised 169, 171
prophecy 120, 152

queen 11, 21, 38, 63–4, 74, 88, 93–8, 100–5, 109, 119–20, 123–8, 146, 159, 164, 182–3; *see also* king
Queensguard, 103, 181

race 17, 26, 30–3, 35, 39–44, 46–7, 55, 85, 97, 133, 154; *see also* people of color
Ramsay Bolton 54–6, 71, 77, 84, 102, 149, 156
rape 4, 35–6, 48–57, 65–7, 69–70, 76, 83–4, 86, 91, 102, 106, 141, 151, 154–6, 159
reality 2, 19, 25, 31, 47, 60, 93, 134, 139, 148, 153, 163, 165, 178, 183–4
Red Priestess *see* Melisandre
The Red Wedding 3, 4, 49
religion 2, 15, 25, 33–4, 49, 69, 93, 152, 165,-6, 185
revenge 3, 35–6, 38, 61, 63, 71, 74, 91, 149, 174
Robb Stark 3, 43, 68, 70–1, 79–81, 139, 168, 172, 176
Robert Baratheon 5, 6, 30, 47, 67–8, 70–3, 77, 81, 106, 167–8, 172, 177, 185

Samwell Tarly 27, 125, 128, 143, 145
Sandor Clegane 61, 74, 82, 102, 149–50, 174
Sansa Stark 13, 43, 49–50, 54–6, 65, 79, 84, 87–8, 90, 92, 97, 102–4, 106, 127–8, 141, 143–4, 149–50, 156, 174, 183
Season 8 1, 12, 20, 23, 29–30, 39, 42, 64, 83–4, 93–4, 99–104, 107, 128, 130, 147, 149–50, 155, 177; *see also* final episode
Seven Kingdoms 12, 22, 37, 41–2, 45, 70, 80, 88, 93, 97–8, 104, 128, 146, 148, 151–2, 163, 166–7, 169–73, 175, 177, 182
sex 16, 35–40, 48, 50–1, 53–7, 59–60, 65–6, 68, 70, 76, 78, 82–6, 91, 102, 143–4, 149, 154–6
shame 25, 50, 75, 104, 139, 141, 151
Shireen Baratheon, 152–3
slavery 21–3, 26, 37–40, 47, 55, 60, 63–4, 77, 98, 121–6, 143, 150, 154, 172, 177
Small Council 19, 62, 103
Song of Ice and Fire, A 1, 5, 32, 47–8, 50–1, 53, 56, 65–9, 85–6, 131, 158–9, 162; *see also* Martin, George R.R.

Sons of the Harpy 10, 37, 110, 123–5
Stannis Baratheon 71–3, 138, 152, 168–71
Stark, House 12, 42–3, 46, 79, 97, 99, 102, 128, 149, 169
stereotypes 30, 47, 51, 55, 58–9, 61, 94, 129, 136, 147, 150, 153–4, 157
subversion 4–5, 47–9, 55, 59, 64, 68, 75, 78, 85, 88, 90, 92–3, 97, 105, 117, 137, 158, 162, 170, 181

Targaryen, House 23, 79, 83, 94, 167, 171
Theon Greyjoy 46, 49, 55–6, 60, 68, 74, 76–8, 92, 103, 149–50, 156
Three-Eyed Raven *see* Bran Stark
Tolkien, J.R.R. 32–3, 47; *see also* Lord of the Rings
trauma 36, 56, 135, 139, 149–51, 153, 155–6
treason 95, 149
triumph 3–5, 43, 55, 61, 181–4
Trump, Donald 2, 27, 87, 89–91, 107
truth 2, 48, 65, 73, 76, 82, 102, 112, 114, 123, 126–8, 161
Tyrion Lannister 4, 22, 40, 56, 62, 68, 71, 73–4, 79, 84, 92, 94–6, 98–9, 103–4, 106–7, 109, 117, 125, 127, 131–2, 136–8, 141–4, 146–9, 151, 156–8, 166, 175–7, 183
Tywin Lannister 68, 70–3, 84, 137–8, 140, 143–4, 156

The Unsullied 34, 37, 40, 68, 75–6, 95, 97–8, 123–4, 126

Varys 18–9, 73, 76–8, 80, 95–6, 99, 127, 150–1, 177
verbal 96, 109, 117–21, 123–5, 127–9
victory 19, 97–8, 109, 126, 152, 175, 182–3
viewers *see* audience
violence 4, 15, 17, 24, 26, 33–5, 48–69, 78, 83–6, 94, 102–3, 109, 126, 133, 151, 153, 155, 156, 183
Viserys Targaryen 34–5, 109, 116–8, 155

The Wall 10–1, 19, 23, 25–6, 28, 33, 42, 44–5, 59, 62, 69, 76, 85–6, 96–7, 107, 145, 158, 165–7, 169–73, 176–7; *see also* Night's Watch
war 4, 14, 18–20, 23, 27–8, 38, 45, 51, 53, 60, 69–71, 74, 80, 92, 94, 96–8, 104, 126, 167, 172–3, 177, 182; *see also* battle
Wars of the Roses 25, 41, 163, 167; *see also* medieval
Weiss, D.B. 7–13, 29, 48, 68, 72, 74, 99, 102, 109, 137, 162, 167, 178, 181–4; *see also* Benioff, David; the writers
Western 22, 26, 33–6, 38–9, 43, 46; *see also* America; Europe
Westeros 14, 18–9, 21–8, 30, 32–4, 38–49, 51, 57, 61–3, 65–7, 70, 72, 76, 78, 80–3, 86, 88–9, 91, 93, 95–8, 103, 106, 109, 116, 119–22, 125, 128, 131, 142, 146–8, 163, 165–78, 182

White Walkers 2, 20, 44–7, 166, 169, 171–2, 175, 177; *see also* Night King
Wildlings 26, 28, 59, 76, 81; *see also* Mance Rayder
winter 7, 11, 28, 45, 86, 91, 166, 169, 173–4, 176, 179, 182
Winterfell 12, 32, 42, 46, 77, 83, 92, 95, 103–4, 141, 167, 172, 182

the writers 21, 92, 99, 101, 103–5, 109, 125, 182; *see also* Benioff, David; Weiss, D.B.

Yara Greyjoy 50, 59–63, 65, 81–2, 88, 95–6, 102–3, 150
Ygritte 26, 59, 62, 81, 88
Yunkai 37, 110, 121–2